PENG

ON

Ian Frazer (left) and Spiro Makrakis at Vothiana in 2002.

Seán Damer hunting high in the White Mountains.

For the Anzac soldiers on the run in Crete from 1941 to 1944, and their Cretan helpers, men, women and children.

ON THE RUN

Anzac Escape and Evasion in Enemy-occupied Crete

SEÁN DAMER
& IAN FRAZER

PENGUIN BOOKS

PENGUIN BOOKS
Published by the Penguin Group
Penguin Group (NZ), 67 Apollo Drive, Rosedale,
Northshore 0632, New Zealand (a division of Pearson New Zealand Ltd)
Penguin Group (USA) Inc., 375 Hudson Street,
New York, New York 10014, USA
Penguin Group (Canada), 90 Eglinton Avenue East, Suite 700, Toronto, Ontario,
M4P 2Y3, Canada (a division of Pearson Penguin Canada Inc.)
Penguin Books Ltd, 80 Strand, London, WC2R 0RL, England
Penguin Ireland, 25 St Stephen's Green, Dublin 2, Ireland (a division of Penguin Books Ltd)
Penguin Group (Australia), 250 Camberwell Road, Camberwell, Victoria 3124,
Australia (a division of Pearson Australia Group Pty Ltd)
Penguin Books India Pvt Ltd, 11, Community Centre,
Panchsheel Park, New Delhi – 110 017, India
Penguin Books (South Africa) (Pty) Ltd, 24 Sturdee Avenue,
Rosebank, Johannesburg 2196, South Africa

Penguin Books Ltd, Registered Offices: 80 Strand,
London, WC2R 0RL, England

First published by Penguin Group (NZ), 2006
This edition published by Penguin Group (NZ), 2007
1 3 5 7 9 10 8 6 4 2

Front cover photo (top) *Tom Moir (2nd from left), and two Cretans, on Crete, May 1943* (Alexander Turnbull Library, ref DA-12587-F);
(bottom) *Pachnes view.* Photographer: Jean Bienvenu, Crete.

Back cover: *The Barge From Crete* by Peter McIntyre (Archives New Zealand/
Te Rua Mahara o te Kāwanatanga, Wellington Office [AAAC 898/NCWA14])
Cover design by Dexter Fry

Designed by Shaun Jury
Typeset by Egan Reid Ltd
Printed in Australia by McPherson's Printing Group

ISBN 978 0 14 300722 7
A catalogue record for this book is available
from the National Library of New Zealand.

Contents

	Foreword	7
	Acknowledgements	9
	Preface	15
CHAPTER 1	Shock and Shame	19
CHAPTER 2	Denying Defeat: The Evaders	34
CHAPTER 3	For You the War is Over: POWs & Escapers	48
CHAPTER 4	MI9, and Crete, in 1941	70
CHAPTER 5	Mixed Fortunes	82
CHAPTER 6	The Long Haul: Winter 1941–1942	113
CHAPTER 7	Summer of Hope	137
CHAPTER 8	Shifting Fortunes: June–December 1942	164
CHAPTER 9	Last Round-up: Christmas 1942–May 1943	181
CHAPTER 10	Discussion	200
CHAPTER 11	Conclusion	214
CHAPTER 12	Epilogue	219

Bibliography 223
Notes 230

APPENDIX 1 Summary of Major Escapes and Evacuations from Crete June 1941–December 1943 245

APPENDIX 2 Roll of Anzac Escapers and Evaders from Crete 1941–1943 249

APPENDIX 3 Alphabetical Lists of All Known Anzac Evaders and Escapers from Crete June 1941–December 1943 264

Index 275

Foreword

I am glad this fascinating book is dedicated to those 'on the run' – the escapers and evaders – the unsung yet truly gallant group of men whose bravery and enterprise was so entirely *personal*. They were given absolutely no training, nor preparation, for the patriotic yet vastly dangerous decisions they took, not even guidance as to where their duty lay. As their exciting stories are unfolded so brilliantly in this

Major-General Sandy Thomas

record we are able to get a glimpse of great bravery and to marvel at the tenacity of some truly wonderful people.

The book's dedication, thank God, also embraces the intrepid Greek and Cretan families, those unassuming but unbelievably brave men and women who risked all for our men. They knew full well that to harbour a Kiwi meant to risk death from the Nazi oppressor – death for the whole family: Mum, Dad, the children, even the baby – no trial, no mercy, just instant death. Yet knowing this, they still opened their homes and their hearts for our countrymen.

There is much in this book to evoke excitement and amusement; there is also an underlying theme for deep thought, for wonder and admiration.

Major-General Sandy Thomas
CB DSO MC ED Silver Star (USA)*

Acknowledgements

We would like to start by paying tribute to the computing, sub-editorial and man-management skills of our wives, Helen Damer and Lala Frazer. Not only have they read every single page of this book several times, and commented cheerfully, helpfully and patiently upon it, but also they have encouraged us at every step of what at times became a long and tortuous project. Their assistance was, as they say in the military, above and beyond the call of duty. We thank them.

The following individuals assisted us with our research, and we are grateful to them: Chris Anderson, Dimitri Anson, Marika Begg, Marina Bennett, Aliki Boufis, Gilbert Cross, Sandra Gorter, John Irwin, Paul London, Jill McAra, George Manousakis, Brendan O'Keefe, John Petris, Bill Rudd, Sonny Sewell, Brian Sims, Ralph Stockbridge, Charles Watkins and Loraine Wilson. We would also like to thank Les O'Neill for drawing all the maps and assisting with other illustrations. Ian would like to thank the following people in Crete for helping him trace his father's movements through Selino: Savas and Fotini Savvas from Paleochora; Spiro and Marika Makrakis from Vothiana; Alex and Liana Makrakis from Hania; Emmanuel Perakis and his wife from Langadas; Eftihis and Calliope Daoundakis from Akladiakes.

For permission to quote hitherto unpublished memoirs, our thanks to Dick Huston's daughters, Toni Lexmond, Gail Sommerton, and Jenny Roberts; Ken Little's daughter, Robyn Perry; Murray McLagan's son, Malcolm; and Bruce 'Bella' Johnston's daughter, Robin Parker, and family.

For permission to reproduce photographs of individual escapers and evaders, we thank Toni Lexmond, Gail Sommerton, and Jenny Roberts, Gisborne: Dick Huston; John Moir, Upper Hutt: Tom Moir; Jean McDevitt, Auckland: Jim McDevitt; Robyn Johnson, Auckland: Bella Johnston; Neville Perkins, Christchurch: Dudley Perkins; the Nathan family, Wellington: Ned Nathan; Phyllis Scott and family, Melbourne: Norman Scott; Malcolm McLagan, Auckland: Murray McLagan; Julia Bracegirdle, Wellington: Peter Winter; Robyn Perry, Auckland: Ken Little; and Arthur Lambert, Whangarei: Vassiliki, and himself. Thanks also to Malcolm McLagan for permission to reproduce his father's sketch of the ox-yoke, and likewise to Robyn Perry for the German reprisal pamphlet.

For permission to reproduce photographs from institutions, we thank the Imperial War Museum, London; the Alexander Turnbull Library, Wellington; the NZ Army Museum & Kippenberger Archive, Waiouru; the Australian War Memorial, Canberra; and the Maritime Museum, Hania, Crete. All of these photographs are fully referenced in the footnotes and captions.

For permission to reproduce archive material, and for assistance with our research, we thank the following institutions and their staff: the Public Record Office, Kew, London; the Imperial War Museum, Lambeth, London; Archives New Zealand, Wellington; the National Library and Alexander Turnbull Library, Wellington; the Hocken Library, Dunedin; the New Zealand Army Museum & Kippenberger Archive, Waiouru; the Australian War Memorial, Canberra; the Australian National Archives.

We are grateful to Murray Elliott for permission to quote from his *Lion of Crete*; to Jean McDevitt to quote from her late husband Jim's *Escape From Crete*; to Bob Anderson to quote from *Stand for New Zealand*; and to Alistair te Ariki Campbell to quote his poem *Retreat: A Marching Song*. Copyright material from the following sources is reproduced with the permission of the quoted publishers: the British Official *History of the Second World War* is Crown Copyright material reproduced with the permission of the Controller of HMSO and the Queen's Printer for Scotland; Foot & Langley's *M.I.9*: PFD; *Australia in the War of 1939-1945* and *Journey to Captivity*: the Australian War Memorial; *Far Above Battle*: Allen & Unwin; *Crete: A Case-Study of an Underdeveloped Area*: Princeton University Press; *Crete: The White Mountains*: Cicerone Press; *The Diaries of Evelyn Waugh*: Orion Publishing Group; *Climax in Crete*: Faber & Faber; Forty's *Battle of Crete* and Pack's *Battle of Crete*: Ian Allen Publishing; *Operation Mercury* and *Anzacs: Stories from New Zealanders at War*: Hodder & Stoughton; *The Struggle for Crete* and *Kia Kaha*: Oxford University Press; *A Sailor's Odyssey* and *Daedalus Returned*: Hutchinson; *A Unique Sort of Battle*: HarperCollins; *Escape From Crete*: Floradale; *Greece to Crete*: Arthur Lambert; *Flowers of Rethymnon*: Kangaroo Press; *Inside Hitler's Greece*: Yale University Press; *Aegean Adventures*: The Book Guild; *A Great Risk in a Good Cause*: Australian Department of Veterans' Affairs; *Brothers at War*: Penguin Group NZ; *Free Lodgings* and *A Near-Run Affair*: Reed; *Officers and Gentlemen* – Penguin Group UK.

'The story of the hundreds of troops who lived for varying spells under the German occupation of Crete is largely unknown. Curiously, since it was an adventure of some proportions, there has been comparatively little published about this lost little corner of the war.'

Harry Gordon: *The Embarrassing Australian: The Story of an Aboriginal Warrior*, page 80.

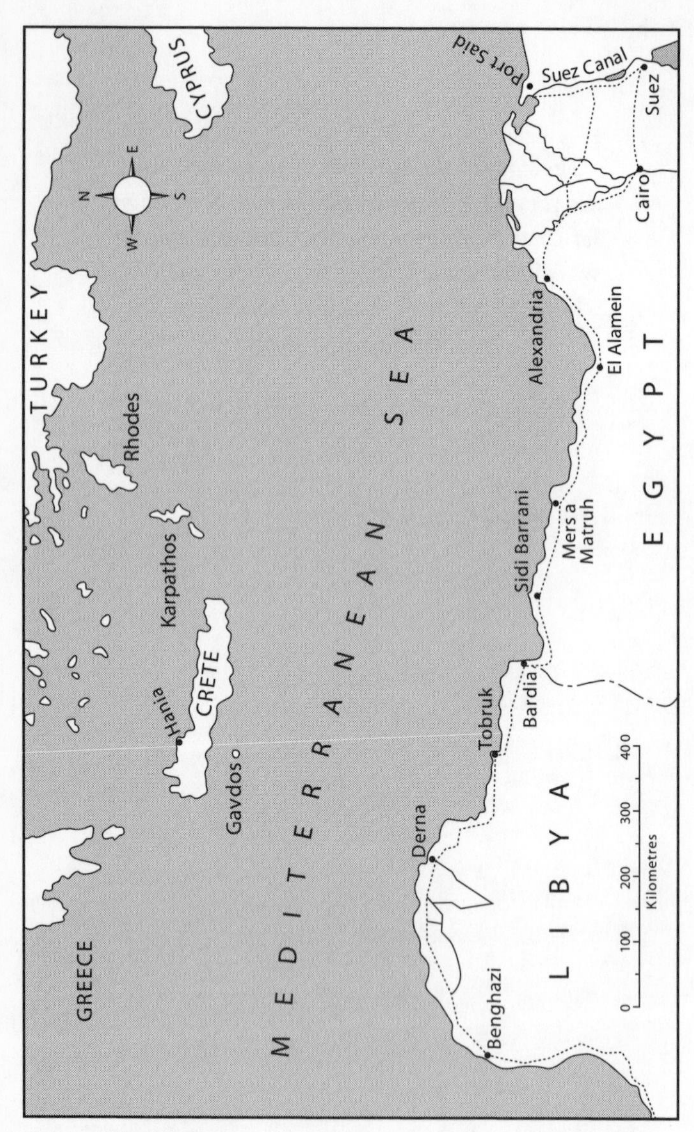

Crete and North Africa

Preface

Seán Damer and Ian Frazer met at the University of Otago in New Zealand in 1999; Seán was a sociologist and Ian an anthropologist. But they soon discovered a mutual obsession with Crete, the 'Great Island' of Greece.

Ian's father, Lieutenant Len Frazer, an Australian Army sapper, had been on the run for a year in the White Mountains following the surrender at the end of the Battle of Crete in 1941. Ian was understandably keen to learn anything which could shed more light upon his father's experiences in Crete, but at that time had only made one preliminary visit to the Great Island.

For his part, Seán had been travelling regularly in Crete since the early 1970s, had led walking parties in the mountains in the early 1980s, had lived in a remote White Mountains village with his Kiwi wife, Helen, from 1985 to 1987 – while conducting an ethnographic study of the local shepherding community – and spoke Greek.

When Ian told Seán that his father had kept a detailed diary throughout his year evading capture, the latter's interest was well and truly aroused, as he had read just about every single book on the Battle of Crete and its aftermath, and the Cretan Resistance. Then he suddenly recalled that in several mountain villages in western Crete, particularly in Koustoyerako in the Selino province, he had been told repeatedly about a fugitive Australian officer during the war and realised that this could only have been Len.

Seán studied Len's diary.[1] Not only did it provide a fascinating insight into the mind of a man on the run, often in extreme physical and mental conditions, but it also offered an equally fascinating look into the culture of the mountain peasantry of western Crete under enemy occupation. Towards the end of 1941, when Len realised that there was a very real chance of his capture by the Germans, he went through his diary and, using an indelible pencil – doubtless army issue! – obliterated the names of all the Cretan villages in which he had received shelter, as well as the identities of all the villagers who had aided him. This was a wise precaution, for the fate of any Cretan who assisted an escaping Allied soldier was the immediate execution of his or her entire family. Hundreds of Cretans were shot in this manner, and photographs of their slaughter are still extant.[2]

However, by dint of a good map, and with his own expert knowledge of the mountain paths, Seán was able to reconstitute the vast majority of the names of the villages, and also those of quite a few of the villagers. He could also deduce the names of local foodstuffs, place names and equipment from Len's phonetic spelling of the Greek. Ian and he began discussing the possibility of publishing the diary as a unique memoir of escapee survival in tough terrain. But they soon discovered that there were quite a few *other* memoirs in existence of this period in Crete, which they began to read systematically. Seán noted that some of the Kiwi soldiers on the run at the same time had encountered an 'Australian officer' hiding out in the mountains, which looked likely to be Len. Ian was able to confirm this surmise by meticulously combing through the various memoirs and triangulating who was in which escapee party, in which place, and at what time, against his father's diary.

The problem with the Anzac memoirs is that several key testimonies were privately published and are not well known.[3] Others were produced by small publishers no longer in existence, or the books are now out of print.[4] Memoirs like Len's manuscript diary, or Dick Huston's manuscript book, have *never* been published, while some have appeared only in Regimental Association magazines, newsletters and the like. Not one of these memoirs had an index in its original form, and only a couple had a map of Crete – usually hopelessly inadequate – and perhaps not surprisingly, many were very hazy about chronology. It is also noteworthy that all of these books were published later on in their authors' lives, often when they were retired. Several contain rather self-conscious discourses on, for example, Cretan history, and grand strategy vis-à-vis the Battle of Crete – knowledge which could not have been available to the authors while they were on the run. There is nothing wrong with this, of course, but at times they constitute rather irritating interruptions to the enthralling narrative of escape and evasion.

It seemed to Ian and Seán, therefore, to be well worth the effort to coordinate these various published and unpublished accounts. It was possible to cross-check them against several sources; namely, the Official British (SOE) Report on the Cretan Resistance,[5] George Psychoundakis's published memoir of the Resistance from a Cretan point of view,[6] the published memoirs of SOE officers Xan Fielding, Billy Moss and Alec Rendel,[7] Murray Elliott's biography of Staff-Sergeant Dudley Perkins,[8] both the Australian and New Zealand *Official Histories* of the campaign in Crete,[9] and numerous unpublished official government and military records in archives and libraries in Australia, New Zealand and the United Kingdom.[10] As their research progressed, it became apparent that all of these sources tell a quite remarkable story. Clearly, this was a book whose time had come.

The title of this book states quite clearly that it is about *Anzac* soldiers on the run. This is quite deliberate on our part. There were also *British* soldiers left behind, whose story is in many ways similar to those of their Anzac comrades-in-arms, but many of them escaped from Crete shortly after the surrender, as we shall see. Thus the Australians and New Zealanders formed a clear majority of the men who were on the run for extended periods of time. This is unsurprising given the Order of Battle in Crete. Our concern is to tell the story of these Dominion troops who had come halfway round the world to fight Fascism in a small country called Greece, about which the vast majority of them knew nothing. It is that fact, together with their exemplary gallantry, both in combat and on the run, which explains the very real and very distinct bond which ensures between Australia and New Zealand, and Crete, to this day. At the time, and in their memoirs, the Australians and New Zealanders referred to themselves as 'British', as will be apparent from some of the quotations which have been reproduced. However, when *we* say 'British' elsewhere in these pages, we mean something or someone to do with the British Isles/United Kingdom, precisely because we wish to maintain the distinction between Australian and New Zealand troops, and those from the UK.

Finally, a word on our system of representing Greek words. The versions of Cretan place names which appear in the various memoirs are frequently wrong – as in 'Sparkia' for 'Sfakia', and 'Galatos' for 'Galatas', for example or make a nonsense of the Greek pronunciation – as in 'Chanea' for 'Hania'. We have followed the conventions of the Modern Greek Studies Association in presenting the words as near to their Greek sound as possible. Thus the south coast village from which the majority of Allied troops were evacuated in May 1941 is properly known as Hora Sfakion, but is widely referred to as Sfakia.

Seán Damer and Ian Frazer
Auckland and Dunedin, 2005

CHAPTER 1

Shock and Shame

Early on the morning of 1 June 1941, the remnants of Creforce, the Australian, British and New Zealand troops on Crete, were ordered to surrender after 12 days of pitched combat. Most were grouped in or around the tiny south coast fishing village of Hora Sfakion, the Royal Navy's evacuation point. New Zealand Gunner James Kinder, who was there, was 'filled with utter horror'. He wrote in his diary:[1]

> One Aussie blew his brains out but that didn't help much and the rest of us prepared for the arrival of the enemy. Most of us were wondering whether the Jerries would feed us, as we were all getting weak with hunger and dysentery which was rife. The latter was the worse of the two and many men were now mere skeletons. We set to work and piled our arms and equipment and then destroyed any papers which might be of use to the enemy.

The experience of these Allied troops involved in the Battle of Crete and its aftermath can only be understood in the light of the expeditionary force sent to mainland Greece earlier in 1941. This was originally known as Lustre Force, and subsequently as 'W' Force.

In April 1939, Britain had guaranteed the sovereignty of Greece in the light of Nazi Germany's occupation of the Czech Sudetenland. However, from a strictly military point of view, Greece had not been

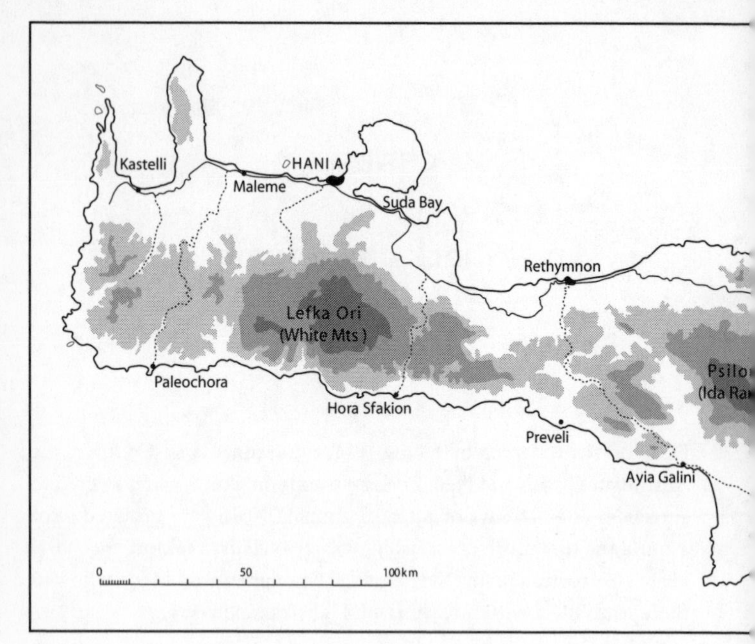

Crete

perceived as a likely theatre of operations; a German invasion was ruled out of the question. But as 1940 dawned, and German intentions in Europe became clearer, Britain committed itself to full-scale support, and General Wavell was sent to Athens. Germany had occupied both Bulgaria and Rumania, and if they attacked in support of their Italian Allies, Greece knew it could not hold out alone. Yet it went out of its way not to provoke the Germans, and did not ask General Wavell for British troops, although Italian arms and trucks captured in the North African campaign were despatched to Greece, along with boots and socks.

When Mussolini invaded Greece in October 1940, Britain immediately sent air support at the request of the Greek government. The Greeks threw the despised Italian *makaronades* – the 'macaroni-bashers'

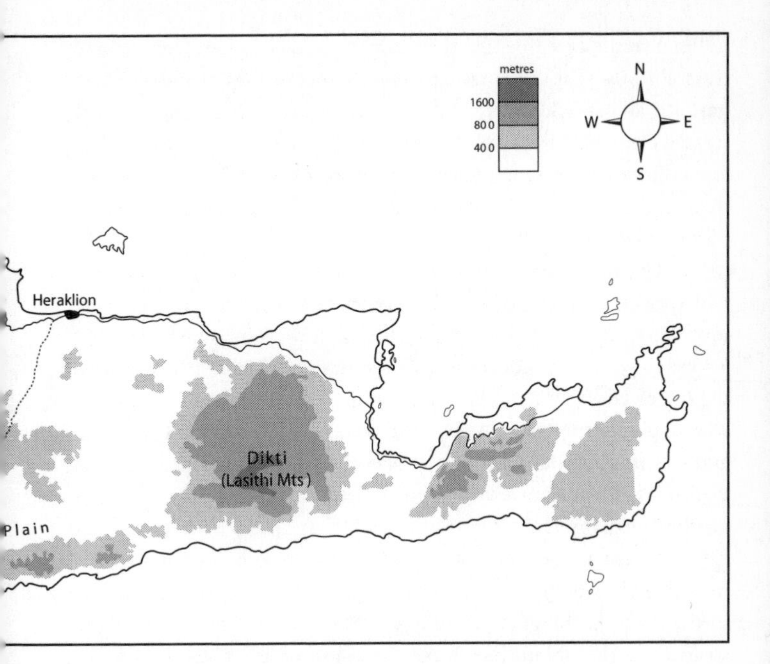

– right out of Greece and pursued them into Albania. However, the ensuing winter proved appalling, and both the Italian and Greek armies were bogged down in deep snow. In February 1941, it became plain that a German attack was imminent, and at the request of the Greeks, and in consultation with Wavell, the British government sent an expeditionary force consisting of one British Armoured Brigade, the New Zealand Division and one Australian division. These fighting troops numbered some 35,000 men, and were deployed in defensive positions in north-eastern Greece, beside three Greek divisions. All the appropriate administrative and support staff, numbering 23,000 men, and RAF aircrew and ground crew were also despatched, the troop movements occurring throughout March 1941. But to some British military observers, this was a nonsensical operation, as it deprived Wavell of some of his best and most experienced fighting units.[2]

Further, the agreement between Britain and both New Zealand and Australia was that the latter's troops were in armies of independent nations, and should be treated accordingly. But Wavell and his staff treated Generals Blamey of Australia and Freyberg of New Zealand as subordinate British generals, and did *not* consult them about deploying their troops, as Tony Simpson demonstrates in his 1981 book *Operation Mercury: The Battle for Crete, 1941*.[3]

The Germans attacked suddenly on 6 April, invading both Yugoslavia and Greece simultaneously. Five German armoured divisions were involved in the attack on Greece, complete with air supremacy and a three-to-one tank advantage. Three days later they had captured the Greek coastal city of Thessaloniki. In spite of heroic resistance in several places, the Greek Army crumbled rapidly, exposing the British and Commonwealth positions. It was all over bar the shouting. The British and Commonwealth troops retired, inflicting heavy casualties on the Germans as they did so. But the fact of the matter was that it was a retreat – dogged, efficient and orderly perhaps, but a retreat nonetheless – in appalling weather. The RAF did what it could, but to the men on the ground, subjected to endless dive-bombing and strafing by the ubiquitous Stukas, it appeared invisible. The 'Adolf Hitler' SS Division turned west, and on 20 April captured the town of Yannina, *behind* the Greek Army fighting in Albania. The Greeks were surrounded, and had no option but to surrender. The British and Commonwealth troops were left in an even more exposed position.

By 21 April, it was clear that further resistance in Greece was impracticable, and the Greek government requested the British withdraw.

Fighting bitter rearguard actions, often using artillery in the first line of defence, and still under constant nerve-wracking aerial attack, the Allied troops withdrew to a series of beaches in southern Greece. Starting on the night of 24 April, the Royal Navy did sterling work in evacuating the troops from Marathon, Porto Rafina and Raftis, but came under German air attack as they headed south, and lost seven ships. Nevertheless, they evacuated some 43,000 Allied troops, although another 15,000 were left behind, either as casualties or prisoners.[4] Of the troops rescued from Greece, about 20,000 exhausted men were disembarked at Souda Bay in Crete. The rest were landed at Alexandria in Egypt – they were the lucky ones. A surprising number of the men left behind managed to find their way to Crete or the Middle East in subsequent weeks, either on Greek caiques, 'borrowed' boats, or with the help of the Royal Navy.

The situation of the troops disembarked on Crete was not encouraging. They had no heavy weapons, no entrenching tools, no transport, no signals, no supplies, and they were exhausted. One officer commented:[5]

> 'W' Force left behind all its equipment. It abandoned more than 8,000 vehicles of one kind and another, all its Anti-Aircraft guns, 25-pounders and most of its mortars and machine-guns. Only a few of its troops managed to smuggle more than their small-arms on board the evacuation ships, since [Admiral] Cunningham's orders to the Navy were to rescue men, not weapons.

On the other hand, the morale of these troops was not bad. They had been forced to retreat, true, but they had been outnumbered and outgunned by a determined enemy with overwhelming air superiority. And they had retreated and been evacuated more or less as fighting units. Some companies of some battalions had become separated from the parent unit and landed in Egypt rather than Crete, but the integrity of the fighting units was maintained, albeit often in substantially lower numbers than had gone to Greece initially. As one New Zealand soldier said:[6]

> The normal number in a battalion was approximately 700 and the 21st [Infantry] Battalion was down to about 240 [on arrival in Crete from Greece]. Those missing were either casualties, taken prisoner or on their way out through the islands, or as some did, through Turkey.

As there is now a substantial literature on the epic Battle of Crete, and as the main turning points are well known, there is no need to rehearse events in detail yet again here. Australian and New Zealand readers are particularly well served by eye-witness accounts, while the *Official Histories* of each nation have the merit of being both clear and well written.[7] Suffice it to say that New Zealand General Bernard Freyberg, the Commander of Creforce – all the Allied troops on Crete – himself knew that Crete would be hard to hold with troops divested of entrenching tools, not to mention all their heavy weapons, and with pitiful air support. Nonetheless, he positioned his troops efficiently to meet the expected main thrust of a German airborne attack, which would be on the airfields at Maleme, west of Hania, Rethimnon and Heraklion. Wavell knew that these would be the main points of attack from ULTRA intelligence, passed this information on to Freyberg, but ordered him first, not to make any dispositions on the basis of ULTRA intelligence *alone*, and secondly, not to mention ULTRA to anyone else on Crete.[8] Another serious problem faced by Freyberg was the knowledge that there might be a seaborne invasion to reinforce the expected parachute drops. Freyberg ordered his men to dig in under the olive trees, camouflage their positions carefully, and wait.

This they did, but as the second week of May rolled into the third, German bombing and strafing increased until it went on all day long. The horror of this continuous, ear-splitting pounding is well remembered by the soldiers on the ground:[9]

> Planes flew over the tree-tops and bombed and machine-gunned us continuously. Unless one has been through an experience such as this, one cannot realise what it is like. All a chap could do was to lie down in his slit trench and say his prayers.

But for all their intensive bombing and air-reconnaissance, the Germans did not actually uncover the strength and dispositions of the Allied infantrymen on the ground.

At Maleme, the expected attack came early in the morning of 20 May, 1941. Initially, the defenders stared with astonishment at the huge airborne invasion fleet, then sprang to their weapons, and began to kill German paratroopers even before they left their planes, in the air, and on the ground. The situation at Rethimnon and Heraklion was identical; the slaughter was appalling. The phrase a 'duck-shoot' appears frequently in the literature. On Day One alone, of 2000 German paratroopers dropped, 1450 were killed outright, out of an estimated total of 4000-plus German dead in Crete. More than 3000 German paratroopers were killed in all.[10]

The New Zealanders, charged with the defence of the Maleme sector, bore the brunt of the fighting, and covered themselves with glory. But, as is now well known, Hill 107 at Maleme was turned by the Germans, the airstrip was taken by pitched fighting, and the west flank of the Allied forces slowly rolled up. The tactical arguments rage to this day. Perhaps Colonel Andrew overlooking Maleme airstrip could have shown more dash in counter-attacking, or at least held his position; perhaps Brigadier Hargest should have shaken off his apparent lethargy; perhaps a reserve battalion should have been committed immediately; perhaps the Greek 5th Regiment at Kastelli should have been summoned; perhaps the coastal defence guns at Souda should have been used to shell Maleme airstrip – but none of these things happened. It has to be remembered that the lack of signalling equipment, combined with total German control of the skies, not to mention the din of battle, all contributed to the turning of the Kiwis' left flank. And, it has to be said, German courage and determination in crash-landing fresh troops on Maleme airstrip, and in the undefended terrain west of the Tavronitis River, meant that Allied defeat was only a matter of time. Heroic actions such as the New Zealanders' storming of enemy-occupied Galatas at bayonet point, the spirited Greek resistance in Prison Valley, and the epic bayonet charge of the Maori Battalion and others at 42nd Street merely prolonged the agony. Freyberg ordered a withdrawal over the White Mountains of western Crete to the tiny coastal village of Hora Sfakion, where the Royal Navy would come to the rescue yet again.

Nobody who was on that retreat, through the villages of Vrisses, Askyfou, and Imbros, has ever forgotten it, and there are many graphic descriptions of the long columns of men staggering over the mountains. Some contain surreal vignettes of badly wounded soldiers gamely heading for Hora Sfakion: soldiers like Gunner Charles Jager of the Australian Artillery marching in bare feet, incredibly, their boots having collapsed or been stolen;[11] shell-shocked soldiers; soldiers who had shed all notions of discipline; soldiers who still marched in organised units; soldiers who to a man were all exhausted, hungry, thirsty and hot. Some died of exhaustion, some simply gave up the ghost, while a determined rearguard kept the Germans at bay, inflicting heavy casualties in the withdrawal.

The young medical officer, Lieutenant Theo Stephanides, remembered it well:[12]

> I knew that I was taking part in a retreat; in fact I wondered if it should not be called more correctly a rout as, on all sides, men were hurrying along in disorder. Most of them had thrown away their rifles, and a number had even discarded their tunics, as it was a hot day . . . Nearly every yard of the road and the ditches on either side were strewn with abandoned arms and accoutrements, blankets, gasmasks, packs, kitbags, sun-helmets, cases and containers of all shapes and sizes, tinned provisions and boxes of cartridges and hand grenades.

And a Maori poet sums it all up in a poem called: *Retreat: A Marching Song*, honouring the indomitable 28th (Maori) Battalion:[13]

White Mountains, I tell you, we're sick
of the sight of you, sick of your
steep road, twisting and turning
like a kaumatua's walking-stick. We have one
aim: to escape the enemy's fingers
tightening around our throats by
withdrawing over your pass; walking
single file on each side of the road,
ready to dive into a ditch whenever
an enemy aircraft appears; stepping over
abandoned equipment, and around teeming
stragglers. We will carry our
wounded, and distribute the loads
of our exhausted comrades among those
with less to carry. Some day we will

make a stand, but where and when, only time
and Tu of the blood-red face will tell.
Meanwhile, old mates, we will take
care of each other. No Maori will be left
behind. We won't rest until we free from
our throats the enemy's stranglehold.

The Royal Navy began evacuating troops from the tiny fishing village of Hora Sfakion on the night of 28 May, the ninth day of the Battle of Crete. That night, somewhat more than a thousand men were embarked, including most of the wounded.[14] An Australian medical officer described these men:[15]

> Walking wounded? What a misnomer! Men wounded in the arms and upper body, doing their best to help even more unfortunate comrades wounded in the legs. Men with broken arms helping men with broken legs, the sightless being led by the more fortunate, even stretcher cases carried by wounded men . . . All this in a comparative silence of pain and stoicism . . . A Greek civilian doctor did what he could with a plentiful supply of aspirin and a few shell dressings.

Several thousand were still making their way down mountain paths and gorges towards the village, while others holed up in caves in the area. Evelyn Waugh provides an acid description of the latter:[16]

> All the caves were full of ragged, starving, neurotic Australians who had run away earlier. Whenever an aircraft was heard, often when it was not, they shouted, 'Aircraft, take cover!' and shot at anyone who moved about. One could hear the wail being passed from cave to cave down the gorge. Some of them had Cretan women living with them in the caves; at night these men sallied forth to raid ration dumps. Some were starving but some had large stores of food they stole in this way.

While it cannot be denied that Waugh was there, on the face of it, it seems most unlikely that Cretan women would have been 'living' with these soldiers, given the conservative morality of the mountain

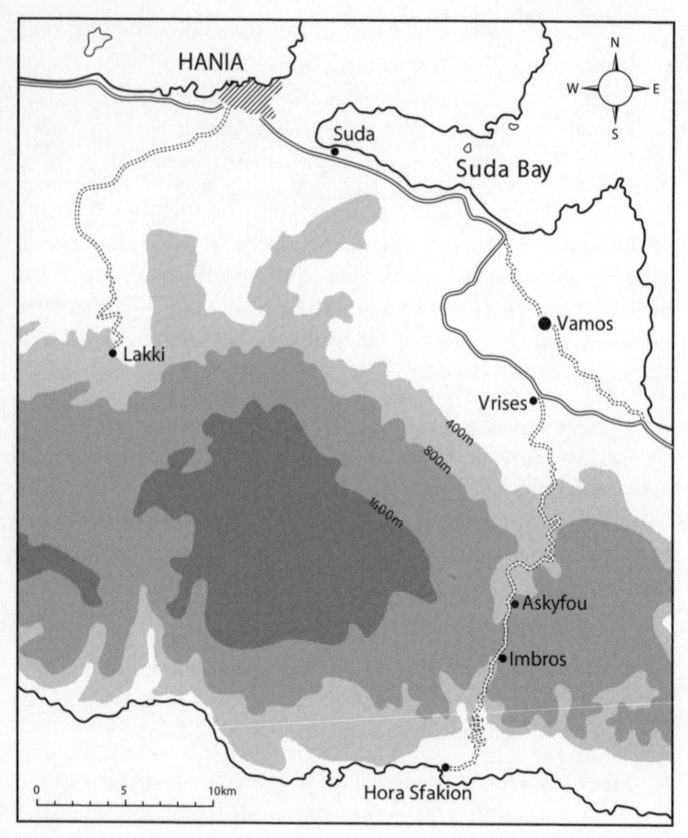

The route of retreat

villagers. The waiting troops were in fact given an astonishing example of the fighting spirit of the local women.[17]

> Near Sfakion a group of armed Cretan women approached the troops waiting evacuation, offering food and wine, and demanding rifles. 'If there is any one of you who can no longer carry his gun, he should either destroy it or hand it over to us, so that the Germans don't get

their hands on it. Tomorrow we'll need it again. The battle has not ended for us.'

The evacuation continued on the nights of the 29th and the 30th, when another 15,000 men were embarked,[18] with troops still staggering down the steep mountain paths towards Hora Sfakion. There was, in fact, considerable confusion in the areas leading down to the beach where troops waited their turn for embarkation, and it is clear that there was some disgraceful behaviour by men pretending to be either Movement Control Officers, Embarkation Officers, or from the fighting units such as the New Zealand 5th Brigade, which were given priority in the evacuation. Further, some non-combatant units became quickly demoralised, as Sergeant Tarrant of the NZ 18th Battalion noted in his diary:[19]

> *Monday – 2nd June [1941]*
> As soon as it was dark, we set off again for the beach [at Sfakia], our party having grown to 50-odd in the meantime. We got mixed up with some Cypriots and felt like shooting the swines as they were absolutely out of control and in a state bordering on panic.

Eighteen-year-old Private (subsequently Sergeant) Sonny Sewell of the Maori Battalion, who was successfully evacuated, put his survival down to an unworldly experience on the retreat:[20]

> I put it down to an episode in Crete. We were just sitting there one day, and I looked down as I felt this thing crawling up my leg. It was a little lizard, about this big. I just put my hand down, and it climbed into my hand. An uncle of mine came over, and said, 'Where did you get that?' I said, 'I just picked it up.' He said, 'You're alright. That's our family guardian. The lizard, the green lizard.' He said, 'You and I will get off this island. You and I will get home without a mark.'

(It is good to report that both Sonny and his uncle did get off Crete safely, and did survive the remainder of the war.)

The last night of the evacuation was 31 May. An eyewitness recalls the final moments:[21]

The last ferries pushed off about half-past-two in the morning. Thousands of men stood watching them go, watching practically their last hope of escape disappear into the darkness of the Mediterranean night. Some of them, men of unconquerable spirit, struck off along the coast or into the hills, hoping to slip through the German cordon which was steadily drawing in around them. Many others slumped down where they had stood and slept to await the coming of day – and the Germans. They knew defeat at last.

A moving musical tribute accompanied these disappearing ferries:[22]

As the last barges pulled out, New Zealand troops both in the barges and on the shore began to sing the 'Maoris' Farewell'. The Australians began to sing the English words . . . 'Now is the hour, when we must say farewell.' The men who had been saved by a matter of minutes and the men who were virtually lost sang it together, and tough, unshaven men wept a little. It was the sort of scene that would undoubtedly have looked hammily, stickily sentimental in a Hollywood war film; on the beach at Sphakia it was spontaneous and natural. For many men on the beach, it was a hymn of unlikely hope.

Evelyn Waugh provides a fictional account of the immediate aftermath:[23]

The golden dawn was changing to unclouded blue. Guy led his section down the rough path to the harbour. The quay was littered with abandoned equipment and the wreckage of bombardment. Among the scrap and waste stood a pile of rations – bully beef and biscuit – and a slow-moving concourse of soldiers foraging. Sergeant Smiley pushed his way through them and passed back half-a-dozen tins. There was a tap of fresh water running to waste in the wall of a ruined building. Guy and his section filled their bottles, drank deep, refilled them, turned off the tap; then breakfasted. The little town was burned, battered, and deserted by its inhabitants. The ghost of an army teemed everywhere. Some were quite apathetic, too weary to eat; others were smashing their rifles on the stones, taking a fierce relish in this symbolic farewell to their arms; an officer stamped on his binoculars; a motor

> bicycle was burning; there was a small group under a sapper Captain doing something to a seedy-looking fishing-boat that lay on its side, out of the water, on the beach. One man sat on the sea-wall methodically stripping down his Bren and throwing the parts separately far into the scum. A very short man was moving from group to group saying: 'Me surrender? Not bloody likely. I'm for the hills. Who's coming with me?' like a preacher exhorting a doomed congregation to flee from the wrath to come.

Although the Royal Navy had performed a near miracle in evacuating some 16,000 troops from Hora Sfakion and elsewhere, it was at appalling cost. Two cruisers and four destroyers were sunk, all by dive-bombing, along with 1828 seamen killed, and 183 wounded.[24] One battleship, two cruisers and four destroyers were also severely damaged.[25]

For the troops left behind, defeat was an awful reality. New Zealand Army Service Corps Driver Peter Winter must have spoken for many men when he said:[26]

> Shocked, shamed and humiliated to a state of abject misery, we milled about the tiny village of Sfakia. Our brains could not cope with the truth. We snarled at each other and hated each other. A fury, like sickness, dulled the senses. My hatred was greater than my hunger.

Lieutenant Colonel Le Souef, the senior Australian medical officer, said much the same:[27]

> There was a certain sullen resignation mixed with consternation and incredulity on every face.

Kiwi Driver Farley agreed:[28]

> God Almighty! What a blow. A Prisoner of War. Me, I had had visions of wounds, death from various causes, including a fight to the finish in the event of a hand to hand go, but a prisoner, never. It was something I had never reckoned on. The realisation was stupefying, dumb-founding. In all my previous existence and I then had nearly 35 years of it, [never] had I received news that knocked me all of a heap as this had.

New Zealand Private Arthur Lambert commented on this:[29]

I think he spoke for all of us; you see, we had never been briefed on the subject, or how to behave in this situation.

Australian Private Jack Ulrick said:[30]

Becoming a prisoner was the last thing anyone thought of – it was really the low card in the deck . . . This was the big low in my life. Here we were badly wounded . . . and when we became prisoners it finally sank in. We thought, 'Well that's bloody lovely. Here's the mob, they've gone – they've cleared out, they've left us here.' That was our feeling – we'd been left behind, the mob had gone. And I think if the Jerries had asked us then we would have joined their flamin' army.

For some poor men – a few like the Australian mentioned at the beginning of this chapter – it was all too much to take, and they shot themselves:[31]

A shot cracks. Shock, or shame, has been too much for the demented Pom. His friend, cradling him with one arm, disgustedly wipes a ghastly mess from his shirt with the other.

Several thousand British, Australian and New Zealand troops were left behind. The official New Zealand War Historian says:[32]

Estimates by those on the spot say about 5000; enemy claims for 1 June were 3000, but by 2 June *5 [German] Mountain Division* was claiming 6500 and this figure seems not unlikely.

While many of these troops were non-combatant, their number also included fighting formations like the 2/7th Australian Battalion, much of a Royal Marines Battalion, and the commandos of Layforce. They had been a major part of the rearguard, and although scheduled for evacuation, were left behind in the confusion of the last night.

These troops were ordered to surrender on the morning of 1 June. The men of the Australian 2/7 Battalion could not believe it, and were about to open fire on the soldiers they saw waving white flags.[33] But the arrival of German mountain troops made the bitter reality evident, and soon a long column of demoralised and dejected Allied troops was climbing back up the tortuous mountain paths it had so recently and so painfully descended.

At the start of the Second World War, there was virtually no training for Allied soldiers in what is now called (i) escape and evasion; (ii) resistance to interrogation; (iii) survival; and (iv) what to say and do if taken prisoner. New Zealand Second Lieutenant Sandy Thomas, badly wounded in the fighting at Galatas, and taken prisoner, remembers that all Kiwi soldiers knew somehow or another that if captured, you were supposed to supply to the enemy your name, rank and number, and nothing else – but this was not the topic of any specific training or instruction as such. Soldiers were not told that it was their *duty* to escape.[34]

In other words, the 6500 or so soldiers who became prisoners of war of the Germans at the beginning of June 1941 in Crete were left entirely to their own devices. The following chapters outline how these men – and their civilian Cretan allies – constructed the devices which not only permitted them to escape, but also to survive in enemy-occupied Crete for, in some cases, up to two years, before eventual evacuation to North Africa, or capture. It is to these men, and the Cretan men, women and children who aided them on the run, that this chronicle is dedicated.

CHAPTER 2

Denying Defeat: The Evaders

Before the stories of the soldiers on the run in Crete are told, we have to make a distinction between two categories of fugitives. They were either *escapers* or *evaders*. The official history of MI9, the secret British wartime organisation responsible for escape and evasion in enemy-occupied territory, makes the distinction plain:

> An escaper is someone who, having been captured, gets away; an evader was never in enemy hands.[1]

This chapter describes initial attempts at evasion by the men left behind on Crete, and offers a preliminary analysis of the early successful ventures.

Exit from Sfakia

Major R. Garrett, RM, who was the officer commanding the Royal Marines in the rearguard, and who had been left behind at Sfakia, was perhaps the most celebrated evader. He seized the initiative and commandeered one of the three abandoned Motor Landing Craft (MLC), which had been used to ferry the troops out from Hora Sfakion to the warships which were evacuating them. However:[2]

> [b]oth engines were out of action, with a wire hawser wound tightly round the port propeller.

Unbeknownst to Garrett, this craft had already been reconnoitered by Australian Lance-Corporal Ian Walker of 2/7 Battalion, who had then gone to collect his own party, which included his officer brother, Lieutenant Keith Walker.[3]

> When I got back to the beach I found that an English Major [Garrett] had taken charge of the barge and he had a party of his own troops. I saw him and asked permission for our party to come aboard and after telling him we could repair the engines he consented.

The craft is described by Lieutenant Walker:[4]

> It was an all steel, flat-bottomed barge about 30' long and 15' wide, and propelled by two Chrysler 6-cylinder engines. The front of the barge was hinged and the rear end was situated [sic] steering wheel and ship's compass.

Happily, he was the:[5]

> Australian officer, an engineer who commanded a Bren carrier platoon, [who] managed to get the starboard engine working.

At 0855 on 1 June, Garrett set sail to the south with a party consisting of:[6]

> 3 English officers, 2 Australians, 23 Australian O.R.s, 8 New Zealanders, 96 British soldiers, 3 Palestinians, 1 Maltese and 1 Greek.

Of the 96 British soldiers, 56 were Garrett's own Marines. Fortunately, the MLC was hidden from the Luftwaffe by a heavy heat haze, and a couple of miles offshore, he picked up a naked New Zealander, Private W. A. Hancox of 1 General Hospital, paddling south on a large plank! Hancox had swum out to sea to pick up an abandoned rowing boat, but it was collected by another party of soldiers before he could reach it.[7]

After three hours, motoring on only one screw (the other was fouled), Garrett reached the island of Gavdos, where they were able to clear the second screw. The crew was organised as follows:[8]

> Major Garrett, skipper; myself [Lt. Keith Walker], Chief Engineer; an English Sergeant, Sgt. Colwell, 2nd Engineer; Cpl. Ian Walker,

3rd Engineer; Lt. McCartney [sic], (the only other Aussie officer), Assistant Navigator; 2nd Lt. Bavie, Royal Navy Quartermaster; plus other N.C.O.s detailed for minor duties.

This pot-pourri of the British Empire set off again that night, the men jam-packed on top of each other. Young Australian Lieutenant Macartney describes the situation:[9]

> At night there was not enough room for everyone to lie down, and many had to snatch their sleep in half-standing positions.

At 0400, the steering gear broke down. Macartney again:[10]

> Repairs took some hours, but shortly after dawn we were under way again. About 9 o'clock the petrol was very low. A four-gallon tin of paraffin was mixed with the few remaining gallons and worked quite satisfactorily. Land was not in sight when the fuel gave out, and having tried dieseline unsuccessfully, we started to drift . . .

The men found another 10-gallon drum of petrol unexpectedly, as Ian Walker recounts:[11]

> On the fourth day out, a ten-gallon drum of petrol was found but after we had restarted the engine, the clutch of the second engine broke down. After failing to effect repairs, we changed the gearbox and clutch from one engine to the other. This was no easy job due to the limited space and the fact that nearly everyone was seasick and weak from the lack of food and water. The ration of half a biscuit, with enough bully beef to cover the surface, and a quarter of a milk tin of water per day, was hardly sufficient to keep everyone on their feet. Any effort to do manual tasks was terrible.

All this time, a rigorous lookout was maintained, and the men tried to attract the attention of passing aircraft by creating an oil slick with the dieseline, and making flares out of the cordite from cartridge cases. Lieutenant Macartney continues the story:[12]

> For the next three days we drifted aimlessly about on the ocean, during which time a despondent Palestinian committed suicide. On the fifth

> day, a sail was made by lacing several blankets together with bootlaces and the barge got under way. However, when she veered off course, the fit men had to jump into the water and push her nose around, so that she could catch the breeze . . . On the sixth day there was no breeze. On the seventh a British soldier died of exposure. By the eighth all men were very weak.

Lieutenant Keith Walker describes an al fresco church parade, when there was only enough of the meagre supplies for two more days:[13]

> On the Sunday morning, Major Garrett conducted the service and it was really marvellous, all knelt and prayed together – all creeds, denominations, Jews, Greeks, and all together. It was great, it seemed to raise the spirits of the lads one hundred percent . . .

The next morning, the 9th of June, at 0230, the exhausted and dehydrated men beached 17 miles west of Sidi Barrani, behind British lines. (The illustration on the back cover of this book is a painting of this episode immortalised by the New Zealand war artist Peter McIntyre.)

A second MLC from Sfakia, skippered by Australian Private Harry Richards, with New Zealand Private A. H. Taylor as engineer, which had in fact passed Garrett's craft earlier, also succeeded in reaching Egypt, with about 60 men on board.[14]

The Commanding Officer of the Australian 2/7 Battalion, which had covered the retreat as a disciplined fighting unit, gave his men the option of waiting for the Germans or striking off in the hope of finding a boat. Substantial elements of this battalion promptly opted for evasion:[15]

> Then, for the first time, the battalion broke up into little pieces. Some headed left along the coast, some right, and some decided that they'd have more hope hiding out in the hills for a few days, until the 'heat' was off.
>
> Other Australians promptly did the same:[16]

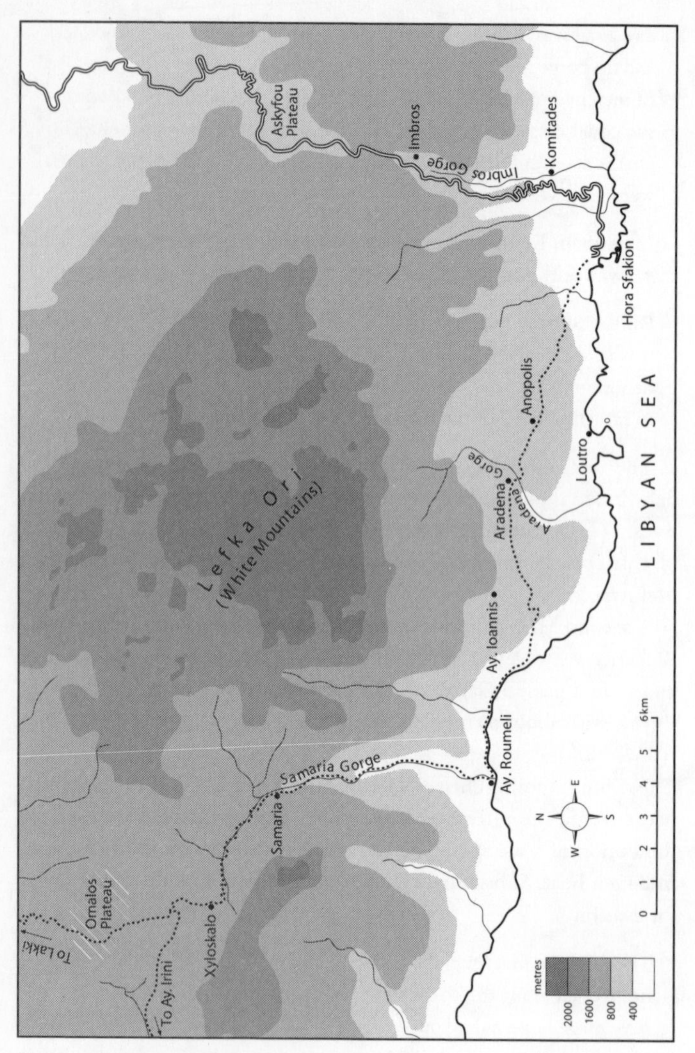

Len's evasion route

On June 1 other 2/2 men also decided to avoid enemy capture, but did so by staying on the island. One group of fifteen joined forces, electing Sergeant Bill Ryan as their leader. Arming themselves with revolvers, taken from the huge pile on Sphakia beach, Ryan's party set off into the mountains, meeting up with Cretan shepherds, who sold them food. On their second day, Ryan's men banded together with other Australian troops, 2/1 and 2/11 escapees from the fighting at Rethymo.

Ian's father, Lieutenant Len Frazer, of the 2/8 Field Company, Royal Australian Engineers, was another evader from Sfakia, albeit one unacknowledged until the publication of this book. Here is how he reacted to the initial order to surrender.[17]

Sunday – 1 June 1941
Lt. Col. Colvin informed us that British intended to capitulate at 0830 hrs, that we should go out of town to avoid casualties. I was staggered. It was 0615 when self plus 6 (3 from 2/8 Field Company – Norm Wiseman, Con Curtain, and Ron Chambers) left. Boys collected frying pan on way out of town, 5 fowls, 2 pieces of stale bread taken off table, a 2 gal. tin, a biscuit tin. Met many Greeks on track, some Australians, Major Regan and his Force HQ (21 AR) making for Agia Roumeli in hope of being picked up by Royal Navy. After hurried conference over old map we decided on the same objective. Agia Roumeli is 1.5 days march. The nearer bay of Loutro we rejected as being too close to Sfakia. Our party in exuberant spirits trecking [sic] in single file to the west with stolen rations and utensils. For some reason very happy. The last few days have been full of uncertainty with no food, no concrete orders, more and more troops flooding into already congested areas. Now we are unfettered, our freedom depending entirely on our own wits.

A final evader from the Sfakia area was Australian Private Vic Solomon of the 2/2 Battalion. He describes what happened when he learned that they were supposed to surrender:[18]

I realised that we were caught like rats in a trap and having to lay down our arms. I wandered around talking to the boys and finally decided to make a break. Darby Munro and myself had persuaded Brookie and

> another chap to come with us, when who should turn up but our old Sergeant-Major Bill Ryan with about a dozen of the boys . . . We got together and elected Bill as our leader, and as there were 16 in our party decided not to let any more join us.

These 16 Australians armed themselves with pistols from a heap of discarded arms, and took off to the east, in the opposite direction to Len Frazer. We shall meet these men again soon.

Exit from Ayia Galini

It should not be forgotten that there were separate actions in the battle of Crete at both Rethimnon and Heraklion, east of Hania. In both areas, British and Australian troops, and their Greek allies, had counter-attacked the German paratroops vigorously, inflicted very heavy casualties on them, and pinned them down. Unaware of what was happening in the Maleme sector, they believed they had the Germans beaten. But at Heraklion, the 14 Infantry Brigade received orders to evacuate on the night of 28/29 May; the Royal Navy was coming to pick them up. This evacuation was carried out silently, and with clockwork precision, and 3486 troops – and four Cretan girlfriends! – were embarked successfully.[19] (Tragically, they were to sustain heavy casualties at sea from dive-bombing.) However, one platoon of the Black Watch, which had blocked the road into Heraklion from the south at Knossos, never received the evacuation order, and they were to turn up in the ranks of both escapers and evaders.

At Rethimnon, there were two Australian infantry battalions, the 2/1st commanded by a Regular Army officer, Lieutenant-Colonel Ian Campbell, and the 2/11th Battalion, commanded by Major Ray Sandover. They were reinforced by two Australian machine-gun platoons, and an ill-equipped and trained Greek regiment. Campbell commanded this makeshift brigade. By 29 May, they knew something was badly wrong when they were told the British had evacuated Heraklion. This reverse was confirmed the next day when large German forces approached and called upon them to surrender. An interesting difference of opinion then took place between the two battalion commanders. Beevor summarises it thus:[20]

> As a regular soldier, however, his [Campbell's] view of the hopeless situation followed the rules of war to negotiated surrender. Sandover, an accountant and businessman, believed that every man should be given the chance to get away, and he proposed to lead those of his men who wanted to try their luck over the hills. The two men . . . agreed to differ and wished each other luck.

Campbell was to be a POW for the rest of the war. Sandover picks up the story:[21]

> We left Battalion HQ at a fast pace intending to make for the south coast . . . The climb is a steep one . . . The party with me was some 20 strong, but there were many others following. Near Timbakion we reached the beach and walked along it to Ay Galini the little fishing village . . . Here we found a large group of Black Watch-Argylls-Yorks & Lancs together with a few RAF and Marines. There were two abandoned landing craft – very little food and a number of wounded.

Thereafter, the story resembles that of Major Garrett. Corporal Mortimer of the 2/11 tells what happened to these craft.[22]

> Both had been washed ashore and were in a damaged condition. One was a 'write-off' with both propellers twisted, the rudder useless and little chance of refloating it. The other had prospects, one propeller was intact, steering gear seemed OK and with the exception of batteries and coils the engines looked OK . . . there were a few trucks up the coast at Timbakion and their batteries may be OK. Basil Avery and I set off to walk up the beach and if OK, bring back the batteries.

These two men – and Mortimer was barefoot – returned with batteries, coils and condensers, while the rest of the party laboured all day with poles trying to lever the salvageable MLC into the water. Just as the engine was repaired and tested, a German three-man motorcycle patrol appeared, and a firefight ensued. This galvanised the launching party and the MLC was soon afloat. Mortimer again:[23]

> With so many helpers to launch the barge and a limited carrying capacity the unenviable task of selecting crew and passengers was left to our C.O. Major Sandover, some 77 all ranks including about 12 from our Battalion.

The MLC took off on 2 June; gallantly, Sandover headed for the hills with the rest of his men. The skipper of the MLC was Private Bishop of the 2/3 Australian Field Regiment, who said:[24]

> It was accepted that I should be in charge because of my experience with yachts and other small craft, so we provisioned our barge with some cooked potatoes from the village vegetable gardens and some bully beef contributed by the Black Watch contingent.

Spare fuel was organised:[25]

> A South African pilot, Sgt McWilliam, known as Big Mac . . . organised a party to drain the tanks of a Glenn Martin aircraft crash landed on the beach nearby.

The barge was well organised, as Mortimer recalls:[26]

> A roll call was held and a roster of jobs drawn up. As it was impossible for all of us to lie down at once numerous lookouts were appointed to watch the left front, front and right front, left and right sides and rear, two to bail and one on the compass.

Although halted by an Italian submarine which took off all the officers, except for one, Lieutenant Bedells of 2/11 Battalion, who had been wounded in the firefight, and a:[27]

> 2nd lieutenant from the Black Watch who had refrained from leaving the barge on the grounds that he had a cold and didn't want to get wet.

And while Flight Lieutenant Gill from the South African Air Force drowned in the transfer, this MLC also eventually reached safety near Mersa Matruh in North Africa.[28]

A completely single-handed evader was Private 'Tich' Carroll, of the 2/11 Australian Battalion, whose story is truly amazing. Carroll was stranded at Ayia Galini, but 'liberated' a 16-foot Greek fishing boat which did not even have rowlocks or oars. Undaunted, he improvised:[29]

> The search for rigging yielded a six ft. length of oregon, which became the mast, a fishing spear with a five ft. handle made a good peak when I broke the centre prong to form the jaws, and the boom I made from four bamboo sticks lashed together. The straps from the ration chocolate tins formed the loop, which allowed the boom to swing on the mast. From the flour mill I borrowed a piece of lightweight canvas for a sail of sorts.

Carroll set sail due south on 11 June, with six tins of chocolate and two gallons of water:[30]

> Several uneventful days passed . . . By now I was pretty badly sunburned and my eyes were badly affected by constant salt spray and the glare of mid-ocean.

On the eighth day, he reckoned he could see land:[31]

> As the sun rose I saw that unmistakeable haze away to the south . . . Taking a chance I altered course and pushed the old tub obliquely across the waves, which were still quite high. In my eagerness to reach land this decision proved my undoing . . . when land looked only a few miles off, the mast smashed a hole in the bottom and my dreams of sailing into Alexandria went with it . . . Tying my tunic to the rudder clamps, I fixed the water tin – almost empty by now – across my shoulders and decided to swim ashore . . . For seven hours I surfed, floated and swam . . . I could see a small stretch of sand between some rocky outcrops, but several jagged rocks were between me and that sand . . . I waited for a really big wave and took off with the water tin braced to take the impact. As I surfed over those sharp, rugged rocks I could almost feel my chest and stomach being ripped asunder. The next moment I was being spun and rolled in all directions. I scrambled clear on my hands and knees and lay there for some time. I couldn't bear the glare of the white sand.

Carroll was behind British lines. What happened when he had recovered – which was remarkably quickly, all things considered – was to prove significant for his comrades-in-arms left behind in Crete.[32]

> On arrival at Mersa Matruh I was taken to see the Camp Commandant, an English Brigadier . . . I told him about the chaps hiding in the mountains [in Crete] and that I was confident that quite a few could be rescued and the sooner the better.

Private Carroll richly deserved the Military Medal he was subsequently awarded.

Wounded Evaders

At this juncture, it is also important to note the existence of a small, but signifiant, subcategory of evaders. These were Commonwealth soldiers who had been wounded, but were never captured, who somehow or another staggered into safety, and were cared for by Cretan families. Three of these men who will reappear in our history were Ned Nathan and Joe Angell, from the 28th Maori Battalion, and Ken Little of the 21st Battalion. Both of the former were wounded in the counter-attack on Maleme airstrip on 22 May 1941. Nathan describes what happened to him:[33]

> I was wounded. I got machine-gun fire in the hip. My worst wound was my face, because I lost the sight of one eye and I lost the use of my jaw. I broke the bone, and that's the injury that caused most of the pain.

But both Nathan and Angell managed to evade capture, and made their way into the interior. Nathan got to Elos and then Sklavopoula where he was attended by a Cretan doctor.

Ken Little was with the Kiwi detachment at Kastelli charged with training and leading a scratch unit formed of the 1st Greek Regiment, plus Greek officer-cadets, plus Cretan irregulars, to defend the town against the imminent German attack. When it came, this composite unit killed 54 German paratroopers, wounded 20 and captured 28 by noon, the latter being lodged in the town jail to protect them from the fury of the local inhabitants.[34] However, a few days later, the jail was hit during a bombing raid, and the prisoners escaped. Ken Little was hit by an explosive bullet fired by a sniper. He recounts what happened:[35]

> it wasn't much later that John Friend found me and alternatively carried and dragged me to a small village called Sfinarion about twelve miles away . . . Here, an old Greek who some thirty years before had been a medical student in Salt Lake City in America, was sent for to tend my wounds. He produced a very large, very old syringe and proceeded to fill it with iodine. It came as quite a surprise to me that nothing untoward became of me after that horrific injection.

As the Germans were by now searching for Allied soldiers in the area, Ken, delirious with shock and in great pain, was moved on the back of a mule to a remote chapel in the mountains. The ex-medical student, known as Johnny, tended to his wounds along with the local priest and village women:[36]

> A local fiery spirit called tsikoudia, an overproof alcohol, was used to swab the two external wounds, after which a tsikoudia-soaked rag was used as a pull-through from one side of my hip to the other. It was absolutely tortuous [sic] and I might add that without a good deal of the tsikoudia inside me, I would not have been a very good patient. However my wounds showed no sign of infection and over the weeks slowly began to heal.

Like Ned Nathan and Joe Angell, Ken Little was completely dependent upon the humanitarianism of Cretan villagers until his wounds eventually healed.

Summary

It is evident from the foregoing testimony that, apart from the wounded, all of these evaders shared a couple of characteristics in common. Firstly, there was a uniform denial of defeat. They might have lost the Battle of Crete, but they had not lost the war. And secondly, they took immediate, imaginative and decisive action. Not surprisingly, the most enterprising troops commandeered all the remaining landing craft. They were not deterred by the fact that these vessels were damaged and unseaworthy. Using their wits and their own resources – for instance, cannibalising army trucks for batteries, coils and condensers, and improvising rigging where none existed – they repaired these craft and made them seaworthy again. It is also noteworthy that the method by which these MLCs were manned was democratic; it was *negotiated* amongst the troops, whether officers or men. The competent Australian engineers bargained a passage with Major Garrett's Royal Marines. Major Sandover selected men from the different units represented at Ayia Galini, but gallantly did not vote himself as senior officer onto the barge. This quick and effective action returned a total of over 300 men to the British, Australian and New Zealand fighting forces in North Africa, within just a couple of weeks of the surrender in Crete – which constitutes a supreme irony given General Weston's original order for *all* troops to surrender, and underlines the heroism of these resourceful evaders.

The soldiers who arrived at Ayia Galini from the fighting at Rethimnon and Heraklion had one distinct advantage over those at Sfakia: they had no Germans in hot pursuit. True, an isolated motorcycle-and-sidecar patrol comprising three men *did* arrive as the Allied soldiers were trying to lever the salvaged MLC into the sea. But in the ensuing firefight these Germans were kept at bay long enough for the troops to float the barge. Further, the Germans were heavily outnumbered, and did not press their attack. This numerical advantage undoubtedly facilitated the local escape, but does not detract from the initiative taken by the British and Commonwealth troops in question.

Furthermore, the manning and sailing of these MLCs in seas, and over distances, for which they were not designed, speaks volumes for the discipline of these troops, and the efficient operation of a chain of command. Major Garrett, as a Royal Marines officer trained with boats, was a natural and effective skipper of his MLC. But elsewhere, as has been seen, a Private soldier who was a peacetime yachtsman was the elected skipper of a second MLC. And at sea, these craft were operated as professionally as if the Royal Navy had supplied the crews: watches and lookouts were established, men with mechanical and engineering skills manned the engine-rooms, food and water was scrupulously rationed, morale was maintained by a church service, and imaginative signalling devices were fashioned. There were no mutinies, there was no nonsense, and if there was any whingeing, it is singularly absent from the memoirs. These evaders were first-class soldiers, who used their own initiative. But they were only a *tiny* minority of the men left behind after the evacuation from Crete. It is to the story of the vast majority that we must now turn.

CHAPTER 3

For You the War is Over: POWs & Escapers

Prisoners of War

The vast majority of the troops left behind at Hora Sfakion surrendered. They were so exhausted and demoralised that the thought of doing anything else simply did not enter their minds. Peter Winter put it like this:[1]

> Why I did not walk off with my rifle and 40 precious rounds I do not know. The thought did not occur to me. Perhaps the Army had done the job of destroying initiative all too well, for there was nothing to stop me.

The enemy which came to round up the Allied soldiers at Sfakia was the 100th Mountain Regiment, Austrian Alpine troops; and initially, relationships were good, as they frequently are between front-line troops, with the Austrians giving out cigarettes, and what rations they could spare. The Australian *Official History* of the Battle of Crete recounts the following incident, as Colonel Walker, the senior officer left on the island, went to surrender to an Austrian officer.[2]

> 'What are you doing here, Australia?' the Austrian said in English. 'One might ask what are you doing here, Austria?' replied Walker. 'We are all Germans,' he said.

But the harsh reality of being prisoners of war soon became apparent.

As the Allied troops trudged painfully back up the mountain path they had so recently descended, Australian Private Charles Jager – who, it will be remembered, had lost his boots – described it like this:[3]

If the retreat of a beaten army is bitter, to retrace these steps is heartbreaking. Every yard is shameful, littered with abandoned gear; rifles, bayonets, ammo, waterbottles, banjos, an officer's blue dress uniform spilling from a suitcase. But as I hop barefoot, picking a tortuous way over stones as sharp as razors, handicapped by stubbed toes, diarrhoea and an empty belly, nothing's so painful as the humiliation of surrender.

Driver Winter again:[4]

The return over the mountains took three grim days. It was sickening to return along the route of our retreat. The bodies of hundreds of our compatriots lay unburied in the olive groves and at the roadside, bloated, flyblown and obscene in the heat of the day.

Private Charles Moorman of 22 Battalion describes a startling incident on the march:[5]

A lot of jokers had dysentery, you name it, somebody had it. This chap collapsed on the side of the road, and one of the guards, he put the boot in to get him up, but he couldn't. He'd had it. So he shot him. And this [German] officer came up, and he was only a young bloke, this [German] Private, and there was a lot of gabbling going on, nobody understood what they said. This officer brings out his Luger, plok! That fixed him. 'You don't shoot an unarmed man.' That was the officer's idea; and that was a German soldier.

Lance-Corporal (subsequently Captain) Fred Irving said:[6]

The day was getting very hot as we were herded back up that terrible track, all 2,000 feet up. It was a chilling, awesome sight seeing all these men, some in very poor condition, struggling to climb that track. When a soldier fell, which many did, the Germans were at them like sheep dogs shouting, 'Up gets march!' A sight I will never forget as long as I live.

Driver Stove describes the desperate search for food:[7]

We passed down a line of broken-down trucks and searched them for food, forgetting that hundreds had been before us with the same desperate need. We did find a few biscuits amongst the filth at the bottom of one of the vehicles and fed it to one of our chaps, who by this time was becoming weaker.

New Zealand Signaller Cosgrave said:[8]

There was no food or drink and the Germans robbed us of watches and rings on the march to the POW camp. It was a bloody shambles.

The column of POWs passed through Hania, which had been savagely bombed. Australian Private Lew Lind, who had been in the fighting at Rethimnon, and marched all the way along the coast, recorded:[9]

As for the town, it was, like Retimo, a place of death and desolation. We could smell the ungathered dead among the ashes and debris, and the streets, except for some groups of loitering Germans, were deserted.

Meanwhile, back in Hora Sfakion, the Germans swiftly demonstrated their attitude to the Cretans:[10]

. . . twenty men – almost all the adult male population above the age of fifteen – were shot, below the waist, and their bodies burned in petrol, the officer in charge dispatching any that survived this treatment with a machine-pistol bullet through the head.

The skulls of these men, complete with bullet-holes, are preserved behind glass in a small monument on the left of the roadside entering Hora Sfakion, just outside the medical clinic. Three of them belong to fellow clansmen of Seán's friend Yiannis Tsitsiridis of Auckland.

The POW Camp

The POW camp, 'Dulag Kreta', was some five miles west of Hania, on the site of the former No. 7 General [Army] Hospital, which had itself also been bombed. Most of the memoirs state that it was at Galatas. This is incorrect. In fact, after a couple of days of initial confusion, there were five separate camp areas. The New Zealanders were held on the coast, *below* Galatas (see map on next page) at Ayios Apostolis, the British were held in two areas close by, the Australians were held near Skines, and the Greeks and Cypriots were held in a separate camp nearby.[11] There was a separate Camp Hospital with five wards containing about 30 beds each. The vast majority of officers, and badly wounded POWs, had been quickly airlifted to Athens by German troop carriers.

The state of the Australian camp at Skines was particularly horrifying:[12]

> This camp was some 16 kilometres inland, a roughly-wired enclosure of sparsely wooded terrain, which had previously housed Italian POWs captured in Greece. Unfortunately during the battle it had been bombed in error and the ground was pockmarked with craters. The first batch of Australians found bits of Italian bodies littering the area, attracting swarms of flies. Although these remnants were immediately collected and buried, the flies stayed on to spread dysentery, and when we arrived [60 per cent of the] men were affected, some seriously.

Initially, at any rate, overall morale in all of these camps was poor:[13]

> A very bad spirit was to be noted among the majority of the troops. The general view voiced was thank goodness I am a prisoner of war. I have had enough. I have been through hell for days at the hands of enemy aircraft and I am going to leave it to someone else to finish it off . . . The majority voiced the opinion that someone was very much to blame and that the island should have been evacuated earlier. The R.A.F. were held very much to blame whereas the Navy were by almost everyone excused from all blame – in fact rumour had it that they had

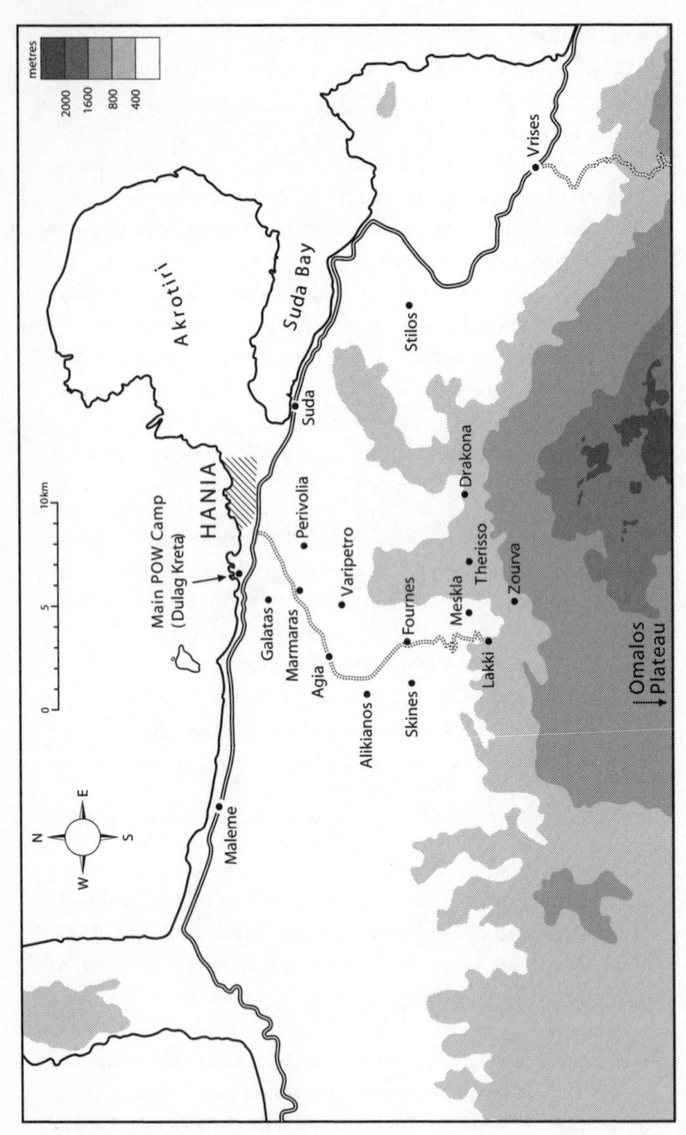

Main POW camp and nearer villages

wanted to evacuate days earlier but the military authorities would not allow it.

This low morale was not helped by the primitive conditions present in all of the camps. Lew Lind again on the Australian camp at Skines:[14]

> we began to sum up our amenities. That did not take long. For example, there was only one well to provide drinking water, and the Greeks shared it with us – more than 3,500 men crowding around for a drink of filthy water. For bathing and washing there was a sewerage drain with about eighteen inches of water in it.

Fred Irving on the Kiwis' camp:[15]

> There were 1,800 New Zealanders for whom the cooks were issued twenty-five tins of bully beef and vegetables to make a stew. Their ladle was a small one and if you got a string of meat you were lucky. Breakfast was equally poor, the porridge was so thin you could drink it.

New Zealand Private Reg Rolfe said:[16]

> This time as a P.O.W. was a terrible experience. The food consisted of lentil soup and mouldy bread for every meal. Everyone was hungry all the time. The latrines were long trenches with a 100mm x 50mm pole to balance on. The winds blew across it to the camp. The flies and the stench were terrible.

Private Leonard Earnshaw (22 NZ Battalion) remembered:[17]

> Conditions in the camp were very primitive. We were riddled with lice and fleas. Every day, we used to take our clothes off and kill as many as we could find, but they'd be there again the next day. And then we had dysentery. It was pretty cold; we just had our shorts and shirts.

New Zealand Driver J. H. Thompson said:[18]

> Almost from the time of arrival at the Camp an epidemic of acute diarrhoea, gastric 'flu and mild dysentery were rife, and, with no provision made for sanitary arrangements, the area surrounding the

Camp quickly degenerated into a filthy condition, especially as the prevailing wind came across the part used for latrines. This deplorable state of affairs was not remarkable as, for the first week, [the] captors had made no attempt to establish any organised routine, nor did the German guards exercise any particular control over the camp.

This is confirmed by Peter Winter:[19]

Not surprisingly, dysentery reached epidemic proportions, until no one could claim to be unaffected. The shallow trenches which served as lavatories were always crowded. Some sufferers slept close to them, finding this more tolerable than the constant trek back and forth . . . Many men wasted away and died . . .

But as Winter himself said of the Kiwi POW camp:[20]

it had one redeeming feature: a glorious stretch of beach was included within its confines. There one could get away from the flies, the dust and the dirt, and the smell was not so bad. Although the sand was only 200 metres from the camp, most of us were in such poor shape that we had to take rest halfway on the daily pilgrimage.

Driver Thompson agreed:[21]

the troops had cause to feel grateful that their camps reached down to the seashore for the facilities of bathing undoubtedly prevented the sickness rate to reach epidemic proportions . . . Not only was this bathing beneficial from a health perspective, but it provided opportunity for exercise and recreation, making the restricted confines of the camp less hard to endure.

The following extract from the original report of Australian Army Medical Corps Lieutenant-Colonel Leslie Le Souef, the Commanding Officer of the Camp Hospital, summarised health conditions as follows:[22]

During the first month in this hospital the diet was totally inadequate in all respects as to quantity and variety. The gross inadequacy of this period was followed by a period during which the diet was supplemented by a small vegetable ration. Since mid-July the diet has again decreased materially in that fresh vegetables are no longer being issued. A slight increase in the preserved meat ration has been made in the last four days. It is noted that grapes have been on issue for the last few weeks and a small issue of tomatoes has also been made. For the nourishment of the serious cases we have been literally depending on the charity of the local inhabitants who have, with great unselfishness, stinted themselves to supply milk and eggs in quantities which must necessarily be small. These gifts are the only means available to the medical Staff for providing seriously ill patients with suitable diets but unfortunately they are totally inadequate in amount for this purpose. As an example can be quoted the fact that the hospital has received in the last 46 days a total of 217 eggs, whereas the minimum requirements for this hospital of 200 beds are 60 eggs a day. Neither rations nor gifts received have permitted the issue of soups and other fluid diets to patients whose conditions demanded them. The effects of the above low diet are now unfortunately becoming increasingly apparent.

1. There is a large percentage of patients within the hospital who will never be restored to normal until an adequate diet is provided. This group of patients consist mainly of cases of dysentry together with a few cases of pulmonary tuberculosis and other chronic ailments.
2. There have been a number of cases occurring in which, in the opinion of all Medical Officers, the low diet has definitely predisposed to the occurrence of disease.
3. Of the 20 deaths occurring in this hospital a large proportion as established by autopsy have been directly or indirectly attributable to malnutrition.

Le Souef, who was to remain a POW for the remainder of the war, was in little doubt that the Germans were deliberately starving their prisoners:[23]

the Germans in a cold, calculated manner had implemented their policy of withholding all but the very sub-basic requirements of our dietetic existence.

But he also noted that the POWs were fortunate in being able to swim in the sea when the Germans let them, and this probably prevented a really serious epidemic in the camp, while facilitating delousing. Nonetheless, 22 soldiers died in these POW camps, five from gunshot wounds, the rest of malaria, dysentery, diarrhoea and poliomyelitis.[24]

However, the health conditions were not the only problems confronting the internees. The Germans used some of the POWs on military works – making sandbag emplacements, and dismantling and repairing crashed German planes at Maleme – which was against the Geneva Convention. Further, some guards had been responsible for random firing into the camps, resulting in the deaths of the five men mentioned above. These incidents were the subject of a formal complaint to the German Commandant by the Senior British Officer, Lieutenant-Colonel Boileau, of the King's Royal Rifle Corps.[25] The German General commanding Crete responded that the hot climate of Crete affected his soldiers' nerves![26]

Under these circumstances, it was hardly surprising that the thoughts of increasing numbers of POWs turned to escape.

Escapers

In the early days of all the camps, the German guards were very relaxed, and deliberately ignored POWs slipping out and foraging for food, especially in the nearby vineyards. Tom Caselli of Layforce said:[27]

> Our guards were the troops we had been fighting and, fair enough, they oftened [sic] turned a blind eye when we went scrounging for edible items.

The New Zealand *Official History* of prisoners of war makes the same point:[28]

> Rations were never sufficient to keep men healthy, and for some weeks the guards winked at prisoners leaving camp to get fruit and other food nearby and allowed Cretans to bring basket-loads to the Camp fence.

Driver Thompson:[29]

The movement of prisoners was practically unrestricted and it was possible for them to go as they pleased to CANEA. Such excursions, as a matter of fact, were encouraged by the guards as they provided a means of supplementing the extremely meagre rations.

Corporal Earnshaw corroborates this lack of restriction:[30]

You may think I'm pulling your leg when I say that for a while the boys were going out of camp during the day and coming back at night, but it was quite true. It was the only way of making up for the food that we did not get in camp. This went on for a couple of weeks before the guards tightened up.

Driver Winter was quick to take advantage:[31]

eventually I made a journey to the capital, Canea, five miles away. Striding along the dusty road I felt fit and well again and happy. The experience of freedom and of going somewhere of my own free will made me joyous and light-hearted. At first I dived for cover when German vehicles approached, but I soon realised that for them, I was just another Cretan peasant. In Canea, I tried to buy food with my small store of drachmae. I returned to camp with a full stomach, laden with food for my friends . . .

But Thompson made an interesting observation:[32]

Just why these men, and others, returned to the camp they were never able to explain, even to themselves. There was, of course, the natural instinct to remain in a body, and that spirit was engendered by the fact that they were all weak and physically exhausted as the results of the privations they had experienced in the preceding few weeks. However, there was no doubt that the psychological effects of frustration and disillusionment had a depressing influence on the men at that time.

But the fighting troops who were the initial camp guards were soon relieved by very unpleasant replacements. Winter again:[33]

A troop of Hitler Youth arrived to assist in guard duties and these strutting young hooligans were likely to shoot at anything that moved. They delighted in baiting the prisoners by offering them food and then tramping it into the ground or eating it themselves.

Fred Irving:[34]

the guards had been changed during the night, and we now had Hitler's Youth group guarding us. They were a bunch of goose-stepping bastards.

So:[35]

After a week things were beginning to get so desperate that three of us started to make plans for escape. My cousin, Cliff Poole, a baker from Dunedin, whom I shall call John, and myself, but of course so were many others.

However, escape was by no means a universal option in these early days of internment. Thompson again:[36]

At this juncture any attempts at escape seemed to be pointless; they were isolated on a mountainous island and there appeared to be no reasonable hope of evading re-capture. They could only expect temporary assistance even if the bewildered and poverty-stricken islanders could be persuaded to give them sanctuary, and the barren, forbidding mountains promised little more than slow starvation. It was no wonder that the spirit of adventure and resoluteness which had characterised their brave endeavours both on the mainland and against the overwhelming odds in the retreat from MALEME aerodrome was now at its lowest ebb.

Kiwi Private Athol Cook, serving with the Australian 1st Infantry Battalion, observed that 'The escapers were very much in the minority. Language was the problem.'[37] Nonetheless, the idea of escape began to be discussed increasingly amongst small pockets of men. The following accounts of escapes are as near chronological as possible.

One of the first to go was New Zealand Driver Arthur Lambert; he had already seen one man die of dysentery and had no intention of becoming the second.[38] His reasoning was simple:[39]

> As I'd been suffering this [dysentery] for a long period I considered my chances of survival in this environment without medical attention weren't good, perhaps my best chance of survival was to escape to the mountains. I recalled that we'd been well received by the Greeks during our escape to Crete, so I decided to leave the camp that night and take my chances in the clean air of the Crete mountains.

Arthur made the break within a week of being put in the camp, along with two other Kiwis:[40]

> Late in the afternoon I decided to do a quick recce of the fence to plan a quick way out, and I found a place where the fence ran over a slit trench. This was ideal – I could crawl under the wire, and through about thirty metres of grapevines, then across a tar-sealed road, and into the vines on the other side, where I was certain a sunken donkey track led up and over a small rise and on to Galatas.

But to his consternation:[41]

> we found the trench had been filled in, so we had to climb over the fence, dive into the vines, crawl to and across the road, and into the vines on the other side. Then we got a fright, a match flared about 50 metres along the road and we could clearly see a German sentry lighting a cigarette! Had he seen us? We will never know.

Lambert was followed shortly afterwards, on the night of 11 June, by Private Geoff Edwards and his mate from the Australian camp:[42]

> We slipped away quietly in the darkness to the dry creek bed where we waited until the sentries passed and our eyes got used to the darkness. Then Bill went first as he was smaller and lighter than me. I lifted the wire for him and he did the same for me. We had to go very slowly on the stony bushy ground at the foot of the hill. I had shorts on so my legs got badly scratched but I didn't notice it at the time as my mind was on that machine-gun at the top of the hill.

The Aussies were followed on about 16 June by Kiwi Reg Rolfe, whose escape proved easier than anticipated:[43]

> For all our planning our escape in the end was simple. A scramble over the barbed wire, into a ditch and through a drainpipe, nobody saw us and we were away.

About the same time, another Kiwi, Lance Bombardier Bruce 'Bella' Johnston of the 5th Field Regiment, Royal NZ Artillery, escaped more by luck than by good judgement. He and a few others were waiting for nightfall so that they could forage some grapes from the vineyards across the road:[44]

> On the evening of my unintentional escape, as we stood by the wire awaiting darkness, the [German] guard Corporal told us we had been very 'naughty' the night before, as the incoming count had been four short of the outgoing, so 'Nix, Nix, Not tonight!' Yours truly and a couple of others, being know-alls, ignored his advice and continued our nightly foray into the grapes. Everything was normal for about a quarter of an hour, then up went the verey lights. Night became day, and the promised colic nearly hit us! Until then I had not realized how small a grapevine was. A period of quiet followed, during which I discovered the light was a distinct advantage in choosing the best fruit. My satisfaction was short-lived though as the guards' next move was to machine gun and hand grenade the vineyard. Casting dignity and discretion to the winds, I took off at a pace I have never achieved since, inland to the more substantial shelter of the olive trees. When things quietened down I tried to return, but owing to the alertness of the guards, it was too dangerous. Here I was – an accidental and unwilling escapee from the German Wehrmacht. I was in a quandary as my dress was only a pair of shorts, no shirt, boots or socks.

June 18 saw the escape of another New Zealander who, as Kapetan Vasilis, was subsequently to become a famous leader of Cretan guerrillas:[45]

> Dudley Perkins was among the earliest of escapers. He had been in the

camp about a fortnight when he and Tom Moir, a staff sergeant in the 5th Field Regiment, were in a group of a dozen prisoners who broke camp on 18 June, crawling in darkness under the wire and disappearing into the olive groves.

Sergeant Moir was also to become a celebrated name amongst the escapers, as we shall see.

Lew Lind shared Arthur Lambert's reasoning for breaking out:[46]

By 24 June I had made up my mind that rather than go mad or die of slow starvation I would try to make a break. After all, a burst of machine-gun bullets would be better than the torture of fading out in this filthy pen.

He actually took off from the Australian camp on 28 June.[47] And in early July, Peter Winter used his loaf, to coin a phrase![48]

Sometimes Cretan women walking along the road threw pieces of bread over the fence. A scramble would ensue and the lucky winner would make for his tent nursing his dusty trophy. These mercy attempts attracted full attention from guards and prisoners alike and, of course, they took place in full daylight. Opportunity came our way when two women with a donkey stopped one day to throw bread into the prison compound. Choice of the right moment, and speed in getting through the wire and across the road, were all that we needed.

About mid-July, New Zealand Private Jim McDevitt also took advantage of a commotion, this time attendant on an unexpected German troop movement:[49]

Cautiously, I lowered myself to the ground . . . Every second was precious to the success of my plan. My hands were trembling as I scooped the warm sand to my side. In next to no time, I had a furrow deep enough to allow my body to squirm its way forward . . . my only path to freedom lay under that barbed wire. I became aware that unseen hands gently lifted the awkward lower strands of wire . . .

Private Charles Jager did the same sort of thing from the Australian Camp:[50]

> Relaxed, with Schmeissers slung over their shoulders and chatting together, a pair of guards approaches and crosses the dry creek bed. Boots clanking on river stones, they pass behind the cook house . . . When they are out of earshot – and rifle-shot – we slither under the wire in the creek, wriggling like goannas among smooth stones big and round as cannon balls.
>
> Leonard Earnshaw took the sea route from the Kiwi Camp:[51]
>
> Barbed wire surrounded the camp, but not out to sea. After getting weaker from lack of good food – I would be giddy if I stood up – I became weak and helpless. About six of us decided to escape. We went out into the sea to avoid the wire, and headed into the mountains.

What happened after the escapees made it out is described by Arthur Lambert:[52]

> I led the way to my Greek friend's house [in Galatas] and knocked. He was surprised and he pulled us quickly inside. I explained, as best I could, our intentions. He understood, and wrote an introduction (on the back of a photo of my brother) to a friend of his who lived in the foothills, packed us some food, and gave us directions to the friend's house.

This friend lived in the village of Therisso. Lambert and his companions arrived there safely,[53] as did Murray MacLagan and Eric Vickers, and many, many others,[54] including Reg Rolfe:[55]

> [The] Cretans gave us more food and that night we slept under olive trees. In the morning we were told the way through a pass to a village where all escaped New Zealanders were directed. It was well secluded in a valley. Access was difficult . . . Amongst the other New Zealanders I met in this village was Bert Gill of 18 Bn . . . Adam Heka of 28 (Maori) Bn. was also there.

Perkins and Moir were similarly aided by locals, although they went in a different direction.[56]

> Perkins and Moir headed west. In a village near Maleme [air]field they found their first benefactor who provided them with food. They ate avidly, but unaccustomed to the oily Greek preparations, suffered afterwards. For two or three days they stayed in hiding and then with the help of a guide, they made their way to the rugged and scantily populated west coast.

Winter's party went south, following the earlier escapers:[57]

> In a small village at the foot of the mountain range we were welcomed with open-handed hospitality typical of the Cretan peasants. All the inhabitants, it seemed, from the very elderly to babies in their mothers' arms, turned out to gaze at us and we were offered food and cigarettes. From the babble of Greek one word, Therisso, was repeated and repeated . . . Therisso was the name of a village in the mountains . . . A lad of about 16 offered to guide us to this Shangri-La. We waited no longer.

McDevitt and his party were also directed to this so-called 'Shangri-La', after meeting a 'Cretan Yank'. He was a local villager who had spent years working in the USA, and had returned with both a modest amount of capital and fractured English.[58]

> A wide path led us through another gorge to a motley collection of stone-built, weather-beaten houses. Most of them had slate roofs. We noticed that all the homes were huddled closely together, as if seeking greater protection from the cruel winter elements. So this was Therisso, our temporary home away up in the mountains! Therisso was probably the last, the loneliest, and the highest settlement in that mountain region.

One of only two English officer escapers and evaders, Miles Hildyard, who kept a diary while on the run, recorded:[59]

> Therisso was always a great stronghold, which the Turks never once reached. It has over fifty [Commonwealth] soldiers living somewhere

outside, and a few whom we met inside. All the women carry them food, and they do some work in return.

A glance at the map on page 52 will make it clear why so many of the men on the run wound up being funnelled through Therisso. On breaking out of the POW camp, the first port of call for many of them, especially New Zealanders like Arthur Lambert who had been stationed in the area, was the village of Galatas. There the locals guided the escapees south on well-established bridle paths, through villages like Marmaras and Varipetro, on to the gorge which led to the village of Therisso. Therisso was difficult to access and was – and still is – secluded. At this time, early summer 1941, when the Germans were not yet active in the mountains, villagers tending their flocks to the north of the village would have been able to give ample warning of approaching vehicles on the solitary dirt road.

Therisso is not itself in the White Mountains; it is in fact located in what locals call the *Riza* – literally, roots – the foothills of the high mountains. But Therisso was connected by a network of *kalderimi* – bridle paths[60] – to other nearby villages in the *Riza* like Zourva and Meskla, and also up to the locals' traditional summer grazing grounds high in the White Mountains, to the south. But Therisso is not just *any* village in the *Riza*; it was the site of the 1905 Rebellion, a signal event in the history of Crete. At that time, Crete was not yet part of the Greek state, but was still nominally a part of the Ottoman Empire, although governed by an international commission of the 'Great Powers' – Britain, France, Italy and Russia – under the governorship of Prince George of Greece (after whom Georgioupolis, east of Hania, is named). This state of affairs infuriated the Cretans as they had risen not once but six times during the 19th-century rebellions against the Turks. So, on 11 March 1905, the Cretan rebels, led by Eleftherios Venizelos, raised the Greek flag in Therisso and declared official *Enosis* – union – with Greece. Sporadic fighting broke out, but matters soon moved onto a diplomatic plane, and *Enosis* was finally achieved in 1913.[61] So, in aiding Australian and New Zealand troops on the run, the villagers of Therisso were merely following their historically-derived tradition as warriors and rebels (this Cretan tradition will be discussed further in the next chapter). In the meantime, Jim McDevitt and Murray McLagan were shown a secret arms dump, cared for by a Kiwi armourer:[62]

> the cache at Therisso contained hundreds of British and German rifles, plus 27 captured machine-guns, seven trench-mortars, as well as thousands of rounds of ammunition.

At this juncture, elementary patterns of concentration of the escapers can be discerned. The bulk of them headed south in the direction of the White Mountains, and were funnelled through Therisso. But some – Perkins and Moir, for example, soon to be followed by Jim McDevitt – headed due west, while others – like Arthur Lambert – decided to strike out on their own, and head east. As we shall see, these decisions were to prove fateful.

Len's Odyssey

After striking out from Sfakia, Len Frazer and his small party of six sappers hung about for four nights in the tiny coastal village of Ayia Roumeli, at the foot of the Gorge of Samaria, waiting in vain for the Royal Navy – which was not about to come. Then, on 6 June, the enemy appeared:[63]

> *Friday – 6 June 1941*
> After breakfast we see 2 boatloads of Germans rowing strongly for Agia Roumeli. We pack up and beat it to valley above village and hide in oleanders. How we love those bushes. The peasants find us, give us food, water, and bring us news after lunch. Three of the party disappointed and discouraged decide to make a break back to Sfakia. They are hungry and scantily clothed.

Note that, although Len is an officer, he is not issuing any orders to these men in his party.

The next night, guided by a local, Len and his three remaining men moved up the gorge. The nocturnal going was tough, as Len records:[64]

> These night mountain walks along steep rocky goat tracks are terribly exhausting and fatiguing. My feet badly blistered and limbs aching . . . The difficult climbing causes us to sweat freely, saturating our clothes. Have no change of clothes and generally fall asleep from exhaustion on bed of cold stones.

They reached the remote, tiny village of Samaria deep in the heart of the gorge, and stayed there for several more days. Len describes their diet and morale:[65]

> *Saturday – 14 June 1941*
> Live on meat and mezithra[66] – boiled wild goat meat, without any salt or bread. Not enough to satisfy our hunger and the nights cold. Meet C.S.M. Carter en route to Agia Roumeli. Going to coast to find small boat which he is prepared to sail with a ground sheet single handed to Egypt. Escaped from Maleme and eulogised German treatment of Australian P.O.W. Promising every man an opportunity to work at his trade in Germany under ideal conditions. Our spirits so low that almost persuaded to give up, to get something better to occupy our minds . . . Everything done to make the captured feel that they should be happier as prisoners.

On 16 June, feeling almost as if they were prisoners in the village of Samaria, surrounded as it is by towering cliffs, Len and his men decided to move on north, and climbed up out of the Gorge onto the Omalos Plateau, 4000 feet above sea level, 11 miles from the Libyan Sea at Ayia Roumeli. That night, he was robbed of his haversack and lost his wallet with his photographs, his writing pad, binoculars and pistol; he suspected a fellow evader – a Kiwi. Within the next couple of days, he had crossed the mountains to the high-level village of Koustoyerako, in the province of Selino, in the west of the main White Mountains massif. This village was to become a noted centre of the Cretan Resistance to the Germans, and one which will feature prominently in this account. There Len met Vasilis Paterakis, one of a legendary family of guerrilla brothers, who gave him some toiletries and money. On 20 June, his men decided to return to the coast in the hope of finding a boat, and Len descended westwards into the Souyia Valley.

By now, he was hearing persistent rumours of boats, but the lack of hard intelligence, the necessity for constant movement, and unreliable sources of food were beginning to affect his morale. On 23 June, he wrote in his diary:[67]

> But I do not care if Germans catch me as I am fed up with the hopelessness of trying to get away and feel that if I am caught Renee [his wife] will know that I am at least alive.

Len's depression is understandable; unlike most of the men on the run, he was an older, 33-year old, married man, with three kids, one of whom – Ian – he had never seen. But at least the weather was good.[68]

> *Thursday – 26 June 1941*
> Cigarettes are very scarce, sold singly and smoked in quarters. People using old motor tyres to sole boots. The summer months – June, July and August – are delightful. It does not rain and is quite comfortable sleeping out without much covering. There is plenty of natural food such as figs, grapes, beans, onions, almonds, mulberries and other fruits.

Len was in fact one of many evaders, escapers and Cretan refugees who were converging on the western slopes of the White Mountains, bringing stories of German actions with them.[69]

> *Monday – 30 June 1941*
> 300 houses in Kandanos were burnt to the ground by the Germans because of resistance. Hardly a house in any untouched village that is not sheltering [Cretan] refugees. The deep generosity of Cretans for their own refugees and the British soldiers is amazing.

Not surprisingly, village houses became crowded. Len recounts sleeping and eating arrangements:[70]

> *Sunday – 13 July 1941*
> Slept with five others, including Cypriot, under one blanket, bed four pillows length, a very bad night, very hot, fleas, mosquitoes, ticks, bugs, ants, etc. Breakfast in Garden of Eden gully, sour cream, milk,

bread, cheese – swim in creek – dinner rice and sour cream, cucumber, roast chicken, *staka* and pears, delightfully served on individual plates. Ken and I were given tremendous helpings. The roast was brought straight from the oven in a large red dish. As usual the men eat while the women watch and serve. The women are delightfully coy, always smiling, and modestly dressed.

The rumours of rescue attempts persisted:[71]

Tuesday – 15 July 1941
[A local] thinks that only hope is to be picked up by Greek sub. Papanikolis stated to be flashing a light and picking troops off coast.

Where this information could have come from is anybody's guess. There *was* a Greek submarine called the *Papanikolis* which was subsequently involved in operations off the south coast of Crete, as will be demonstrated, but at this juncture it was not operating in local waters. It seems that the Cretan habit of telling people what they wanted to hear was asserting itself, and it was one which came to infuriate Len. However, shortly afterwards, Len returned to Koustoyerako. There he met Vasilis Paterakis's brothers Manolis and Kostas; they were not men prone to exaggerate for effect. Len comments:[72]

Thursday – 24 July 1941
They tell of 8 soldiers who 3 days ago stole row boat at ★★★★★ and made away. They tell us that there is a Capt in Apon with 10,000 [drachmae] and 4 men trying to get a boat and a sailor.[73]

Len and the others evaders in this area raised 18,830 drachmae between them, but it was not long before reality struck:[74]

Friday – 26 July 1941
V. returns with bad news. The G[ermans] have registered all the boats, and 4 of the 5 owners will not sell. It appears that the Greeks have lied to us for it is doubtful if at any time all 5 owners agreed to sell. Very disappointed. I could cry. ★★★★★ is sad and organize plan to steal boat. We sleep 6 in one bed. Not so good.

By the end of July, Len is becoming despondent, not surprisingly, as it is his wife's and eldest son's birthdays – and, of course, they have had no news of him for nearly two months now:[75]

> *Thursday – 31 July 1941*
> Renee's and Kevin's birthday. Please God tell them that I am alive, that they may be happy, and that I may see them soon.

The Wounded Men

Meanwhile, the wounded soldiers, including Ned Nathan, Joe Angell and Ken Little, were still being sheltered and nursed faithfully by Cretan villagers. Ken Little describes how they hid him from German search parties:[76]

> Whenever a patrol made its way towards the hamlet, I would be lowered by rope into a cave, the entrance to which was simply a hole in the ground. Once safely onto the cave floor about twelve feet below a flagstone would be placed over the opening. I hated it down there, but as a hidey-hole, it was perfect.

We will hear more about how these wounded men fared in subsequent chapters.

CHAPTER 4

MI9, and Crete, in 1941

MI9

In the first couple of weeks of June,1941, the first evaders who had escaped from Crete using their own initiative began to stagger ashore in Egypt. These men reported that hundreds of Australian, British and New Zealand soldiers were still at large on the island. This galvanised MI9, the secret British organisation responsible for assisting both escapers and evaders in enemy-occupied Europe, into action. Its sole member at Middle East Headquarters, Lieutenant-Colonel Dudley Clarke, had his hands full arranging the debriefing of the evaders, and planning how to rescue an unknown number of escapees on the run in Crete. The records state: 'June 17th, 1941: Plans started for the attempted rescue of troops left behind in Crete.'[1]

According to its published history, MI9's wartime aims were:[2]

> to aid escapers, by tools and training, to escape; to train potential evaders to evade; to encourage secret routes along which either could travel; and to glean such intelligence as was to be found in prisoner-of-war camps.

This history has a somewhat self-congratulatory air – it exudes more than a hint of 'Jolly Good Chaps from Good Regiments doing Splendid Work in Bloody Awful Conditions'. However, unpublished sources in the Public Record Office in Kew, London, reveal that there were no escape networks anywhere in Greece, including Crete, at all. The manuscript history of Special Operations Executive (SOE) during the war, in a section entitled 'M.I.9 Activities in the Eastern Mediterranean 1941–1945', states:[3]

> On the outbreak of war in 1939 there was no M.I.9 organisation whatsoever in the Middle East, nor were there any officers familiar with M.I.9 work, and it is extremely fortunate from the escape angle that no operations occurred in this theatre for nearly two years.

Further, a 1945 report, 'Summary of M.I.9 Activities in the Eastern Mediterranean', states:[4]

> M.I.9 in this area grew up piecemeal and, particularly at the start, was largely an ad hoc organisation formed to meet the varying and pressing needs as they arose. This is particularly true of the East African, First Western Desert, and Greece and Crete campaigns . . . In the European area, particularly in the early stages, M.I.9 escape and evasion operations were carried out to a large extent through the medium of the two other large secret organisations, M.I.6 and S.O.E.

This was certainly the case in Crete, which is hardly surprising, for when MI9 was established in Middle East Headquarters in January 1941, this report notes that it had precisely one member – Lieutenant-Colonel Clarke – and that his main employment was actually in *other* top-secret areas. The report further observes:[5]

> There was no general plan for preventive training in the Middle East, nor was there a full distribution of escape devices.

In other words, as has been noted earlier, the escapers and evaders in Crete were left literally to their own devices. MI9, therefore, had to expand rapidly, and expand it did. It both borrowed personnel from Special Operations Executive, and recruited from among the men who had reached North Africa. From SOE, Clarke acquired Major A. C. Simonds, a man experienced in clandestine operations, to take charge of 'N' Section, responsible for escape and evasion, in September 1941.[6]

In terms of the successful evaders, the report states:[7]

> The idea of using 'a thief to catch a thief' (this, although apposite, is hardly complimentary to the gallant men who volunteered) came from the eagerness and enthusiasm of escapers and evaders who volunteered to return to help their less fortunate comrades. In innumerable cases interrogation reports contained in their concluding sentences:
>
> This officer (or O.R.) wishes to volunteer to return to Crete, where he thinks he can be of use to rescue other escapers. The most outstanding advantage of using ex-escapers was that of 'cover'. An ex-escaper returning on M.I.9 duty, and carefully briefed, had an almost watertight 'cover story', unless such personnel made a mistake when recaptured, it was almost impossible for the enemy to break their story. The main outline of all such stories was that they were escapers who had escaped from one of the numerous transit camps in Greece or Crete, and had been at large ever since. An 'escaper', because that justified the wearing of plain clothes.

The report goes on to list the following Anzac escapers and evaders used subsequently by MI9 in Greece and Crete: 2/Lt J. W. C. Craig, 22 Bn; Lt Greenway, 2/11 Engineers, AIF; Sgt J. A. Redpath, 19 Army Transport, 2 NZEF; Sgt A. P. Empson, 18 Bn; Pte Bazely, 2/5 Bn, AIF.[8] There were many others not listed, such as the Australian soldier G. D. Atkinson captured with a party of 22 evaders on the Greek island of Antiparos in early 1942,[9] and Kiwi Staff Sergeant Tom Moir, who was awarded a DCM for his exploits on Crete.[10] The escapers and evaders also constituted a source of personnel for other secret organisations, particularly SOE, as shall be seen.

A third source of personnel for MI9 in the Middle East was Greeks. In this regard, the report contains an ungenerous comment:[11]

> M.I.9 was fortunate in having the services of large numbers of gallant Greeks who volunteered to carry out escape and rescue work for them. Such volunteers fortunately did not count against the British wartime establishment.

The latter sentence means that the 'gallant Greeks' were not paid for their pains! By the end of the war, in fact, MI9 had seven Greek HQ staff, and 12 Greek operational staff.[12]

The Numbers Game

Even now, in 2005, it is impossible to give an absolutely accurate figure of the numbers of soldiers on the run in Crete in the couple of months following the battle. However, there does appear to be a rough convergence of estimates. Kiriakopoulos says that there were about a thousand, but does not provide a source for that figure.[13] Kokonas, a usually reliable source, in his history of SOE in Crete says 'over 1,000' in two different places.[14] Long, in the *Official History* of Australia at War, quotes a contemporary estimate of '600 Australians and 400 New Zealanders living in villages in western Crete'.[15] The post-escape report of Captain Embrey of the Australian 2/1 Battalion, who was taken prisoner, and subsequently escaped, submits:[16]

> In using the word British, I include all our troops – I saw not more than 20 Englishmen, but I consider that about 600 Australians and about 400 New Zealanders are living in the villages of Western CRETE.

Ned Nathan, himself an evader on the run, suggests 'there were about 1,500 New Zealanders, Australians and Britishers in the mountains'.[17] A 1945 SOE report states: 'Over 1,000 British troops remained behind in May 1941 after the evacuation of the island.'[18] Another evader, Reg Saunders, who was on the run for more than a year, said in an interview for the Australian Sound Archives:[19]

> I reckon round about eight hundred to nine hundred, probably, on the whole of Crete – all over Crete. Some of them never got captured.

And Major Xan Fielding, the SOE agent responsible for western Crete, said:[20]

> 'There were then about a thousand Allied stragglers wandering about the island, most of whom had made for the south coast in the hope of finding a boat to take them to Africa.'

A major reason for the difficulty in computing the precise number is that we simply do not know how many men broke out of the POW camps. However, it clearly must have been in the hundreds overall. There seems little reason, then, to doubt that there *were* about a thousand men on the run in the summer of 1941. While we will deal with the numbers successfully evacuated in subsequent chapters, it is to be noted at this juncture that quite a few of these men were captured by the Germans; some men, usually very ill, returned voluntarily to the camps in search of medical attention, or gave themselves up; a small number were actually executed; and a few died of illness.

Crete in 1941

The Crete from which MI9 had to evacuate the thousand or so troops on the run was a *very* different place to their native Australia or New Zealand. Fortunately, a detailed picture of the island in this era is provided by a post-war study undertaken by the Rockefeller Foundation in the late 1940s, and published in 1953.[21] Although it *was* a post-war study, it provides much data for earlier periods, and the situation it delineates can be taken to have obtained in Crete during the interwar years.

Crete is a mountainous island, with four distinct massifs taking up two-thirds of the land area: the Levka Ori, the White Mountains, in the west; the Psiloritis or Ida range in the centre; the Lassithi or Dikti range east of Psiloritis; and the Sitia range in the far east. These limestone mountains soar to well over 8000 feet at their highest points in the White Mountains and Psiloritis ranges, are of a *karst* landform, and are barren, rocky, dry and savage to a degree. Over half the village communities on the island lay at 1000 feet or above, and because limestone is porous and soaks up rainfall, water was a major problem in pre-war Crete.

In 1940, with a population of 438,239,[22] Crete was a peasant society, dominated by peasant forms of agricultural production, peasant ways of thinking, where the inhabitants lived in hundreds of peasant villages and farmed smallholdings. Even the very small Cretan middle class – the doctors, lawyers, teachers and merchants – all had immediate and real connections with their villages of origin, to which they were fiercely loyal. In these villages, the small size of the holdings frequently meant subsistence production and simple commodity exchange, although not insubstantial surpluses of agricultural produce were marketed in the northern coastal towns of Heraklion, Rethimnon and Hania.

The study describes a society whose 'economy was almost untouched by modern technology'.[23] More than half the farms had less than $20 worth of implements and equipment, usually wooden saddles for their donkeys, and wooden ploughs and harrows. There were only 37 tractors on the whole island.[24]

Yet that same society was characterised by a culture with deep roots stretching back to Minoan times, 3000 BC, and earlier, in legend, to the birth of Zeus himself. That culture was and is redolent of a strong local patriotism, *pallikariá* – a warrior spirit, a fierce independence, and great dignity and charm – accompanied by a formidable *filoxenía* – literally, love of strangers – expressed in an almost overwhelming sense of hospitality.[25] The Cretans, both men and women, are also notably intelligent and strikingly handsome people. They fought the Dorians, the Romans, the Barbary Corsairs (Saracens), the Venetians, the Turks, and now, the Germans. The Saracens ruled Crete for more than a century, from AD 832, the Venetians from 1204 to 1669, the Turks from 1669 until 1897. As we have already noted, in the 19th century alone, the Cretans rose in arms six times against the Turks, the 'Great Rebellion' being that of 1866, when substantial tracts of the island were reduced to depopulated wastelands.[26] Crete only became a part of the Greek state in 1913. But 'Greece, before World War II, had the lowest per capita national income of any country in Europe'.[27] In a word, the rural people of Crete, which meant the vast majority, were poor, and their lives were hard. To the many men from rural backgrounds in Australia and New Zealand, where they had just experienced the exigencies of the Depression, this was a state of affairs to which they could relate. They could understand the effort needed to clear rocky land, and the back-breaking labour involved in activites such as milking sheep, and cheese-making.

There was a dark side to this culture though, albeit one not usually visible to outsiders. The Cretan men were, and still are, prone to sheep-stealing – to a degree where it could almost be said to be the national sport. They are also embroiled in bloody vendettas of astonishing complexity and longevity, and within living memory, also indulged in bride-snatching (although, anthropologically speaking, there was more than a hint of negotiated consent in this latter practice!). The men on the run were to encounter both fugitives from vendettas, and sheep-stealing, and indeed were not wholly innocent of the latter misdemeanour themselves, on the odd occasion.

The pre-war diet of Crete was maintained throughout the war, when possible, and remained unchanged for years after its end. The Rockefeller study characterised the basic foods as: 'olives, cereal grains, pulses, wild greens and herbs, fruits, goat meat and milk, game, and fish in limited quantities. Bread was served with every meal.'[28] But several items are inexplicably missing from the Rockefeller diet. The first is cheese – the famous Cretan *graviera*, a hard cheese, or the soft *misithra* and *anthotiri*, all made from goat's or sheep's milk, and what we would now call completely organic. The second is chickens and eggs. And the third is sheep meat and milk. Although most families had a few goats or sheep, they were mainly kept for milk, and mutton or goat's meat was reserved for special occasions. It is small wonder that the Cretans were a hardy and vigorous people, especially the men involved in shepherding in the savage terrain of the massifs like the Psiloritis or the White Mountains. But 30 per cent of them were illiterate.[29]

In the 1940s, rural Cretan houses were very small, usually one-storeyed, stone-built, white-washed structures with two or three rooms with high ceilings and shuttered, unglazed windows, and, in the mountain villages, an earth floor. Animals – the donkey, a few goats, hens – were frequently kept in the house in a partitioned-off corner, or in an adjacent room. Running water was unknown, as was electricity. Winter rainwater was drained off the roofs through pipes into an underground *sterna*, a drystone tank or cistern, and raised by hand in a bucket. Light was provided by oil lamps. Toilets as such were primitive privies. Furniture was basic and solid, the only decoration being rugs ands mats woven by the village women on hand-looms. And 'Ninety-two percent of the families used open fires for cooking.'[30]

Communications were difficult. The only sealed road ran along the north coast of the island between Heraklion and Hania, and during the war years, there were perhaps 800 miles of gravel road, mostly very rough, on the entire island. Only a very few mountain villages had roads leading up to them from the north coast, while communication between villages was via the criss-crossing bridle paths or *kalderimi* already mentioned. In western Crete, the only metalled roads were those which ran down to Hora Sfakion (nearly), and Paleochora. When Seán lived in the Sfakiot village of Askyfou in the White Mountains in the mid-1980s, older villagers could remember that in the pre-war years it was a two-day journey by mule or donkey to the provincial capital, Hania, and they thought nothing of it. It now takes one hour by car.

Hardened as they were by their Depression experiences, the Kiwi and Aussie soldiers who stumbled into this situation were nevertheless taken aback by what they saw as primitive conditions. Kiwi Bella Johnston said: 'They seemed in some ways not far removed from medieval times.'[31] Lew Lind remarked:[32]

> Cretan customs at this time were almost biblical. It was quite common on arriving at a Cretan home for the lady of the house to remove one's shoes and socks and bathe one's feet in warm water and olive oil.

Fellow Australian Charles Jager describes a house where he was sheltered:[33]

> Inside, his dwelling is a refuge from the winter for man and beast. A wooden floor, instead of tamped earth, is a good indication of our host's affluence. Outside, his wife cooks what she grows or kills in the lime-washed dome of a wood-burning oven, and draws water from an ancient well. They eat well but live hard; without electricity – and their sanitation is a truffling sow and her piglets. Crete is raw, vibrant, cruel. Not for the squeamish.

And this, as Jager says, was an *affluent* house. The majority of the dwellings had earth floors, the thick stone-and-rubble walls were cold and damp, and even in the 1980s, many women were still cooking outside over an open fire of twigs. But it has to be remembered that in the pre-war years the Overseas Experience or OE, so common among post-war generations of Australians and Kiwis, was most unusual, so these soldiers had no comparative experience with other European countries.

One particular institution in Crete which was to prove very important to the men on the run was the Greek Orthodox Church. As the Rockefeller report notes:[34]

> Part of being a Greek is being a member of the Greek Orthodox Church.

In 1941, the ubiquitous Orthodox priests and monks in Crete were recruited overwhelmingly from the peasantry, and the majority lacked higher education. Nevertheless, they were important people in their parishes, where priests were usually married men. Further, as the report emphasises:[35]

> The church is closely associated with the history of the country . . . Greek nationalism is nourished by the church; patriotism and loyalty to the church are almost indistinguishable.

The theology of contemporary Orthodoxy stressed the role of the *nikokyria*, the housewife, as both the cornerstone and servant of her family. This implied a strict division of labour in which there could be no doubt that women were subservient to men. All the fugitive men remarked on this gender distinction. Peter Winter put it like this, referring to a 16-year-old girl, and a young woman of 21, in the household in Meskla where he was sheltered:[36]

> Tarsula [Tassoula] and the lovely Iphigeneia were shy and unobtrusive as was expected in this community. They fetched and carried, washed and mended my clothes, set chairs for me in the shade during the heat of the day and poured water into my cupped hands for me to wash. I too, was shy and diffident in their presence. I was unused to being treated as a kind of god . . . It was a man's world. One of the villagers had a single sentence in English which he loved to air: 'Let the *womens*

do it.' Women did all the chores, they did not eat until the men were fed and they waited on them hand and foot.

The Rockefeller report is even more specific:[37]

> Particularly in the rural communities, Cretan women worked harder than Cretan men. Managing a Cretan home seemed frequently to require caring for children, cooking, cleaning, spinning, weaving blankets and clothing fabrics, sewing, embroidering, making garments and helping with farming activities . . .

Seán can report that, in the 1980s, the situation had altered little in the mountain villages.

However, a perception of local economic and social conditions as *uniformly* biblical is in fact misplaced. While local conditions may have been primitive relative to agricultural conditions in contemporary Australia or New Zealand, Crete was what social scientists call a region of 'uneven development'. That is to say, the harbingers of a more advanced society were already in place. One of the most obvious of these was the phenomenon of the 'Returned Yank'. These were Cretan men who had migrated to the United States earlier in the century and returned with some capital, some knowledge of the English language, and some experience of life in an industrialised capitalist society. The men on the run bumped into these Yanks continuously. For example, Australians Charles Jager, Geoff Ruddick, Len Frazer and Lew Lind, and Kiwis Dick Huston, Herb Stove, Ken Little, Peter Winter and Jim McDevitt all mention meeting such men, who frequently assisted as interpreters and guides. These returned migrants would subsequently prove to be key players in the development of peripheral Greek society, particularly in the islands.[38]

Be that as it may, the antipodean escapers and evaders were not social scientists, they were mainly country boys, and they proved to be singularly unsqueamish in relating to Cretan culture, appreciated the hard life of the mountain peasantry and, at the suggestion of their hosts, adopted both Cretan costume and Greek names. Thus, for example, Charles Jager become Kiriakos, Norm Delaney became

Manolis, Ned Nathan became Andreas, Joe Angell became Yiannis, Bella Johnston became Prokopis, Ken Little became Pavlos, Arthur Lambert became Thanassis and Jim McDevitt became Dimitris. Some – Kiwis Ned Nathan, Joe Angell, Bella Johnston, Dick Huston, Jim McDevitt, and Australian Reg Saunders – learned Greek, and became proficient speakers of the Cretan dialect, good enough to fool the Germans on several occasions. It should also be noted that both Nathan and Angell were Maori soldiers from the 28th Battalion, Johnston was a Maori from 5 Field Regiment, while Reg Saunders was an Australian Aboriginal from the 2/7th Battalion.

The traditional male dress which some of the men on the run also adopted was handsome, although worn more in the mountain villages than in the towns of the north coast. From top to bottom, it comprised: the *sariki*, or black tasselled headband; the *vrachas*, or baggy trousers with concertinas of folds between the legs (called 'crap-catchers' by the Kiwis), held in place by a cummerbund; and *stivania*, the knee-high jackboots. An alternative to the *vrachas* were *gilotes*, which closely resembled riding breeches. And the shepherds wore a thick hooded cloak made of woven goat's hair called a *kapota*, and carried a *katsouna*, or crook. The men on the run were not to know that, in fact, this dashing costume derived from the 228 years of Turkish occupation – and indeed, it would have been impolitic to mention it!

It is hardly surprising, then, that some villages almost became Anzac clubs. Therisso, Meskla, Ayia Irini, Epanohori and Koustoyerako are cases in point. Peter Winter describes the situation in Therisso:[39]

> Sheltered by mountains on four sides, Therisso was situated in a green valley on the banks of a sparkling mountain stream. It looked a paradise indeed – the prettiest village in the world. Huge walnut and plane trees bordered the stream, while quaint stone houses peeped from under the green branches of olive trees that grew on the slopes on either side . . . Unfortunately there was one great disadvantage to our Utopia. It was ideally suited to the role of hide-out but already far too many of our fellow prisoners of war had found this delightful valley and made

it their own. Not surprisingly, they were jealous of their right to claim that they were there first.

As the men moved around the mountain villages seeking food and shelter, they kept bumping into other groups and individuals, even in the remotest locations. The following story is simply irresistible:[40]

> An Australian private, seeking the south coast of Crete during an evasion which had started well – he was already in plain clothes of a ramshackle sort – found out that he had to cross a main road under constant German watch. He had no time to wait for dark. The only hope of cover seemed to be a shepherd. He came upon a dozen sheep in the charge of a shaggy biped bundle of rags, before whose face he crackled his only inducement; a white five pound note. The bundle at first said nothing, but repeatedly lifted his head sharply, in the Greek sign for 'No'. When an hour's attempt to chaffer had produced no more result, the bundle remarked in broad Glasgow Scotch, 'Gae and find yer own bluidy sheep. I've spent half a day getting this damn lot.'

CHAPTER 5

Mixed Fortunes

Dispersal

As large numbers of soldiers escaped from internment in Dulag Kreta and spread slowly through the villages and hamlets of western and central Crete, it was like a second invasion, albeit one which was clandestine and completely unrehearsed. Unlike the German airborne invasion of several weeks earlier, these invaders were unarmed, poorly equipped, physically run-down and desperate to leave the island. They had little idea how they might get away though. Rumours abounded – stories about Royal Navy submarines patrolling the south coast, fishing villages with small boats that might be sailed to Egypt, caiques involved in inter-island trading. But these were only rumours, and there was still the problem of working out how to survive in the meantime.

However unusual it was to see so many starved and bedraggled soldiers, Cretan villagers responded quickly and generously with the basic assistance that they required, readily sharing food and civilian clothes, and providing reliable contacts to those who wanted to move on. Northern villages were very hospitable and more than willing to adopt some men on a long-term basis. Within a few days of escaping, for example, Peter Winter found himself staying with a family at the village of Meskla. Very weak and run-down when he arrived, Winter recovered quickly on a diet of fresh fruit and vegetables, olive oil, eggs and home-cooked bread. In fact, he had only been with the family a short time when they were urging him to marry their eldest daughter and make his home on Crete.[1] Reluctantly, Winter and a number of other escapees staying in the same village decided to leave after several weeks, and check out the rumours of men getting off the island by submarine or small boat. It was a decision they were to regret very quickly because, as they headed for the far west port town of Kastelli, they were recaptured.

Every northern village took in some escapers and gave them food and shelter, but there were limits to the number they could cope with. The majority of escapers stayed only briefly before moving on. The tendency was to make for the south coast but this depended on finding mates to go with, places to hide as they travelled, and people to assist them on the way. As it transpired, the direction that they took, whether they went south-east or south-west, made a huge difference to their chances of getting off the island in the months ahead. All the evacuations carried out by MI9 in 1941–42 took place on the south coast, around the centre of the island. Only those escapers who happened to be in or near those districts had any chance of being included.

Nevertheless, the friendliness of the Cretans and their willingness to help out was identical on both sides of the White Mountains. Local Resistance leaders cooperated closely with each other and formed networks of safe houses through which the roaming soldiers found food and good hiding places. Later on, when organised evacuations began, some of these networks became established escape routes – the most well known being the 'High Spy Route' through the Amari[2] – via which fugitives were guided to pre-arranged pick-up points. In other cases, the networks were used simply to provide support, share information, and test out possible means of escape. In this chapter we will look at the way in which these networks developed, and the very different outcomes that unfolded either side of the White Mountains, in the summer of 1941.

Evaders in Lotus Land

Following the surrender of the troops at Hora Sfakion and Rethimnon, a good number of the evaders – mostly Australian with a few British –

spent the weeks of June and early July in the mountains south of Rethimnon. Later, they were joined by escapers filtering south-east from villages around Hania, increasing their numbers considerably. They were fortunate in finding themselves in a particularly prolific and hospitable part of Crete, where there was much goodwill to all soldiers who had been involved in the defence of the island. In the rich valley lying between the Mt Ida range to the east and the slopes of Mt Kedros to the west was the district or eparchy of Amari, so bountiful and popular with British SOE agents that they subsequently gave it the codename of 'Lotus Land'.[3]

Local Resistance leaders in the Amari and in the neighbouring eparchy of Ayios Vasileios (St Basil), organised quickly to share the burden of supporting the evaders and doing whatever was required to facilitate their escape. Indeed, in the Nomos (prefecture) of Rethimnon, in which these regions are located, the Resistance was arguably the earliest organised in Crete. The core of this Resistance was Reserve and Gendarmerie officers, ordinary Cretan villagers, and Greek Orthodox priests like Father Agathangelos Lagouvardos, the Abbot of the Holy Monastery of St John at Preveli, a 14th-century monastery located on the Ayios Vasileios coast almost directly south of Rethimnon. These local resistance leaders set up the Independent Organisation of Escape and Intelligence.[4] Some of the evaders were hidden in the precincts of the monastery:[5]

> Nearly 150 British took refuge into [sic] the monastery complex, since the beginning of June, where they stayed all day long. During the nights they were sending SOS messages from the coast hoping that these would be picked up by some of the submarines patrolling in the area, to come and rescue them.

Others were spread around neighbouring villages: Mirthios, Asomatos, Drimiskos, Vatos, Gianiou and Frati.[6] Australian veterans of the Rethimnon fighting were prominent among the men hiding in and around the monastery, including a group of 2/11 Battalion soldiers led by Captain Jackson. As a consequence of the active role taken by the local Resistance, including Father Lagouvardos, Ayios Vasileios had one of the highest concentrations of evaders and escapers in all of western and central Crete in the first months of the occupation.

One of the groups that found its way there was Vic Solomon's party of Australian 2/2 Battalion soldiers, whose rapid departure from Hora Sfakion was described in Chapter Two. As Solomon relates it, they could not believe the hospitality shown to them as they made their way through the mountains:[7]

> we came to a village where the inhabitants made a great fuss over us. Separating us into twos and threes they took us to their homes and fed us like fighting cocks and found us a domicile for the night in a stone enclosure used for wheat threshing. Next morning the food began to arrive and what a variety! There was goat's milk, all kinds of fruit, three or four kinds of vegetables all cooked in olive oil, rye bread, cheese, olives and even cakes. Some of us made ourselves sick we ate so much.

As they continued, there was no let-up to this generosity:[8]

> It appeared as though three families had agreed to support us between them. The variety of food was great, all cooked in olive oil, and apart from that we used a quart of oil a day for salads and for soaking the bread in it. Fruit was plentiful, we had grapes, figs, pears, and apples, a bottle of wine on Sundays and ouzo all the week. We had cheese from goat's milk, not to mention the vast quantities of olives we consumed. They brought us shaving gear and even took our clothes away to wash them.

Even though they had little idea where they were, Solomon's party had been guided close enough to Preveli by mid-July to be within the network of 'safe' villages connected to the monastery. Through their Cretan guides they were put in touch with other Australians, and seven days later received a message to join the first group of evaders being taken off Crete by submarine.

What needs to be stressed here is that well before MI9 had even landed its first agent on Crete, the Cretan Resistance, which had burst spontaneously into action on Day One of the German invasion, had deployed a sophisticated network entirely of its own construction to look after the men on the run and channel them into safe havens like the Preveli Monastery.

Selino: Many Boats, Few Escapes

At the same time as evaders and escapers were converging on Preveli in late June and early July, there were large numbers pushing into Western Crete. All their attention was given over to finding any boat at all that might get them to North Africa. It was the most frequent topic of conversation, not to mention rumour, speculation and frustration among every group of soldiers gathered in that area, and it is easy to see why. West Crete has a long southern and western coastline with several fishing villages and one small port. There seemed to be numerous boats around and North Africa was tantalisingly close. Len Frazer did the calculations on a piece of scrap paper (page 88) using Elafonissos in the south-west corner of Crete to calculate the distances across the Libyan Sea.[9] The nearest landfall was only 200 miles away – this would take less than three days travelling at three knots.[10]

The problem was that German troops had occupied the small port town of Paleochora by 25 May and, from early June onwards, had moved quickly to secure the rest of the south-west coast. They destroyed lots of small boats, registered those that remained and put them under close surveillance. In some cases they insisted on accompanying fishermen every time they put out to sea. Further, they warned all boat owners of swift retribution against them, their families and their villages, should any be caught assisting Allied soldiers to get off the island. Turning Crete into a fortress did not deter the men hiding in the hills however; it only made their mission more hazardous. In most cases, escapers tried to negotiate with boat owners and offered to purchase the craft they needed, but if necessary, they were prepared to steal them.

On 16 June, in the only escape from south-west Crete which was successful that summer, two Australians and two New Zealanders stole an abandoned rowing boat from the beach at Souyia and half-rowed, half-sailed it to the North African coast, completing the voyage in

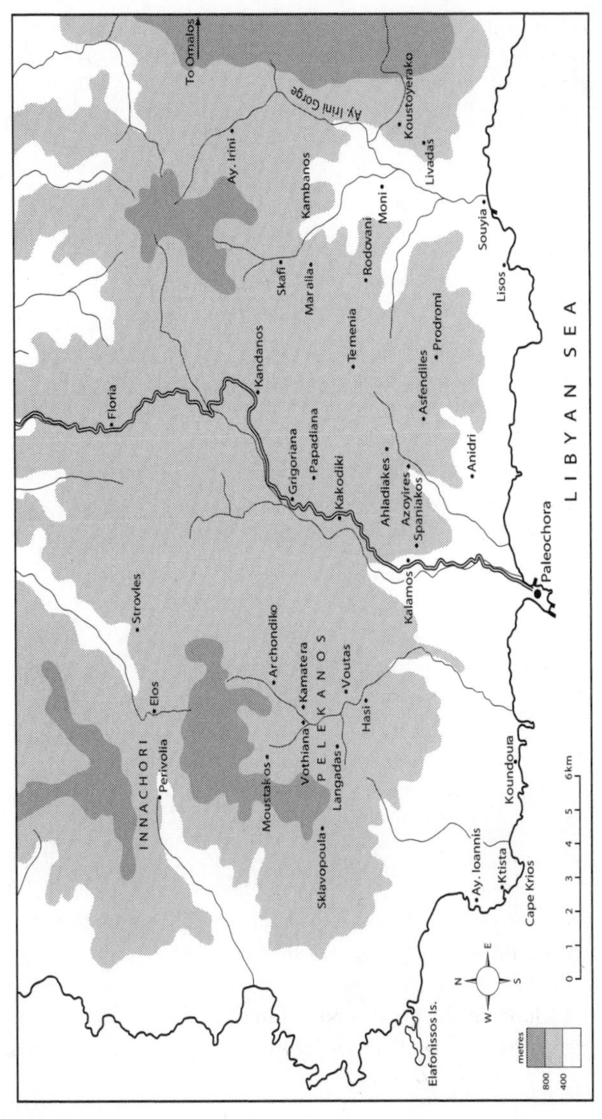

South-west Crete

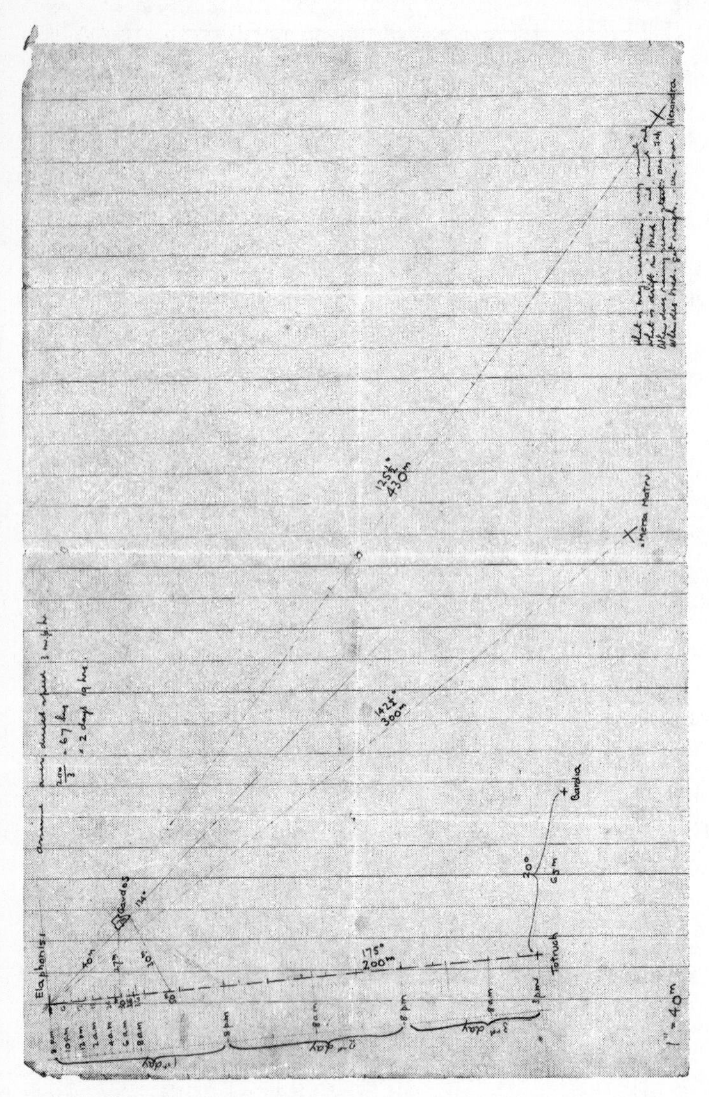

Diagram from Len's diary

just under four days. It was an audacious effort as the boat was barely holding together. They were not to know it, but the boat had already been paid for and taken to sea by a mixed crew of Australians and New Zealanders three weeks earlier. On that occasion there were seven aboard and they were forced to give up when planks came loose and the boat began leaking badly.[11] The new crew of Corporal R. R. Gordon and Private R. G. Buchecker of Australian 2/7 Battalion, Private D. N. McQuarrie of 18 NZ Battalion, and Private B. B. Carter of 27 NZ MG Battalion staked out the vessel for several days, waited for a moonlit night, and pushed it out to sea. Corporal Gordon recounts what ensued:[12]

> In order to give Gavdhos Island a wide berth, we rowed south all day and, when nightfall came, were at a point about eight kilometres to the west of Gavdhos. When a fresh breeze sprang up, we were able to hoist our sail and changed course to a south easterly direction, maintaining this until the night of July 18/19 when the weather got too rough for comfort. We then decided to head south in the hope that the escarpment in Libya had been passed. Our guess proved to be correct and we made landfall at Sidi Barrani at 2030 hours on the night of July 19, 1941.

The 'sail' in question was a blanket rigged on an oar! The soldiers who welcomed them were flabbergasted when they saw the condition of their boat:[13]

> Soldiers waded out to help the escapers, but when they grasped the boat the top planking came away. Next day when others tried it out to find how such a broken-down craft had stood up to the long and hard voyage, the dinghy fell to pieces.

Private Buchecker and Corporal Gordon were awarded the MM for this daring escape.

Most other attempts to secure small boats involved trying to make deals with their owners. None of them were successful. Time and again, discussions started with Cretan boat owners, an agreement was made, fund-raising commenced, crews were selected, and, when it came time to claim the boat, the deal fell through. Mostly it was because of worries about the repercussions of being caught – at best losing their boats, at worst execution of them and their families.

Len Frazer was involved in several of these failed arrangements, starting from the time that he and his party first reached Ayia Irini in Selino, arriving on 16 June. Separating from his companions temporarily, Len soon found himself in Koustoyerako, high above the east side of the Ayia Irini valley, with another bunch of New Zealanders and Australians scouting for likely boats in and around Souyia (including the one that was given a trial, rejected and then stolen by Buchecker's group). When those schemes stalled, he and several of this group moved to Ahladiakes to position themselves for some motor boats at Paleochora. In one case where a considerable sum of money was demanded (15,000 drachma, or roughly 34 pounds), they didn't have enough money of their own, so started to collect funds from local villagers. With their own funds and the villagers' donations, they collected some 18,000 drachmae in three days. But they had no sooner got the money together, selected their crew, gathered provisions, received a tearful farewell from all the villagers, and prepared to claim the boat, when the deal fell through.[14]

For Len, the only consolation of living through all these disappointments was that it was the height of summer, and Selino villages were at their most abundant. He described Ahladiakes as being like a 'Garden of Eden', nestling in a secluded valley with a small stream, vegetable gardens and lots of fruit and nut trees. Food was plentiful and readily shared with the visitors. Their clothes were washed and mended, and in every other way they were treated like special guests. Len was unused to all the attention and just a little frustrated. It seemed as if he could do anything except the one thing he wanted above all else, and that was to get off the island.

Lew Lind – and many others – waxed positively lyrical about the landscape:[15]

> In perfect weather our eyes met beauty in every direction, the very air being scented with the perfume of wild herbs and the rich crops

of distant farms. Here and there, amid the luscious green of trees and flowering bushes, sparkling streams weaved gaily down the valleys. Against all was the background of an endless chain of mountains. It was impossible to associate war with this panorama of peace and loveliness; impossible to associate human slaughter and strife with the life of the goatherd and his family who lived in a hut halfway down our mountainside. The music of the goat bells mingled soothingly with the songs of these happy, harmless people, attuning our thoughts to all that was best and good.

However, others who were hiding in Selino that summer – and there were large numbers of them – had a tougher time of it. Jim McDevitt had gathered with several other 'footloose evaders' – mostly New Zealanders but some Australians – in the hills above the village of Skafi, on the western side of the Ayia Irini valley. Being careful not to overburden villagers, they tried living off the land:[16]

> Our daily routine consisted, in part, of foraging for weeds [horta] of various kinds, which we then prepared and boiled in our al fresco kitchen. One of the additions to our diet during those days was an ornamental flowering plant called the nasturtium. Sometimes we boiled the leaves of this plant and on other occasions we cut up the leaves into a salad . . . We made our lives more bearable by organising community sing-songs, singing our hearts out for hours on end, just as we had done during our captive days at Galatos . . . From time to time, we varied our entertainment programme, cutting back on our singing and turning to story-telling. Everyone talked about his job back in civvy street.

Charles Jager emphasised the reality of being on the run, however beautiful the landscape, and however generous the Cretan villagers:[17]

> But it's a Spartan's life [sic]. We are still prisoners on an island. Sleeping rough in the bush, or bedded down on the winnowed husks of an *aloni* – the village threshing floor – awakened by the bustling of hens scratching among the husks for a grain of rye, we blink at the first shafts of sunlight and pull on our boots. Always being on the alert

sharpens us up. Gossip can be lethal and so we stay only one night in one place, even on the most comfortable threshing floor. Although we put our faith in the villagers and they in us, deep down we are being worn ragged.

McDevitt, Jager and their mates were reasonably safe for the rest of that summer, but towards the end of August there were ominous signs that the relative security would not last. German Fieseler-Storch planes started reconnaissance flights over the White Mountains, suggesting the possibility of large-scale raids. Tipped off about this prospect, McDevitt's group decided it would be better to disperse. From then on all they could do was hide, and wait.

The Northeners

In the meantime, New Zealanders Dick Huston and Colin Ratcliffe (19 Battalion), and Jack Symes (Divisional Petrol Company), had also broken out of the POW compound, some time in late June. They formed a distinct subset of the men who remained in western Crete. In actual fact, they, and the couple of men who subsequently joined them, appear to be the only group which stayed in the northern part of western Crete, within eight kilometres of Hania town. They were to remain based in the one area of the *Riza*, the foothills of the White Mountains, in the rough rectangle formed by the villages of Perivolia, Therisso, Meskla and Fournes, for two years. But that is to anticipate their story. They were initially sheltered in the village of Perivolia, where an English-speaking woman, Eleni, offered them some advice about survival in the Cretan uplands:[18]

> She gave us some very good advice which I think helped us for the rest of our stay on Crete, to always look mournful and hungry especially in front of Greek women and we could be sure of their sympathy. She warned us not to play around with Greek girls if we did stay in the mountains and more especially in the mountain villages, for if we wanted our throats cut, this was the surest way to get it done . . .
>
> One other thing Eleni advised before we left . . . was not to be too

> inquisitive about Greek names. As she said, if you did not know the names you could not tell the names if you were recaptured. Of course we insisted that we would never tell but she said that the Germans had ways and means but did not elaborate.

The three Kiwis headed south into the higher hills, and found a well-camouflaged cave, which became their base. They systematically explored the barren plateau above them – shepherding territory – always with a scout out front, and found the ancient north-facing fortifications of *Kastellos*, south-by-east of the village of Varipetro. Meanwhile they made their cave as comfortable as possible:[19]

> We found a number of parachutes, conveniently rolled and stacked together as if to be picked up the next day, and carted them up to the plateau and hid them. We also found three canisters, unfortunately empty, and although we did not have an immediate use for them carried them up to the top too. Being of lightweight alloy they were not heavy to carry and later they compensated us for the effort in no small way. At this time we were preparing for a long stay on the island in case we did not get off, though reasonably confident we could find a boat. Why we did these things instead of going straight to the south coast, I cannot explain, but whatever the reason it was the right thing to do as it transpired.

After about ten days exploring the plateau, Huston and Ratcliffe descended very carefully to the nearest village, which was Varipetro. They encountered a suspicious local woman who, on learning that they were from *Nea Zilandia*, immediately took them to her house, where her son Mitsos – who insisted on being called 'Jim' – spoke some English. Dick Huston promptly became 'Dimitris' and Colin Ratcliffe 'Adonis'. From this point onwards, these men were exceptionally careful about what contacts they had with this one family in Varipetro:[20]

> we made a little rule that we would not sleep with families in case we were captured in the house and the family executed.

This group learned how to move cross-country without being seen;

how to locate water; how to deal with local shepherds and, as we shall see, bandits; how to live off the land as far as possible; and in the case of Huston in particular, how to speak the Cretan dialect of Greek. They even made a foray to south-western Crete in quest of a boat, but found the area 'crammed with escaped prisoners,' and full of 'rumours that could get us into trouble', as has already been shown, so they made their way back up north to the security of their cave and their 'support family' in Varipetro. As the weeks passed, their troglodyte existence became more routinised:[21]

> As time went on we gradually became organized. Dry foods we kept and did not eat but put aside for the winter when given to us or we had dried ourselves. In case we had to vacate the cave in a hurry we set up emergency caches in the German canisters at different places up on the plateau. We used silk or was it nylon from the parachutes to wrap the dry stores in and place in the canisters . . . We found out from the good Greeks who were the bad Greeks and we stole from their gardens especially anything that could be dried and stored away. We were encouraged to do this by the good Greeks and I think were led astray at times but as we were beginning to develop the instincts like animals our consciences forgave our stealing. The ladies from Varipetro had supplied us with some needles and as the three of us had been taught how to sew when young we could keep our clothes in some sort of order. We used the silken ropes on the parachutes, after un-ravelling them, for thread.

We shall encounter this hardy group again, but their decision to stay put in the north of Crete meant that they missed out completely on the rescues now to be discussed.

Rescue at Preveli

It was a completely different story back in Ayios Vasileios. Early on the morning of 22 July, reacting to the intelligence brought to North Africa by the successful early evaders, a Royal Navy submarine, HMS *Thrasher*, landed Lieutenant-Commander Francis Pool, RNR, and a Cretan guide, Stratis Liparakis, on Limni Beach, just a few kilometres from the

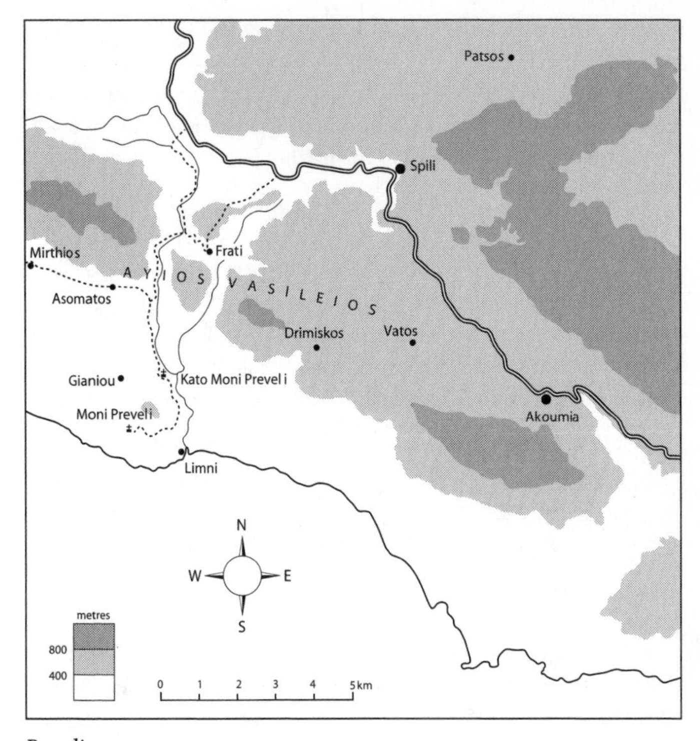

Preveli

lower part of St John's Monastery at Preveli.[22] Pool was familiar with the island and could speak Greek; before the war he had managed the Imperial Airways flying-boat station at Spinalonga in north-eastern Crete.[23] He actually worked for SOE, but was 'borrowed' by MI9 for this operation.[24] His primary mission was to pick up Commonwealth soldiers who had gathered in the Preveli area, but commensurate with SOE strategy, he also proposed to meet with local Resistance leaders. Pool made his way to the monastery and immediately formulated plans with Father Agathangelos Lagouvardos and other Resistance leaders for the evacuation of soldiers hiding in and around the monastery. A strict routine was established when the evacuation took place, with the departing soldiers leaving all clothes, boots and gear on the beach before they boarded.

From a naval point of view, these operations were extremely hazardous. Admiral Cunningham, the Royal Navy's Mediterranean Commander-in-Chief, delineates the hazards:[25]

> The steep, rocky coast, too, was practically uncharted from the point of view of operations close inshore, and the beaches used often consisted of little more than a few yards of rough shingle at the mouth of some precipitous ravine. Moonless nights were usually chosen, and moving in to within 50 or 100 yards of the shore through shallows studded with rocks was dangerous in the extreme, particularly in winter with a heavy sea running, or with the iron-bound coast blanketed in thick mist.

The story of this operation is told in HMS *Thrasher*'s 'Report of Second War Patrol', for the period of 22 to 31st July 1941, by the captain, Lieutenant-Commander P. J. Cowell, DSC.[26] This is the first time this excerpt from the submarine's log has been published:

Saturday 26th July

1730 Off Limni beach. Observed beaches through periscope, and drew a contour map of the mountains so that the bay could be identified in the night. Wind North, Force 7 in gusts. Remained dived in vicinity.

2145 Surfaced, and approached beach; found weather unsuitable for launching folboat.[27] Withdrew to seaward to charge.

2220 Saw light on hillside (adjacent to Limni Bay) flashing 'S.O.S. Please send help'. This was repeated at intervals throughout the night. Arranged code with Lieutenant Commander Pool, R.N.R. He agreed to contact the signaller and send me a coded signal with the number of men and time, so that I could rescue them the next night. Signal to be made at 2330, 27th July.

Sunday 27th July

0030 Approached beach and lay off about 250 yards from shore. Lieutenant Commander Pool, R.N.R., and one Commando manned boat on port fore plane. Submarine was trimmed until

Troops disembarking in Crete from Greece
(*Imperial War Museum Negative Number A10216*).

IMPERIAL WAR MUSEUM

General Freyberg (*Imperial War Museum Negative Number E3020E*).

IMPERIAL WAR MUSEUM

NZ soldiers in trench on Crete (*Imperial War Museum Negative Number E3025E*).

IMPERIAL WAR MUSEUM

HMS *Thrasher* (*Imperial War Museum Negative Number FL9745*)

The retreat to Sfakia (*Waiouru Army Museum Reference Number DA 10330*).

IMPERIAL WAR MUSEUM

The last well before Sfakia (*Imperial War Museum Negative Number HU17836*).

WAIOURU ARMY MUSEUM

Waiting embarkation at Sfakia (*Waiouru Army Museum Reference Number DA 10331*).

WAIOURU ARMY MUSEUM

Successful evacuees (*Waiouru Army Museum Reference Number DA 8168*).

IMPERIAL WAR MUSEUM

HMAS *Kimberley* picking up successful evaders.

IMPERIAL WAR MUSEUM

Wounded Maori soldier coming ashore at Alexandria (*Imperial War Museum Negative Number E3285*).

AUSTRALIAN WAR MEMORIAL MUSEUM

A group of Australians who were on the MLC captained by Major Garrett soon after they arrived in Alexandria, Egypt, June 1941. L–R. *Back row*: Sig L. K. Camm, L/Cpl H. Lang, Sgt G. Cockman, L/Cpl J. Lester, Dvr F. J. Wain, Dvr A. B. Hall, Pte R. King, Pte C. H. Steele. *Front row*: Sig B. F. I. R. T. Smith, Cpl I. W. Walker, Cpl E. F. W. Kirby, Cpl H. G. B. Nugent, unknown and unknown. (*Australian War Memorial Negative Number 023727*).

AUSTRALIAN WAR MEMORIAL MUSEUM

A group of Australians who were on the MLC captained by Private Richards soon after they arrived in Alexandria, Egypt, June 1941. L–R. *Front row*: Pte J. A. Gordon, Pte H. Richards, L/Cpl G. J. McMillan and Pte J. C. Thompson. *Back row*: Pte A. C. Jackson, Pte R. N. Doran, Dvr J. L. Smith and Pte R. J. Host. (*Australian War Memorial Negative Number 023722*).

Lt Len Frazer, 1941.

AUTHOR FAMILY ARCHIVE

AUTHOR FAMILY ARCHIVE

Frazer Family, 1945, young Ian in the front.

IMPERIAL WAR MUSEUM

Site of the 7th General Field Hospital/British–New Zealand POW Camp (*Imperial War Museum Negative Number HU10200*).

WAIOURU ARMY MUSEUM

Individual POW tag.

plane dipped and boat paddled off. Wind was still very gusty, gusts down the valley of about Force 6. Boat paddled for about 35 minutes and was blown back to the ship by every gust. Attempt abandoned, withdrew to seaward to charge.

0245 Wind dropped, returned to beach, lay off 150 yards from shore, and landed Lieutenant Commander Pool, R.N.R. Boat returned and landed Greek guide. On reaching shore boat was holed by a rock. It sank just before reaching the ship, in a gust of wind. Lieutenant G. S. Clarabut dived over the side and assisted the Commando to salve the boat. One tommy gun was lost, much to the regret of the Commando. Boat broke up while being hoisted inboard.

Withdrew to seaward to await next night.

2300 Sighted three pairs of green stars over Gavdo Island.

2330 Three miles off Limni Bay, received signal that 46 men would be on the beach at 0100, Monday 28th July.

Proceeded inshore and embarked 62 British soldiers, 5 naval ratings and 11 Greeks.

Details of Embarkation in Appendix 1.

Monday 28th July

0210 Operation completed, set course for Alexandria, as it was impossible to patrol with so many men on board, diving by day.

The laconic prose of the naval log should not detract attention from the remarkable seamanship required to pinpoint a small beach in the middle of the night on an enemy-occupied island, and to manoeuvre the submarine to maintain a steady position against the movement of the sea, on the one hand, and a powerful katabatic wind sweeping down from the mountains, on the other. Nor should it detract from the courage and sheer physical stamina of the SBS (Special Boat Squadron) commandos who had to paddle the folboat inshore. Nor from the almost superhuman efforts of the naval personnel to embark exhausted troops, many of whom could not swim. The actual chaotic situation on the beach on which the Royal Navy had to impose control is described in detail in the Appendix to *Thrasher*'s War Patrol:

Monday 28th July

0020 Broke charge and proceeded inshore slowly on Main Motors.

0045 Stopped motors and proceeded slowly towards beach.

0050 Touched bottom Forward, checked way of ship, and let her rest with bow just aground, 75 yards from beach.

Launched folboat manned by two heavily armed Commandos carrying forty lifebelts; boat proceeded to shore carrying rocket line, the inboard end of which was attached to a 3' grass line. On reaching shore they hauled the grass line across to the beach and signalled that there were 70 men to come off.

It had been arranged with the Commandos that 11 swimmers should be sent off to the ship, and that the remainder dressed in lifebelts should be hauled across on the grass [floating] line. The signal came off that only five swimmers had started. These men arrived and stated that there were 75 more ashore.

A delay followed and Lieutenant G. S. Clarabut was sent ashore as Beach Officer. He found a good deal of disorganization. A great many non-swimmers thought that they should be taken off in the boat and the rest were all saying ceremonious goodbyes to the Greeks who had befriended them. Boat had orders to take none. One Commando remained ashore to protect rear, and the other in the boat shepherded the swimmers in the water.

After persuasion, the men started swimming off again holding on to the grass line, but unfortunately those who thought they were drowning turned back to the shore and hauled the shore end of the grass back into the sea. However the operation continued amidst a great deal of shouting for help, and cheering. The noise was most alarming and impossible to stop. Lieutenant Clarabut came off to report the situation, but he did not get ashore again for some time, because every time he set off he had to rescue someone and pull him to the ship. The skill of these men in forcing their heads underwater when they were properly dressed in lifebelts was remarkable.

The greatest credit is due to Lieutenant Clarabut at this time, he saved at least ten men singlehanded. The evacuees did not help one another, it was a question of 'Sauve qui peut'.

When only twenty men remained ashore traffic eased. The grass was reestablished ashore, the men were dressed in lifebelts and told that the grass was going to be hauled off to the ship, with or without them. The ship would then leave. They came.

Many fell off the grass on the way, but all were saved by Lieutenant Clarabut and the two Commandos, one swimming and one in the boat.

It took all available hands to hook them out of the water. As they were naked they were not easily classifiable on deck. Several Greeks came off in this batch, but unfortunately by the time the Control room interrogation party had sorted them out I had left the beach.

0210 Came astern and proceeded to seaward at 14 knots. The most noteworthy point is that not one single man was drowned and that all organized troops were brought off.

The air photographs carried were invaluable.

The extremely accurate navigation of Lieutenant Vine, R.N.R. went a long way to making the evacuation a success.

It is an interesting coincidence that the 'help' messages flashed from the hills were the first to have been made for some weeks, and that although a constant lookout was maintained 'Thrasher' was not sighted until the folboat arrived at the beach.

Lieutenant Commander in Command.

Australian Geoffrey Edwards describes what it was like from the point of view of an evacuee:[28]

I pulled myself along the rope to the sub. Halfway out there the soldier in front of me panicked as he couldn't swim a stroke and he started splashing around and shouting out. A sailor quickly quietened him with a terrific punch to the jaw and then guided him along. As I climbed down the conning tower I got the old claustrophobic feeling but couldn't do much about it as someone just above me was pushing me down, so down into the sub I went. We were packed in like sardines but the crew were marvellous. It wasn't long before we had a lovely hot cup of tea and freshly cut sandwiches. We surfaced the next night to get some fresh air through the sub. We slipped into Alexandria harbour in typical naval style, no fuss or bother, and were told not to mention our escape from Crete as it could jeopardise the next trip that was now being organized.

In this operation, 39 Australian, 20 British, and 3 New Zealand troops, and 5 Royal Navy ratings were evacuated, along with 11 Greeks, a total of 78. The following morning the monks pushed flocks of sheep onto the beach to remove all trace of what had taken place.[29]

When HMS *Thrasher* left, Lieutenant-Commander Pool remained on the island to start talks with local Cretan leaders and organise a second evacuation. He continued to work closely with Father Agathangelos and the network of villages connected to the monastery. Pool spent the next three weeks in the interior with the Abbot putting the word around on the 'Cretan wireless' about another evacuation, to be arranged in August. This news was carried as far as the prison camp near Hania and led to even more escapes. The submarine used for the second evacuation was HMS *Torbay*, captained by Commander A.C.C. Meiers, RN.[30]

Among those who joined the second evacuation were some of the original evaders. They included Major Sandover and the last of the Australian 2/11 Battalion soldiers who had got away from Rethimnon. After seeing their comrades off at Ayia Galini at the beginning of June (see Chapter Two), they had found refuge in a village called Apodoulou, in the Amari Valley. There, Sandover had a secret meeting with Pool and learnt of the plans for the second evacuation. As the senior officer, he played the leading role in organising the embarkation when the *Torbay* arrived.[31]

The big difference between the first and second evacuation was that there was now a much larger contingent of escapers than evaders. The way in which escapers were guided from village to village shows how quickly and effectively Cretan support was mobilised once the news of Pool's evacuation plans started to get around. George Psychoundakis, who later became famous as a runner for British SOE agents operating in Crete, came from Asi Gonia, one of the villages on the main escape route between western and central Crete. He details the activity that was set in train by the first evacuation at Preveli:[32]

> So the flight of the English to Africa began. Every day a new party reached the village and every day I was their guide. I would lead them to the villages of Arolithi, Alones or Kali-Sykia and hand them over to others of our people to help them on their way. At Alones I could put them into the hands of any villager I met because all of them were good and all eager to help; and, best of all, they knew how to keep their mouths shut. Their village priest, Father John Alevizakis was a golden-hearted man and a true patriot . . . At Kali-Sykia I would guide them to the house of Stamati Tavroulakis, a fellow-villager of mine, and to several other houses. Up in the mountains above our village, at a place called Vourvoure, lived another fellow villager of ours, the Infantry Lieutenant-Colonel Andrea Papadakis. He had a fine property there and a fine house where the English often lay in hiding.

This demonstrates that Psychoundakis only had to activate pre-existing social networks to pass these men safely and quickly through Asia Gonia and on to villages further east.

Corporal Burgoyne of the Australian 2/2 Battalion describes the experience of a small group of Australians being guided through the same part of Crete.[33]

> The people gave us a guide and we went half a day's march to the other village. From then on the people always sent word ahead to say we were coming. Whenever we got there the whole village had turned out and had a meal waiting for us, usually in the village square . . . And this happened every day for a couple of weeks. They'd provide us with a guide and send a message on ahead to say, 'There's three Australian troops coming down. Look after them.' And boy did they look after us! We always had somewhere to stop.

Not everyone took a direct route to Preveli. Perhaps the most circuitous journey was that adopted by Lew Lind after he escaped from the POW camp. Starting in the Maleme area, he traversed the island three times, from north to south, south to north, and north to south again, before finally reaching – in a wholly serendipitous fashion – a village near Preveli.[34]

Other escapers to spend time in Western Crete before reaching Preveli were four sappers from Len Frazer's unit, the 2/8 Field Company. Three of them escaped from the POW camp where they had been taken after the surrender at Hora Sfakion; the fourth was one of the original members of Len's evasion party. They were all in Selino until early August, then decided to push eastwards, three of them following the coast in a small stolen rowing boat, the fourth making a wide circuit to the north. They only reached the vicinity of Preveli and learnt about the forthcoming evacuation within a few days of it taking place.[35]

Lew Lind documented the surreal appearance of this large group of Allied soldiers:[36]

> If you had searched the world, I don't suppose you could have seen anything more ludicrous than the appearance of some of our New Zealanders. Their sartorial styles were many and weird, dating down through the years to the naughty nineties. Several strutted about in straw college hats cocked well over the eye; another sported a bowler hat which he seemed to regard as a halo to his long beard; a few wore caps of strange shape; and there were two Kiwis walking about in ancient Turkish costume, turban, shirt, droopy-bottomed trousers and leather knee-boots complete. And, of course, everybody carried a walking-stick in the Greek fashion.

If members of the 2 NZEF were heavily underrepresented in the first evacuation on HMS *Thrasher*, they certainly made up for it the second time. When HMS *Torbay* pulled away from Preveli on 20 August there were 62 members of the 2 NZEF on board, the largest number that would ever come off Crete in one operation in the two years of evacuating stragglers, and roughly half the number on this submarine.[37] Most of them were escapers from Galatas prison camp and they comprised a wide cross-section of all the 2 NZEF units that fought on Crete. They did not always have the seemingly untroubled experience that Burgoyne describes getting to Preveli, reaching the south coast by a wide range of different routes and any number of near misses from German patrols.[38] One helpful soldier turned his hand to farm work while he was waiting for the second evacuation:[39]

> We filled in time by helping the farmers with their ploughing, becoming quite good at using a two cow, single furrow wooden plough. We also helped with the harvesting of the grape crop.

The total number of soldiers taken off on HMS *Torbay* was 125, and the majority of those (104) were Australians and New Zealanders. It was a record for the number of people boarded on one submarine.[40] Corporal Earnshaw describes the excitement of being among the men who were taken off:[41]

> Well, we weren't taking any chances, so as soon as darkness fell, we headed for the beach just as a long black object surfaced one hundred yards out to sea. What a glorious sight, and what a feeling of pride to see a British ship right at Jerry's back door. A small boat came ashore and then returned to the sub to enquire if we were to go aboard. Just imagine our feelings sitting on that sandy beach, sweating with a mixture of anxiety and excitement. However, that was not all our rather overstrained nerves had to suffer. All eyes were fastened on that long black outline, patiently waiting to see the small boat heading shoreward, but such was not the case. Instead, we saw that dark object slowly disappear into the black night, and with it went all our hopes of escape. So confounded were we that we remained peering into the darkness, unable to fathom such behaviour. Many were the prayers offered during those few minutes. After a while, the dark outline appeared again on our left, and came within fifty yards of the shore. This manoeuvre had been carried out in order to find a spot sheltered from the wind. A line and life-jackets were brought ashore to assist the non-swimmers, and shedding boots and clothes, and carrying any personal belongings, a swimmer and non-swimmer set off together. On reaching the ship we were hoisted aboard and given a cheery welcome

by the crew. Down below we were given towels and dry shorts, and a tot of rum. Cigarettes were freely distributed by the crew, and there was an air of goodwill among all.

Because of the large number of men collected for evacuation, HMS *Torbay* went back in again the following night. There were still too many to be embarked, so the men drew lots.

Earnshaw sums it all up as far as the lucky ones were concerned: 'What a glorious sensation that was, and to have seen these happy faces would have done you good!'

As does Lew Lind:[42]

> Once inside, a dozen cigarettes were thrust into my eager hands, and I was able to look about in the dim light. The ship was terrifically crowded. Naked men, coated with oil and grease, sprawled everywhere. They all wore an expression of deep contentment and were smoking avidly.

Three days later, on 22 August, they were in Alexandria. These two operations had evacuated a total of 203 personnel from Crete, of whom perhaps 180 were Commonwealth soldiers or sailors, the rest being Greeks.

However, a high price was exacted for these two evacuations at Preveli. After being tipped off about the second evacuation, German forces surrounded the monastery on 25 August, arrested some of the monks and ransacked the premises, taking away all moveable property, their livestock, and produce stored there. They then put the premises under permanent surveillance, effectively closing down the Preveli escape route.[43] It was a devastating end to what were two highly successful operations in the early months of the occupation. Fortunately, the Abbot escaped before the raid took place, and was later spirited away to Cairo.

There were still many more escapers hiding in Ayios Vasileios who were unable to get off on HMS *Torbay*. They were waiting for a third submarine evacuation, planned for Preveli in September. But with the monastery empty and under constant watch, that mission had to be cancelled and the men relocated. There were 120 hiding in and around the village of Frati under the care of Manolis Vassilakis. With the help of several guides they were moved to Patsos under Yorgos Harokopos, and from there fed slowly through the Amari in the direction of the more isolated coastline below the Messara Plain.[44] Again, there was nothing for it but to hide and wait.

North by North-west

Among the large number of escapers that passed through Selino, a small detachment shifted their sights elsewhere rather than persist with the increasingly unfavourable small-boat lottery being played out along the southern coast. In some cases, like Lew Lind, they headed east to the other side of the White Mountains and were lucky enough to get off on HMS *Torbay*. Others took a new direction altogether, heading north to try their luck with boats crossing from Crete to mainland Greece. Heading for the mainland would not be any less dangerous than Crete but there might be more boats available making the run to Egypt. There was also the possibility of heading east through the Aegean Islands to Turkey.

One party that gave up on Selino and aimed north was a small (and rather exclusive) group of officers, British and Australian, led by a Greek, Lieutenant-Commander Emmanuel Vernikos, RNR, better known to the men on the run as Captain Emilios. Vernikos is described in the MI9 Summary History as a merchant marine skipper, who commanded the *Irene Vernikos* in Souda Bay, tending the boom.[45] For the short time he was in Selino, Vernikos tried to convince all the wandering soldiers he met that he could get them off the island. In the end he only took three officers with him, crossing to the Greek mainland from the Rodopos Peninsula, then sailing by small boat through the Cyclades and on to Turkey, and thence Egypt.[46] These three officers were Miles Hildyard and Michael Woodbine Parish of the Sherwood Rangers, a Nottinghamshire Yeomanry regiment, and Fred Embrey of the 2/1 Australian Infantry Battalion.

Brief mention must be made here of these first two officers. They were among the very few Englishmen in the surprisingly low number

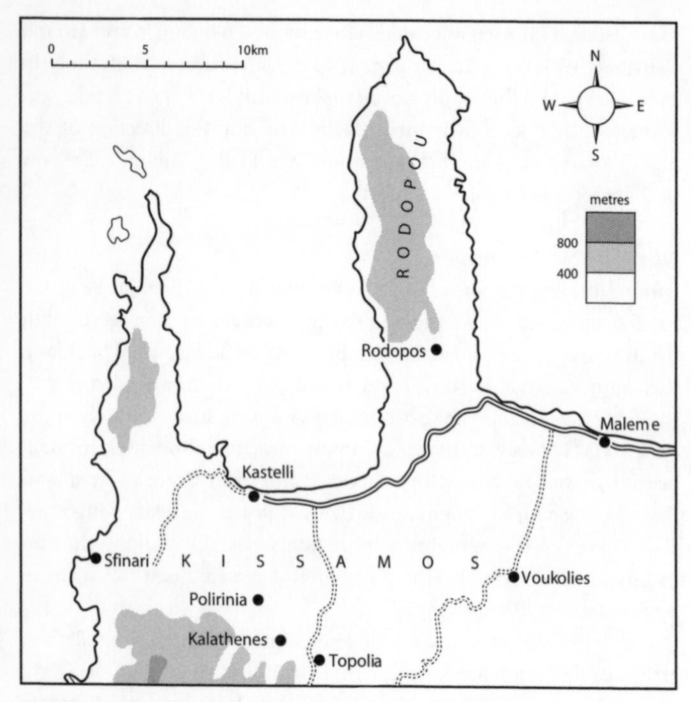

North-west Crete

of officers represented in the thousand or so escapers and evaders. Their memoir leads ineluctably to the conclusion that these two officers were of the kind referred to as 'Ruperts' by British squaddies.[47] Reading between the lines, it is plain that they were shuttled around by either Cretan villagers, or Australian and New Zealand soldiers. On meeting some of the former, Hildyard says:[48]

> Now, sitting alone on a rock with three of them, I discovered how very much easier to talk to they were than our own men. Completely democratic, without any class consciousness, they were perfectly reasonable companions, where an English soldier would have been either dumb or tiresome.

However, these same Australians, men from the 2/2 Battalion, tell a different story:[49]

> One of the Pommies complained about the straw in the bread. And I dunno whether I said it, or a mate said 'Look, their kids are going without that bread to give you a bloody feed.' And he didn't realize that. He said 'It's hard eating.' We said 'They're not getting it – they're giving it to you.' That's why we didn't like them. We didn't really get on together. They tried to pull the English gentlemen on us and we were only ignorant Diggers sort of thing. But we reckoned we were better soldiers than they were, even though they were officers. In the end we were glad to see the end of them.

These two English gentlemen failed equally to impress the New Zealand soldiers. Fred Irving (23 Battalion) describes meeting them:[50]

> It was at this time that two British Army officers joined our group, and immediately started to order us about, they were smartly told we had got here by our own initiative and they could go and get stuffed.

Both of these officers gave Vernikos a cheque for fifty pounds to pay for their escape to mainland Greece – the only recorded instance of payment in order to get off Crete.[51]

An infinitely more impressive escape effort, at much the same time, was that made by Kiwi Sergeant Redpath. Redpath was hanging around Ayia Irini and Epanohori in late July, completely fed up after several failed attempts at getting a boat in Selino, when he heard about caiques making secret crossings between mainland Greece and Crete. This intelligence was passed on by Cretan soldiers, recently returned to their homes on the island after serving with the 5th Crete Division on the Albanian front. After fighting with great distinction against the Italian invaders, this division had found itself stranded after the German invasion of Greece and the Greek surrender in April 1941. Those who could, made their way back home.[52]

Redpath persuaded eight other escapees, Australians (including Charles Jager) and New Zealanders, to accompany him to the Rodopos Peninsula in north-western Crete. Initially he planned to board one of these caiques on its return journey, seize it while at sea, and force the crew to divert to the south. After getting to Rodopos they had to wait 11 days for a boat. However, once it arrived and they forced their way on board, they decided to make for the Peloponnese rather than try and hijack the boat. Redpath and his party reached Cape Maleas on 13 August and made for the Neapolis area. They spent nearly two months there hiding from Italian forces, were joined by a lot more escapees, made two unsuccessful attempts at hijacking caiques until finally, on their third attempt, seized a boat that they were able to sail to North Africa.[53]

Waiting Game

Despite the resounding successes in getting off the island from June through to August, there were still large numbers of Australians and New Zealanders left behind; and they were no more certain of getting away than they had been when the enemy occupation began. German garrison forces were tightening their grip on the island, and issuing tough warnings against any who might be engaged in assisting Allied soldiers. The lack of certainty, and the risk that their presence posed for villagers, saw most of the men adopt a fugitive lifestyle whereby they kept constantly on the move, only spending a short time in any one location, living off the land and supplementing that with food provided by their protectors. While they were on the move, they always travelled at night and only visited people after dark. When resting, they avoided staying in houses or villages, but found shelter in the surrounding hills, using caves, shepherds' huts, olive groves and various other shelter for protection.

This lifestyle did not preclude close personal relationships with Cretan families, however. Most fugitives, like Dick Huston's group, had their favourite calling places where generosity was automatic and unconditional, but they were careful not to overuse them, rotating between them depending on enemy movements, the state of food supplies, and the presence of other fugitives in the district. The principal maxim on both sides was secrecy at all times. As their lives became more and more intertwined, Cretans and Anzacs tacitly accepted that for their mutual protection they had to conceal everything.

Atrocity and Massacre

When the Germans were about to invade Crete, they were told that the Cretans were Germanophiles and would rally to their support against the British and Commonwealth forces. However, the Germans cannot have been familiar with the history outlined in Chapter Four, because from the very first minute of the invasion, Cretan men, women and children joined their compatriots in uniform, or attached themselves as irregulars to British and Commonwealth units, or simply formed their own bands of *franc-tireurs*. Armed with ancient muskets or shotguns, and more often, knives, sickles, shepherd's crooks and rocks, they fell upon the Germans, killing them wherever they found them. Not only were the Germans astonished at the slaughter of their elite paratroops – often before they even hit the ground – but they were also astounded by the ferocity of the Cretan civilians' resistance. Very early on in the battle, on 23 May, when pitched fighting was still taking place, General Ringel issued the following proclamation:[54]

> THE GREEK POPULATION, IN CIVILIAN OR GERMAN UNIFORM, IS TAKING PART IN THE FIGHTING. THEY ARE MUTILATING AND ROBBING THE CORPSES OF OUR GERMAN SOLDIERS. ANY GREEK CIVILIAN TAKEN WITH A FIREARM IN HIS HANDS IS TO BE SHOT IMMEDIATELY. HOSTAGES (MEN BETWEEN 18 AND 55) ARE TO BE TAKEN FROM THEIR VILLAGES AND IF ACTS OF HOSTILITY TAKE PLACE AGAINST THE GERMAN ARMY WILL BE SHOT. TEN GREEKS WILL DIE FOR EVERY GERMAN.

This grim proclamation was endorsed by General Student, who subsequently, on 31 May, issued an equally implacable order for wholesale reprisals.[55] Needless to say, there were no Cretans fighting in *German* uniform.

It did not take long before the atrocities started. A group of 42 villagers from the Heraklion area was executed without trial as early as 24 May.[56] On 2 June, 60 men from the village of Kontomari, near Maleme, were executed by firing squad.[57] At Kandanos, where the locals, after three days' fighting, had wiped out a motorcycle thrust

To the population and the military forces on Crete

It has been brought to the notice of the German Supreme Command that German soldiers who fell into the hands of the enemy on the island of Crete have been illtreated and even mutilated in a most infomous and inhuman manner.

As a punishment and reprisal therefore is announced as follows :

1) Whosoever commits such crimes against international laws on German prisoners of war will be punished in the manner of his own cruel action, no matter be he or she a man or a woman.

2) Localities near which such crimes have been perpetrated will be burned down. The population will be held responsible.

3) Beyond those measures further and sharper reprisals will be held in store.

The German Supreme Command

This chilling pamphlet was air-dropped on all villages bordering on the battlefield in May 1941

towards Paleochora on 25 May and then fled to the hills, the Germans returned on 3 June, executed the remaining seven villagers and burned the village to the ground.[58] (This was the atrocity which Len Frazer had heard about up in the mountains, via the 'Cretan telegraph' – see Chapter Three.) At Kastelli, where a 72-strong German company had lost 54 men to a mixed force of the 1st Greek Regiment and Cretan irregulars, 200 local men were slaughtered.[59]

This last massacre happened because the Germans alleged that Cretan irregulars had mutilated their paratroops (see pamphlet on page 110). A subsequent German enquiry found that only 25 cases of mutilation were reported on the whole island, and as Beevor reports, '. . . almost all of those had almost certainly been inflicted after death'.[60] The fact of the matter is that most of what the Germans saw as 'mutilations' were inflicted by the primitive weaponry carried by the irregulars, with stab wounds and caved-in heads being frequent, exacerbated by the effect of heat upon dead bodies.

Similar blood baths took place all over western Crete, particularly in the areas where the fighting had been heaviest. One source says that 2000-plus Cretans were executed in June 1941 alone.[61] The Cretans were then warned that the penalty for harbouring men on the run was death – of the whole family involved. The first systematic terror related to this edict occurred on 1 August, in the villages of Skines, Fournes and Aliakianou, south of Hania, which were destroyed, with the butchering of 145 men and 2 women.[62] Peter Winter, who, as we have seen, had escaped from the POW camp – and a potential arranged marriage! – eyewitnessed the latter massacres after being recaptured near Kastelli:[63]

> We were led away to a point where we could see the Cretans who had already been 'court-martialled' being tied in rows of six before being led to a dry river-bed and shot. One old man who could not keep pace was untied and allowed to hobble alone to his death. The scene was so unreal one did not feel particularly threatened or even shocked: there was merely a kind of numbness. Our turn in the death procession was getting close when the interpreter strolled over and offered us cigarettes. He talked casually for a time, then said it had been decided not to shoot us that day. Reprisals for the Cretan civilians' resistance to the German invasion and for their mutilation of some of the parachutists was his explanation of the scenes we witnessed. 'It is for soldiers to fight, not civilians,' he announced blandly as a burst of machine-gun fire dealt with another six peasants.

On the same day, there was a similar massacre in the Souda area:[64]

> The Suda Valley massacre of 1st August 1941 was a busy affair, 108 men shot at daylight, including several priests and a Kiwi sick in bed with malaria, and all with no names and no questions asked.

Now there could be no doubt in anyone's mind about what was going to eventuate if the Germans found Cretans harbouring Anzac soldiers on the run. Lew Lind's 'human slaughter and strife' had arrived with a vengeance, quite literally.

CHAPTER 6

The Long Haul: Winter 1941–1942

Tightening the Noose

In the first three months of the occupation, German reprisals and attempts to catch escapees were largely confined to the northern coast of Crete, especially villages in and around the battlefields between Kastelli and Heraklion. In western Crete, there were small garrisons at Paleochora and Askyfou, and a listening post at Souyia, but little presence elsewhere. So long as the men on the run took basic precautions – travelling only at night, keeping out of villages as much as possible – they could move about fairly freely.

In early September this state of affairs changed dramatically. Well aware that there were large numbers of escapees in the mountains, the Germans made their first large-scale sweep through the interior with heavily armed patrols and Fieseler Storch spotter planes. They picked up fugitives – and executed villagers – as they went. There was advance warning about the raids through the 'Cretan wireless' and every effort was made to find good hiding places, but many men were caught in this action.

Len Frazer was still in the Ahladiakes area when the German sweep started, and was taken to a cave in the hills just outside the village. Jim McDevitt had also reached Ahladiakes from Skafi, and they ended up in the same cave, along with a third man by the name of George, from a Cypriot army unit.[1] They were all under the protection of Manolis Daoundakis and his family, at enormous risk to themselves.

The three men were no sooner lodged in their hide-out than they were virtually imprisoned there. Completely unaware that there were any stragglers in the vicinity, a small German detachment set up an observation post immediately opposite the cave, armed with a machine gun that covered everything in view. The cave dwellers were effectively sealed in. They were visited at night by members of the Daoundakis family who kept them supplied with food and blankets, and also brought the latest news of troop movements in the area. As the days wore on, Manolis Daoundakis became quite ingenious, if not foolhardy in his efforts, at keeping them informed. Grazing his goats around the cave, he would sing *mantinades*, traditional Cretan songs, incorporating coded messages.[2] Hence they learned of the large-scale arrests and executions taking place in nearby Paleochora.

The imprisonment in the cave lasted for a fortnight, with one close shave after another as the three troglodytes looked for ways to relieve their boredom. Becoming impatient, Len nearly blew their cover by leaving too early, but was quickly pushed into another cave by Manolis's mother.[3] Finally, the Germans decamped and returned to base, and the trio were free to move around in the light once more.

Others were not so lucky. Large numbers of Commonwealth soldiers were recaptured, and scores of villagers were executed. In a German report held in the British Public Records Office,[4] there is a brief summary of a raid that took place on the Omalos Plateau.

> The Tribunals found 110 men guilty, amongst which 39 civilians and 6 British personnel, all sentenced for attempting resistance, and immediately shot . . . 77 British military personnel were captured.

Note that these German 'Tribunals' summarily executed Commonwealth soldiers as well as Cretan civilians. Most of the civilians arrested in the Selino district were taken to Paleochora and confined in an abandoned oil factory on the outskirts of town. They were then arraigned before a provisional court, but this was a mockery; there was never any intention of giving the Cretans a fair trial. Executions were carried out daily over the first 10 days of September; at least 29 were killed in this way.[5] Mark Mazower, the historian of the German occupation of Greece, explains the ruthless logic behind these executions:[6]

> One of the basic assumptions behind German Occupation policy was that 'terror had to be answered with terror' to force the population to withdraw its support from the insurgents.

Not just insurgents, but escapers and evaders as well. What had started in May, and had been sanctioned at the highest levels, was being continued, and would be continued throughout the occupation. General Student's orders were still being followed:[7]

> All operations are to be carried out with great speed, leaving aside all formalities and certainly dispensing with special courts . . . These are not meant for beasts and murderers.

Although there are no reliable figures for the number of Commonwealth soldiers recaptured in September, or the numbers of soldiers and civilians who were executed, we estimate that at least one hundred soldiers were rounded up. However, what we do know is that, on Crete, this German policy did not have the intended impact. There were still large numbers of men on the run, and Cretan families continued to protect and feed them as best they could. There was now much greater vigilance than previously, but relations between soldiers and villagers remained as strong as ever.

Fugitives and Their Friends

Once German troops withdrew from Selino villages in mid-September there were renewed attempts among the escapers and evaders to find ways of getting to Egypt. Within a short time, persistent rumours began circulating of an evacuation being planned for the end of the month. By 30 September, large numbers of Australians and New Zealanders had gathered in the far south-west corner of the island, close to Cape Krios, all hopeful of a boat that would finally take them off Crete. Cape Krios is a rocky headland with steep cliffs on the seaward side (see Map on page 87). Not far north are two small beaches in between the cliffs providing good shelter for small boats. On the slopes above one of the beaches, in amongst the loose rock and low coastal vegetation, there is a small white-washed church, the Chapel of Ayios Ioannis (John the Baptist). Further north still, there is a large bay, at the far end of which is the small uninhabited island of Elafonissos. This is a remote and isolated region of Crete, largely unfrequented except for shepherds and their goats.

The soldiers who gathered there arrived in small groups, mostly at night or early morning, coming cross-country on shepherd's paths from various parts of western Crete. By some accounts there were up to 60 men congregated in the area by 30 September.[8] The rumour was that at least one caique, and possibly two, would be calling to take Commonwealth soldiers to Egypt. The person whom they believed would bring all this about was a Cretan known only as Kapetan Yorgos – Captain George.[9]

Len was one of the few people to actually meet the Captain. This was on 23 September 1941:[10]

> After lunch go with guide to next village. Well received eat and drink taken over by C. who knows abt boat and who has satisfied himself I am not a spy. Go to town meet boat captain, [who] ask[s] for my identification papers, [and] says that boat will go in 3–4 days. I [am] to look after [the] Engl. 40 and 30.

The '40 and 30' refers to the capacity of the boats. Len was quoted 20 pounds a head, and expected to organise payment when they reached Alexandria. Other versions of this story say that the boat was up for purchase, and that lots of fund-raising went on before the soldiers were due to meet Captain George.[11] Ken Little provides a slightly fuller account of this enigmatic figure:[12]

> Captain George . . . was something of a black marketeer, dealing mainly in supplying soap and cigarettes . . . Anyway, Captain George went from village to village collecting money from his supporters to buy a boat and it was during this time that we met him. He was a real character, I would not have liked to have been his enemy.

Meanwhile, food was short amongst these waiting soldiers, except for the few scraps which they brought with them and what they could forage from the surrounding hillsides and rocky foreshore. And they quickly discovered that they were not the only ones hoping for a ride to Egypt. Soon after their arrival, another would-be passenger appeared – a heavily armed bandit, Yiannis Glabedakis, who had escaped from Galatas prison during the invasion and been hiding out in the mountains ever since. He had been sentenced to 15 years for murder before the war.[13] A much more pleasant surprise was the unexpected appearance of a prominent Cretan landholder from the distant village of Vothiana, Alex Makrakis – another 'Returned Yank' – bringing a donkeyload of basic supplies.[14] Makrakis knew about the arrangement with Captain George and wanted to give all the men – some of whom he was sheltering at the time – a good send-off. Considering it was a six-hour journey on narrow bridle paths from his village to the coast, they all appreciated this generous gesture.

However, days passed without any sign of Captain George, and then word arrived that he wouldn't be coming. This is how Private Murray McLagan of the NZ 5th Field Regiment tells it:[15]

> Then tragedy! News came through that the Greek from whom we were buying the boat had taken both it and our cash. Some may say that we had been careless but the boat was in a port occupied by German troops, and, of course, it was impossible for us to supervise the fitting out of the boat and we had been assured of the honesty of the boatman. Failure! Dismay beat in the heart of every man as we heard this saddening news. Would we ever escape now [?] The Germans had every boat under guard so what hope had we of obtaining one . . .

Len Frazer, who went to Cape Krios with Alex Makrakis, also recorded this incident in his diary:[16]

> 1 [October]. Up early and set out with A. for coast. breakfast on honey and cheese. A. falls and camera is broken. pick up B & B go to church. I sleep on the altar.[17] No boat comes, we are many.

SOLDIERS

OF THE

ROYAL BRITISH ARMY, NAVY, AIR FORCE!

There are MANY OF YOU STILL HIDING in the mountains, valleys and villages.

You have to PRESENT yourself AT ONCE TO THE GERMAN TROOPS.

Every OPPOSITION will be completely USELESS!

Every ATTEMPT TO FLEE will be in VAIN.

The COMMING WINTER will force you to leave the mountains.

Only soldiers, who PRESENT themselves AT ONCE, will be sure of a HONOURABLE AND SOLDIERLIKE CAPTIVITY OF WAR. On the contrary who is met in civil clothes will be treated as a spy.

THE COMMANDER OF KRETA

German surrender pamphlet

2. J. and I spend day in gully. eat dry fruit and nuts. Go to church at night sleep outside – No boat.
3. Back to gully. J. has skin disease caused by Mos. [mosquitoes] for over week. Aeroplanes are spoil sports. We go back to 'different' home. – pamphlet 5½ hours walk, 2 hrs sleep.
4. We are stumped. Get some tucker and sleep all day in old house and later at water.

> 5. Bert brings cobbers and we are many.[18] Meet Doc. W. Hear that Capt G. who went to get boat has got married instead. The mentality of these people is beyond my comp. The hopes of getting away are rare. I think a lot of home and wonder that if I have to stay here two years or so if Renee will marry again. Consider this a silly thought. Sleep between sheets with John.

The aeroplanes referred to here were German seaplanes searching for stragglers from the air. The 'pamphlet' was part of a big leaflet drop by the Germans urging the fugitives to give themselves up.

The line in the pamphlet which worried some men was the last one, promising an 'honourable and soldierlike captivity' if they gave themselves up straight away, but threatening to treat as spies anyone caught dressed in civilian clothes. For many of those who gathered hopefully at Cape Krios, the experience with Captain George and the continuing harassment by German forces constituted a reality shock. Winter was fast approaching (as the pamphlet reminded them), and their options had virtually dried up. Rumours to the contrary, no British agent had surfaced in western Crete since the occupation began, and there seemed little chance of being rescued in the foreseeable future. Not surprisingly, some – again an unknown number – gave themselves up at this time,[19] as Murray McLagan recounts:[20]

> Many, considering their chances of escape hopeless, gave themselves up to German patrols while others, including my friend Vic, marched into German posts and surrendered themselves to the troops.

One of the contributing factors to the surrender of these men – besides being in despair of rescue – was the pitiful state of their boots. Weeks of being constantly on the move, travelling cross-country on rough mountain tracks, had taken their toll and reduced their footwear to shreds. If they hadn't found a replacement pair or been lucky enough to have them repaired, they were reduced to bare feet or wooden clogs, greatly limiting their ability to survive.

For those that did not give themselves up, the will to keep going and avoid capture depended essentially on forming close relations with

Cretan families. In some cases this started very early, just as soon as they left the prison camp in between June and August, but for others it took several weeks, and some considerable wandering through western and central Crete, before they were befriended in this way. The bonds that were formed with supportive families were so close that the men concerned were treated virtually as family members.

Kiwi Sapper Len Beere was making his way back to the north coast on his own, thinking seriously of giving himself up after the debacle at Cape Krios. Cooking himself some chestnuts, he met a young girl who persuaded him to accompany her to the family house in the village of Strovles.[21] The young girl's parents, Spiro and Anastasia Vakakis, persuaded Beere to stay with them. Initially he lived inside as a member of the household, sharing in the farm work. Later, when it became too risky to stay on indoors, he moved out and found shelter in the nearby hills. His last hiding place was two hours' walk from the village, but despite this, his friends continued to feed him and look after his basic needs. This close relationship continued until he was finally evacuated in May 1943.[22]

Another straggler with a similar experience was Murray McLagan. He had not travelled very far from Cape Krios, heading back eastwards along the coast, before he was taken in by a family at Koundoura. He ended up relying on them for the next 18 months.[23] During this time, he worked as a shepherd, milked goats and sheep, and undertook other routine farmwork. Feeling obliged to make more of a contribution to the household, he devised a way of making stock chains out of stolen telephone wire, setting up a small workshop in a cave some distance from the village. He became so good at this art that he was able to barter the chains (and other handcrafts) for food and make himself more independent. Like Len Beere, he found a place where he was accepted and protected while waiting for help in order to get away.

Privates Reg Rolfe and Bert Gill both found families in the village of Vothiana, deep inside western Selino. Bert Gill lived with the Makrakis family, and Reg Rolfe with the Pondikakis family, alternating between the two Pondikakis brothers, Manolis and Theodore.[24] Two other New

Zealanders, Sergeant Tom Moir and Gunner Dudley Perkins (both from 4th Field Regt.), hid in the village of Moustakos, only a short distance from Vothiana.[25]

Not far away from them were Jim McDevitt, and Corporal Ned Nathan of 28th (Maori) Battalion. Nathan had become friendly with two closely related families at Sklavopoula, the Torakis family and the Papantonakis family. He had originally found his way to Sklavopoula in late May after evading capture in the aftermath of fighting around Maleme and Hania.[26] Badly wounded at the time, he approached the Torakis family for medical assistance. He didn't stay long on that occasion, but returned there three months later after spending time at Koustoyerako and Prodromi. McDevitt was invited to Sklavopoula by Iphigenia Papantonakis (known as Fifi), the wife of the Chief Medical Officer for Crete.[27] McDevitt had accompanied Gill, Rolfe and John Kerr back to Vothiana after the episode at Cape Krios, and Fifi stepped in to take some of the pressure off the Makrakis household. In time, Fifi became a legendary host to New Zealand stragglers, looking after 25 of them at various times during the first two years of the occupation.[28]

The men who were in concealment around Vothiana, Moustakos and Sklavopoula were particularly determined in the hunt for a boat. They were desperate to get to Egypt and prepared to take big risks to do so. It didn't matter if winter was coming and ocean conditions were against small boats, they would keep trying. On one occasion, Perkins and Moir stole a four-metre boat about five kilometres north of Elafonissos.[29] Sailing it south to the little island, they hid it while they gathered some supplies and equipment for the voyage. But before they could put out to sea again the owners caught up with them and demanded their boat back. The Kiwis had no choice but to return it.

Later on, Kerr (who discovered the boat), Rolfe, Gill, Moir and Perkins put to sea again; this time in a boat that had been abandoned and needed some repairs to make it seaworthy.[30] They repaired the boat as best they could in the shelter of Elafonissos, and made a sail out of blankets. There was no rudder, but three oars between five of them. When they eventually set sail and reached the open sea, they were engulfed by a violent storm. They soon abandoned the attempt but it

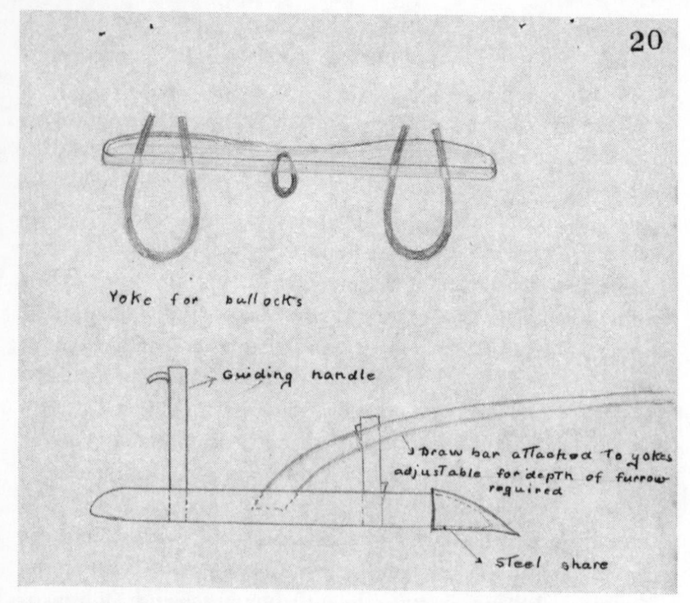

Murray McLagan's sketch of yoke and plough used by oxen on Crete

took them nine hours of baling and rowing to get back to land again. When they recovered, they decided it was vital to find a bigger vessel.

There were other attempts that winter, but it was not until April 1942 that all these efforts finally met their reward and one small party of eight men at last cleared the coast and made it to North Africa.[31]

Slightly to the east, Lance Bombardier Bella Johnston had based himself in the village of Asfendiles, six kilometres north-east of Paleochora. His dark Maori features permitted him to pass as a local:[32]

> To augment our cigarette ration, I was going into Paleochora and selling oranges to the Germans. This was no great risk, as my colouring and appearance made it easy to pass myself off as a Greek. Furthermore, my sketchy knowledge of Greek was vastly superior to the Germans.

But as winter was approaching, Johnston was worried about his lack of adequate footwear, so decided to give himself up, beg, borrow or steal some boots, and escape again. But when he went down to Paleochora he couldn't find a German to whom he could surrender, the Cretan Police didn't want to know about it, and so he repaired to the local *kafeneion* (café) for a wine-drinking session. Johnston was one of the few men who did not have a fake identity card, so he knew he was in trouble when a German officer and two privates came into the *kafeneion* demanding ID:[33]

> When the officer came to me the conversation went as follows.
> Officer – 'Pou Enna Taftortita' (Where is your pass?)
> Me – 'Venesse' (Have Not)
> Officer – 'Pou' (Where?)
> Me – 'Spiti mou' (My house)
> Officer – 'Pou Enna Spiti' (Where is your house?)
> Me – '32 Wanganui Avenue, Auckland NZ. What are you going to do about it?'
> I have never seen a more dumbfounded look, particularly as we were practically nodding acquaintances. During my sojourn as a fruiterer the officer was one of my best customers. Off I was marched to the local jail where the Police implored me not to do a bunk, as the officer with typical German practicality had told them: 'See he is here in the morning or we will shoot the lot of you.'

We are happy to report that Johnston arrived safely in the POW camp, where, as he puts it, he 'collected' a pair of boots and promptly escaped again – with two mates! In his own words:[34]

> About this time I gained a certain notoriety, by having a price of 4,000 Drachmae put on my head.
> N.B. 4,000 Drachmae was roughly the price of a very ordinary pair of boots.

Success and Failure in Central Crete

It was outlined earlier how escapees who travelled eastwards from the villages of Therisso and Drakona benefited from a network of Cretan villages where sympathetic families fed, clothed and hid them, and passed them on from one safe house to the next, in the direction of the Amari Valley. The first two evacuations in July and August took the pressure off local communities temporarily, but large numbers of escapees remained. The southern districts of the Rethimnon and Heraklion prefectures, and especially the Amari, still harboured the largest concentration of stragglers of any area on the island.[35] Before his evacuation, the Abbot of Preveli, Agathangelos Lagouvardos, had played a major role in coordinating the movements and protection of these soldiers; so did the schoolmaster of Gerakari, Alexandros Kokonas, and a man who ran an olive oil pressing business and later became a prominent guerrilla leader in the Heraklion region, Kapetan Yorgos Petrakoyorgos.[36]

The key problem for the men on the run was that their rescue had relatively little priority in Middle East Headquarters in Cairo. Much greater priority was given to supporting the Resistance on Crete, particularly after Lieutenant-Commander Francis Pool returned in late August, as SOE was keen to see a united resistance movement.[37] One of the escapees rescued by Pool on *Torbay* was Lieutenant (later Major) Jack Smith-Hughes, who had fought on Crete with the Royal Army Service Corps.[38] While at large, he met Lieutenant-Colonel Andreas Papadakis, who helped him to escape.[39] Papadakis had established an organisation for the liberation of Crete in the early days of the occupation, and put himself at the head of it. It was called *Anotate Epitrope Apelevtheroseos Kritis* (AEAK), or the Supreme Committee for the Liberation of Crete.[40]

Once he reached Cairo, Smith-Hughes was recruited by SOE for further service on Crete, returning on 9 October 1941 on the submarine HMS *Thunderbolt*, skippered by Lieutenant-Commander Cecil Crouch.[41] Smith-Hughes was accompanied by an ISLD[42] operative, Sergeant (later Captain) Ralph Stockbridge, who was being sent to the island as a wireless operator. They landed at Tsoutsouros Bay, near the village of Akhendria, and immediately made their way westwards to meet up with Papadakis and establish a headquarters at his house.

Smith-Hughes's principal task was to liaise with guerrilla leaders and encourage greater cooperation between them. But in addition, he was also charged with preparing another group of stragglers for evacuation. This time it was proposed to utilise the same boats being used to transport agents, arms and supplies to Crete. There were two vessels involved, HMS *Hedgehog*, a converted trawler, and HMS *Escampador*, a caique, skippered by Lieutenant-Commanders John Campbell and Mike Cumberlege respectively.[43]

Seven weeks after he landed, on 23 November 1941, Smith-Hughes oversaw another large evacuation of escapers and evaders at a small beach called Treis Ekklessies, located on an isolated part of the south coast (directly south of Heraklion). While both vessels travelled to Crete, only HMS *Hedgehog* boarded soldiers for the return trip to Alexandria. HMS *Escampador* was carrying another agent, Captain Monty Woodhouse, who would, in due course, take over from Smith-Hughes. Woodhouse was startled by the nature of his arrival:[44]

> Expecting a clandestine landing, Woodhouse found a reception committee of bewildering size. Apart from Jack Smith-Hughes, there were the three main guerilla kapitans of central Crete: Manoli Bandouvas, his *frère ennemi*, Petrakogeorges and Satanas, together with scores of British and Anzac soldiers clamouring for evacuation. A number had acquired Cretan girlfriends and wanted to take them to Egypt.

Of those scores of soldiers that Woodhouse encountered, 86 were boarded for the trip back. They included 28 Australians, 28 New Zealanders, 11 British, and 16 Cypriots.[45] Whether any of the 'Cretan girlfriends' were also taken on board is not recorded. However, not all of the stragglers who had heard of this evacuation were physically able to reach the south coast. For example, Arthur Lambert, who was hiding near the village of Lambini, nine kilometres north-east of Preveli, in November 1941, had been afflicted with yellow jaundice, which he was to have for three months.[46] He had teamed up with Australians Sergeant Reg Saunders, an Aboriginal, of the 2/7th Battalion, and George Burgess of the 2/3rd, whom he describes:[47]

> Both were six feet tall, a pair of the finest, most decent men I've ever met.

A young local woman, Vassiliki, was looking after them. Burgess subsequently took off on his own.

The news of the evacuation, and a German raiding party, arrived simultaneously. After a series of hair-raising escapes, Lambert and Saunders set off for the coast. Lambert's boots were now soleless, so he discarded them and continued barefoot, but soon realised that there was no chance of covering the twenty kilometres to the pick-up point in that state. He describes what happened next.[48]

> I said, 'Reg, my feet are in bad way, so I'll stay here. I've given you my brothers' unit and army numbers and when you get to Egypt please contact one or both, tell them I'm alive and well, and I'll try to catch the next sub.' Reg was silent for a moment, then he squatted down in front of me and said, 'Get on my back.' I said, 'Reg, you're a great guy, but you couldn't carry me 20 kilometres.' He replied, 'I would give it a bloody good go!' I said, 'Go, Reg, go! I'll be okay.' Reg got to his feet, turned to the guide, and said in Greek, 'Thanassi (my Greek name) and I have decided to stay. We like it here, so let's go back to the village.' And to me, 'Do you think I would walk out on you? *Never!*'

The onset of winter made for worsening conditions on the south coast. It was planned that *Hedgehog* would do another trip in late December/early January, dropping more Intelligence personnel and picking up another load of stragglers. Woodhouse would round these men up and have them waiting at Treis Ekklessies. Among the SOE agents being sent to Crete was Captain Xan Fielding, the first to be assigned to western Crete.

As it turned out, *Hedgehog* departed Alexandria but never made it to Crete. It struck a storm mid-ocean and was forced to return.[49] The agents, with their supplies, immediately secured another vessel, the submarine HMS *Torbay*, under Lieutenant-Commander Meirs, to transport them to their destination. However, bad weather prevented

Vassiliki, Arthur Lambert's helper from the village of Lambini, in 1981

both the *Torbay* and a Greek submarine from carrying out further evacuation, and around 120 men waiting at Treis Ekklessies were left stranded.

This time, equipped with a pair of shoes made by the Lambini cobbler, Lambert had made it, and was waiting to be taken off. He had come to know Woodhouse well and remembers him advising them that there would be another vessel coming for the pick-up, but that there would be 20 fewer spaces than originally planned.[50] Generously, Lambert volunteered to stand aside, but in the event he need not have bothered. Shortly afterwards, news arrived that the Germans had got wind of the evacuation plans and were already on their way. Everyone was ordered to clear out rapidly and head back to the safety of the mountains. Lambert and six others, including Saunders and Burgess, immediately made off east, towards Lasithi.[51]

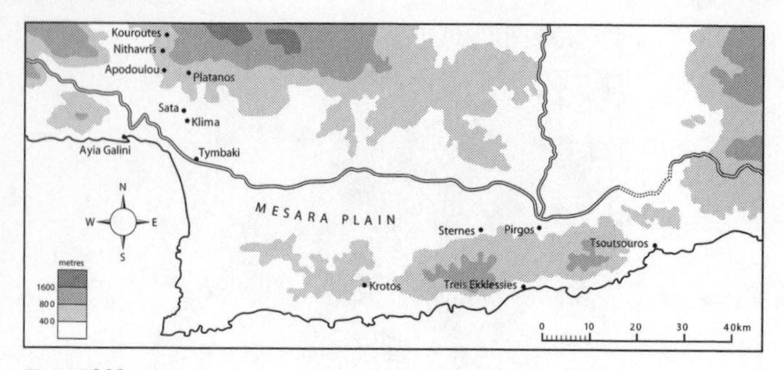

Treis Ekklessies

This was, in fact, the third time that Lambert had just missed out on getting off the island. The first time was at Preveli, when he was mistakenly advised not to go to the pick-up point; the second time was in November when, as we have seen, not only did he have jaundice, but also his bare feet simply could not carry him to join the evacuation group being organised by Smith-Hughes.

When Xan Fielding went to meet Woodhouse on the day that he landed, he came across a large group of Australians drowning their sorrows:[52]

> For a moment I felt as though we had entered an Anzac encampment. The chorus of *Waltzing Matilda* filled the dusk as loudly as a wireless switched on at full blast against a background of yowling, spluttering atmospherics composed of typical Antipodean sounds of revelry; and through the open door of the village coffee-shop I saw a horde of frenzied giants in tattered khaki and slouch hats. All these men had hoped to be evacuated from Three Churches two days before and were now, understandably enough, drowning their disappointment – an easy feat in Crete, where wine and raki were both more plentiful than food.

The disappointment on this occasion was compounded by the atrocious conditions that everyone faced. It was mid-winter,and the island was in the grip of one of the worst winters in living memory.[53]

All food reserves were used up; if they had not been requisitioned by the occupation forces, they had already been shared with the visitors. Most families throughout Crete were reduced to surviving on the food of last resort – carob beans, snails and *horta*. Although steps were taken by local guerrilla leaders to redistribute the fugitives caught out at Treis Ekklessies through adjacent districts of south-central Crete, many either gave themselves up or were captured, during the winter of 1941–1942.[54] George Psychoundakis, the 'Cretan Runner', describes this winter:[55]

> Everybody suffered from hunger during the Occupation, but 1942 was the worst, especially the winter [i.e. 1941–1942], when we nearly starved. It was then that the snail kingdom suffered the fiercest inroads. Every night, armed with oil dips and torches, the villagers would set out in hundreds in search of the priceless treasure which was the most luxurious fare to be found in house or inn.

Years later, the late Flight Sergeant Pilot Paddy McDonough, RAF, the father of Seán's good friend Roisin McDonough, told him about seeing these lights as he piloted his bomber over the White Mountains to attack the airfields at Maleme or Heraklion – and wondering what they could have been.

Before they dispersed, Woodhouse tried to assure the men on the run that he would work strenuously for their evacuation, but he was also very critical of his superiors. Lambert remembers some cutting remarks in his closing comments:[56]

> The authorities don't appear to care about you in Egypt but if they could see you as I do now perhaps they might help. I can picture at this minute the officers' mess in Alexandria; by now they will have finished a five-course dinner, and will be enjoying brandy and cigars. In front of me are over 100 half-starved brave men in rags and broken boots, infested with lice and no way of getting rid of them.

In passing, Woodhouse was one of the very few British officers on Crete who was respected uniformly by these Australian and New Zealand soldiers. He stayed on at the island until mid-April when he was relieved by Captain (later Major) Tom Dunbabin.

Throughout that dreadful winter there was little change in the plight of the men on the run. They felt utterly abandoned, as if the rescue effort, such as it was, had now ground to a complete standstill.[57] It is not difficult to understand how this feeling arose. Grand strategy in Middle East Headquarters was actually more concerned with stopping and defeating the Afrika Korps than with worrying about the fate of a few hundred escaped prisoners in Crete, miserable as they might have been. But for these Australians and New Zealanders, the news which really caused their morale to plummet was of the Japanese surprise attack on Pearl Harbor on 7 December 1941, and the subsequent fall of the allegedly impregnable Singapore. This brought the war to their doorstep back home, and here they were marooned and starving on Crete, without any inkling of how the struggle in Europe might go for the Allies. It is hardly surprising that some of these men gave themselves up at this juncture. The shattering news is mentioned in many of the memoirs. Here is how Murray McLagan perceived it:[58]

> No news leaked through to me about the progress of war in the Pacific and the first news of the Japs having entered the war was the disaster at Pearl Harbour, then came the news of the fall of impregnable Singapore. To us who had no news of the strategics of the Japs leading up to the Fall of Singapore this was a terrific blow to our morale and optimism.

The Northeners

Meanwhile, back up north, Dick Huston, Colin Ratcliffe and Jack Symes had by now become expert cavemen. Observing how local women gathered snails after it rained, they began to imitate them.[59]

> All through the summer months, the snails glue themselves to the underside of rocks but come out when it rains and do what the bride and groom had been doing . . . The snails on Crete were large and twelve snails each made an excellent meal. Certainly they were messy things to cook, needing about four boilings to get rid of the slime, but as we all took turns at cooking, it was not considered to be much of a chore.

Huston, through observation and copying, had mastered the body-language of Cretan men, as well as a modicum of the Greek language.[60]

> Because I looked like a Greek, could act like a Greek and could use a lot of words in Greek, nouns mostly but the adjectives were coming along too, I became confident about moving around on the plateau in the daytime.

One day, tracking a German patrol up on the plateau, he had a startling encounter:[61]

> When I was sure that the [patrol's] target was not going to be our cave, but most likely Therisso, I started to retrace my steps when a white conical rock spoke to me saying, 'Yassoo'. I am sure my heart almost stopped beating when the rock stood up and I had met my first bandit. He certainly looked the part, being armed with a rifle, a German Mauser, two pistols in his sash and two ugly looking knives in the sash as well. I knew he was not a shepherd because shepherds do not carry weapons like that but keep them concealed in hide-outs. He was not the sort of person I would like to have opposed, he looked tough and he looked as though he was part of these hills . . . I was to meet this man on many occasions and we became quite good friends later on when we could trust each other. The reason he had looked like a rock when I first saw him was because he had on his 'Kapoti', a huge cloak of wool. It had no arms to it but a big hood, so when you knelt or crouched down with the hood up and the cloak around you, you looked exactly like one of the conical rocks, and provided you did not move, became part of the landscape.

This bandit, Kiriakos, was to bring Dick and Colin *kapotis* of their own to wear, which served them in good stead during that hard winter, a winter which was so awful that more than 40 years after the event, the villagers of Askyfou were to recall it for Seán with a frisson of horror, using one Greek word, *pina* (hunger), emphatically. Huston describes the consequences:[62]

> It was not an easy winter for us but I think it was a worse winter for the Greek people. With our stored food the early part of the winter was not too bad for us but the Greek people were not allowed to hoard so had no reserves. In most of the villages the people were existing on *horta*, and every day you could see the women out picking *horta* which was just a weed.[63] As the weed became scarce near the villages the women had to search further afield and some even came up to Kastellos. I think the Greek people were saved by the fact that they had olive oil, perhaps not in abundance but enough to smooth the bitter flavour of the weed. To us it was terrible to visit a village and watch your hosts eating *horta* while we were served something better. It made us feel very humble. Of course we protested to no avail for at Varipetro in particular, they became really offended if we did not accept their fare . . . Before the gardens and the grain came on again we were reduced to a diet of snails and *horta*.

Huston describes the outcomes of living like this, like hunted animals, on a poor diet:[64]

> In the six weeks we lived on this diet we all lost about a stone and a half in weight. Yet we still felt we were better off than those poor blokes in P.O.W. camps. We were always able to get olive oil and wine and both helped us to survive the winter, the oil to richen our poor fare, the wine not only as a drink but to lift our depression at times . . . Another thing that linked us to animals was that our senses sharpened. For instance, when asleep, you were not really asleep but were aware of what was going on around you through sound and you analysed the sounds you heard in your sleep and if you thought it was a danger sound, you were alert in an instant. Hearing became very acute as did smell. Our eyesight improved too and it was possible to pick up movement from long distances.

Endurance

Although Dick Huston and his mates did not know it, another escaper was living in even worse cave conditions not that far away, to the east. Private Norman Scott, a bandsman in the Australian 2/8th Battalion, was holed up in a cave in the hills above the church of Samonas, seven kilometres due south of Souda Bay, and four kilometres west and south of the village of Neo Horio, in the Apokoronas district.

Norm, as he was known, had already had his share of adventures.[65] He had been on the ill-fated Operation Lustre in mainland Greece, had been evacuated from Kalamata on the *Costa Rica* in a convoy bound for Alexandria, but this convoy was bombed and his ship sunk. Norm and all the other troops aboard were safely transferred to a destroyer and put ashore on Crete. His battalion was involved in the fighting during the battle, but was forced to surrender on 1 June along with all the others. Norm wound up in a POW camp, but escaped with two mates on 26 June. They made it to the south of Crete, but seeing no hope of evacuation, gave themselves up. Back in the POW camp, the food was so terrible that Norm decided to escape again. In actual fact, he broke out of this camp a total of five times!

In late summer 1941, Norm was holed up in a cave above Samonas with some other Australians. But on 1 September, he became paralysed. For six months he was completely paralysed, suffering excruciating pain in his legs, and helpless. Nobody thought he could possibly survive the winter; his mates had moved south, with his blessing, when news of possible evacuation filtered north. But he was tended faithfully by a young Cretan woman, Irini Lagonikakis, from the nearby village of Neo Horio, who – rain, hail, sleet or snow – trekked to Norm's cave twice a week throughout that winter, dodging German patrols, to bring him food. Thus Norm Scott also became all too familiar with that winter's diet of *horta* and snails. At times he considered giving himself up, but decided it would be better to stay where he was.

The Far East

After the debacle at Treis Ekklessies, Arthur Lambert and six mates had struck out east, with the last words of Captain Woodhouse ringing in their ears: 'Boys, avoid capture and wherever you are my agents will find you. One way or another, I'll get you off this island!'

This band wound up in the Dikti Mountains in the prefecture of Lasithi, in eastern Crete. They were one of the very few groups of escapers who traversed this area, which, by agreement with the

Germans, was garrisoned by the despised Italians, and where, in marked contrast to central and western Crete, they were not made welcome by locals. Lambert describes their route:[66]

> Our path led up and around the 'Oros Dikti' mountains, and for a few hours was above the snowline; it wasn't until days later that I discovered the damage that the snow had done to my shoes – the soles were parting with the uppers! It was now the middle of winter and we were encountering snow often, yet considered going back unwise, as the Italians would be looking for us. So we decided to continue round the north side of the Oros Dikti mountains, and then head west into the country we were familiar with, and where we knew that we would be well received. The path led through a pass, and when we reached the crest the view below robbed us of speech. There was a circular plain ringed with snow-covered peaks and some red-roofed villages. The plain was covered with hundreds of black four-bladed windmills, and it was like a scene from another planet. This was [the] Lasithi [plateau].

Arthur Lambert's group in fact completely circumnavigated the Dikti Mountains on foot, in mid-winter, in freezing conditions, with pouring rain nearly every day, dodging Italians at each and every turn. It is hardly surprising that Lambert was stricken down with bad flu as a consequence.

Fugitives and Friends Celebrate

As has been stressed, those fugitives who had been able to establish a 'special relationship' with Cretan families stood not only a better chance of eventual evacuation, but had also access to more regular supplies of food and clothing, and even medical attention. For the lucky ones, it involved getting their feet under the table quite literally. Thus, while poor Arthur Lambert and his party were struggling through the snowy wastelands of Lasithi, and while Dick Huston and his mates, and Norm Scott, survived on snails and *horta* in their caves in northern Crete, Jim McDevitt and Ned Nathan enjoyed both comfortable quarters, and a series of parties over Christmas and New Year, in that winter of 1941–1942. McDevitt enthuses over the celebrations in Sklavopoula:[67]

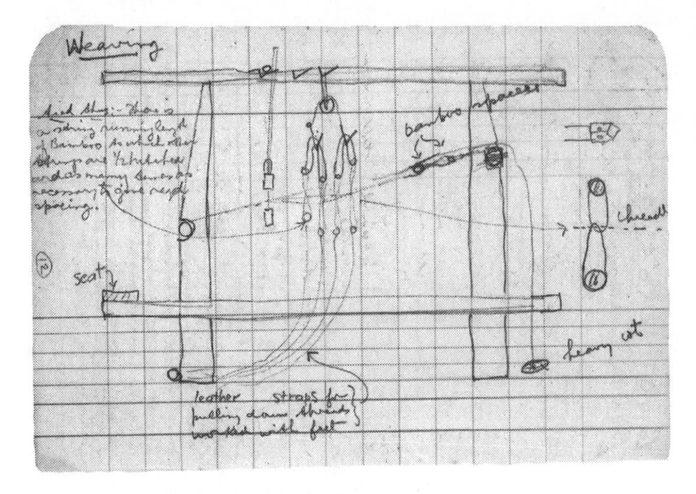

Diagram of hand loom from Len's diary

On Christmas Eve [1941], Evangelos and Fifi turned on a very merry party, or 'glendi'. They refused to let the war get them down. Our other fellow evaders, roaming the surrounding hills and southern shoreline were not forgotten when the invitations went out. What wonderful hospitality! The spacious room where Ned and I often slept was quickly transformed in appearance to accommodate the guests. Furniture was stacked to one side and it became known as 'The Cabaret'. There was ample room for dancing. Music was supplied by a big, old-fashioned gramophone. Ned helped out with extras on a borrowed guitar. Wine was served by a bevy of charming young ladies. These refreshments helped us to overcome our natural shyness to take to the floor. We showed our friends how such rollicking numbers as the 'Lambeth Walk' and 'Boomps-a-Daisy' should be performed.

Only a couple of kilometres away, in the village of Vothiana, Len Frazer had been invited to spend Christmas with the family of Alex Makrakis, the generous 'Returned Yank' we have already encountered in connection with the Cape Krios disappointment. Len's diary entry for Christmas Day reflects his homesickness more than his appreciation of the hospitality of his hosts.[68]

> *Thursday – 25 December 1941*
> Breakfast: tomato and olives. Go to church. Dinner: boiled pork and egg and lemon soup. Go to get hair cut and get a piece of pork as well. Man, wife and 4 children live in room 9 by 9. Refugees. Try another scheme to get word home.

The very next day, Boxing Day, Len left Vothiana and headed east for Azoyires, a village where he had already spent some time, and where he knew a friendly Cretan family. This move proved to hold considerable significance for Len's eventual fortunes, as we shall see. In the meantime, the weather remained appalling. But, as Jim McDevitt astutely observed:[69]

> It was indeed a good thing for the people of the Selinos villages that the bitterly cold conditions kept the Nazi search parties tied to their comfortable bases.

CHAPTER 7

Summer of Hope

The situation in Crete in early 1942 was not optimistic, either for the men on the run or their Cretan hosts. The SOE's final report on the Cretan Resistance notes that the failure of the Treis Ekklessies mission, general hunger, bad weather, British reverses in North Africa, forced labour, and the landing of substantial German reinforcements on the island all of which:[1]

> had a calamitous effect on Cretan morale. This was exploited by the enemy counter-espionage which now succeeded in enrolling considerable numbers of local agents.

This report continues:[2]

> There were still about 300 Imperial troops left in CRETE. Many were captured by enemy search parties following the TREIS EKKLESSIES failure, but surveillance was poor and a number of them succeeded in escaping from gaol or hospital. Those at large were now in rags and bootless, and were faced with a severe winter in the open. Most parts of CRETE went very hungry in the winter of 1941–42, and in the western half of the island bread ran out in January. But in spite of dangers and privations the peasants were ready to share their last crust with an Englishman.

The Cretan Resistance and/or individual families continued to feed and shelter the Anzac men on the run despite increasing numbers of arrests and executions; torture of suspects was by now routine.

There was greater optimism in Cairo, however. Woodhouse returned there in April 1942 and made his report. Although his original report has proved untraceable, it is plain that Woodhouse made no bones about the pitiful conditions of the stranded men, and the attempts made to evacuate them. This is clear from a review of it by an anonymous SOE staff officer:[3]

> I can well appreciate the conditions and experiences which have given birth to the tragic tone in which it is presented.

The review continues:

> Capt. WOODHOUSE's report deals with an extremely difficult operation [Treis Ekklessies] carried out in circumstances that could scarcely be more unfavourable. The period of the operation coincided with an almost unbroken series of naval and military reverses elsewhere; no craft capable of reaching the island were available; weather conditions were at their worst and prevented the operation of our own slender seaborne resources; aircraft were hard to come by and the weather usually precluded their regular and accurate intervention; signal equipment and personnel were almost non-existent. All this time the enemy was in complete control of the island. He possessed excellent material for propaganda among a people violently unstable in temperament and ripe for reaction as the long months of our enforced inactivity drew on. In addition, we believe that the enemy expected to be attacked and tightened up his control of the island. It should also be noted that Capt. WOODHOUSE had to work among a notoriously difficult section of the CRETAN population.

Nevertheless, this patronising review goes on, the SOE/MI9 organisation in Crete was still intact, Captain Xan Fielding had been landed to take over western Crete, intelligence continued to roll in, there had been no casualties amongst agents, another wireless link had been installed, the weather was getting better, and the British advance in Cyrenaica had given the organisation a forward base which cut the distance to Crete by nearly 50 per cent. Amongst its immediate objectives, SOE proposed:[4]

> To evacuate BRITISH stragglers. This would have a direct and important propaganda effect and will do a great deal to create confidence.

In April, Captain Tom Dunbabin was landed in Crete to restore confidence amongst the inhabitants by arranging the evacuation of the last of the stragglers.[5] It is difficult to avoid the impression that, for SOE Headquarters, the morale of the Cretan Resistance was more important than the fate of the men on the run.

In fact, the military bureaucracy charged with supporting, rescuing and debriefing these men had already begun to expand at Middle East Headquarters. On 25 February 1942, 'N' section of MI9 was established with two subsections – the Escape Section and the Preventive Training Section under the command of the recently promoted Lieutenant-Colonel Simonds.[6] Utilising the information brought back by escapers and evacuees, Preventive Training for all troops was intensified. The Army Interrogation Office (AIO) was also formed in this month, and took over all interrogation of escapers and evaders from MI9.[7]

These interrogations of evacuees were very thorough. For example, the report on the interrogation of Sergeant F. Davis of NZ 18 Battalion, who was evacuated on HMS *Thrasher* on the night of 27/28 July 1941, contains sections on conditions in, and organisation of, the POW Camp, ration-scales, prisoners' units and morale, German units and troop movements, enemy aircraft and shipping, and the morale and organisation of the Cretans.[8] Subsequent interrogations also inquired about safe villages and houses, the names of both patriotic and treacherous Cretans, enemy dispositions, the numbers and locations of stragglers, and a wide range of other intelligence material. Crete was effectively used as a floating aircraft carrier, supply base and hospital for the German North African campaign, and both locals and stragglers could glean some idea of how the fighting was going by the numbers of wounded being flown in, and the amount of reinforcements being flown out, as Murray McLagan noted.[9]

However, for the men on the run in Crete, all they knew from listening to clandestine radios was that Rommel had attacked the Eighth Army on 21 January 1941, and Benghazi had been evacuated on the 25th, although Tobruk still held out. Extracts from Len Frazer's diary for January and early February give a good picture of what it was like for him in Azoyires.[10]

Thursday – 1 January 1942

Breakfast: cheese, tea and doughnuts. Dinner: rice, egg and lemon soup and boiled pork. There is 20 years difference between Markos and wife. She was 14 years old when they married. Last night hot bath in wooden tub, and shave. Snowed all day. German attempts to control prices all ludicrous. Prices rise 100 fold. Conditions very bad in Athens. New Year's greeting is Chronon Polar [*Chronia Polla*]. Tea: pork sausage and shillopita, with cheese and butter.

Saturday – 3 January 1942

Breakfast: Tea and mizetra [misithra cheese]. Dinner: celery leaves and boiled pork. Tea: hordrow soup. I am afraid that I will have to insult this lady to stop her stuffing me with food.

Sunday – 4 January 1942

Breakfast: tea and mizetra. Dinner: boiled peas (Begalia) and egg. Tea: peas and Lakilsoonas [kalitsounia?]. Visit and have a row with my hostess. Annoys me. She has the brains of a louse. Talks scandal all day and parades my private affairs. The Greeks love this sort of talk and argument. Fed up, I walk out. Hear that Bardia has fallen and 1100 British prisoners rescued.

Tuesday – 6 January 1942

Breakfast: tea and mizetra. Dinner: rice soup and pork. Raining all day. Markos dances a folk dance to amuse me and break the tension. Go to brother's place, schoolteacher, speaks very good English. Eat pig ears and fresh cabbage for tea. Meet George [a Cypriot soldier on the run] and we discuss boat prospects. I promise him a trip to Australia and a job if he gets me a boat. Hard bed.

Tuesday – 13 January 1942
Markos comes home trembling. Germans troops in Paly. [Paleochora] have been beating up respectable citizens with sticks and wrecking certain places because they say they like English. It has rained every day this month. Good tea, fowl and potato. Take a quinine tablet.

Sunday – 18 January to Wednesday, 21 January 1942
Head heavy and have a cough. Sleep with Greeks. Can get Greek news only. Hear that Sol. and Hellfire fallen and now at Al Ajaila. People here are intelligent but bad. Bed and food. Play chess. Schoolteacher beats me. Rain every day. Place full of lice. Heels fixed.

Monday – 26 January 1942
Markos goes to Canea for soap, salt and matches for villagers . . . The woman here is very annoying, tantalizing. No brains. Always wanting to play with fire . . .

Saturday – 31 January 1942
Very sad. Heard that Germans are in Bengazi. This may add another year on to the war and my exile . . . This blasted woman tried to kiss me.

Sunday – 1 February and Monday, 2 February 1942
Had a two hour fight with woman [Markos's wife]. She wanted to more than kiss me. I annoyed her with my knees very much. She is ignorant and ugly, no brains . . . Rain every day this year and sea is pretty rough, blast it. Markos has not yet returned. His wife even had the cheek to ask me if I had another friend . . .

Tuesday – 3 February 1942
Got fed up and walked out. Renee alone is worth 1,000,000 of this blasted woman. Cry under the olives. Go to old teacher and have a lesson. Bad news.

However, when Markos did return from Hania, he brought a letter for Len. This was from a local, 'Cougas', who had been an interpreter at the Royal Navy base at Souda Bay, and whom Len had met earlier. The letter informed Len that two of his mates had been evacuated the previous Christmas Day by submarine, and were safe in Egypt, but that

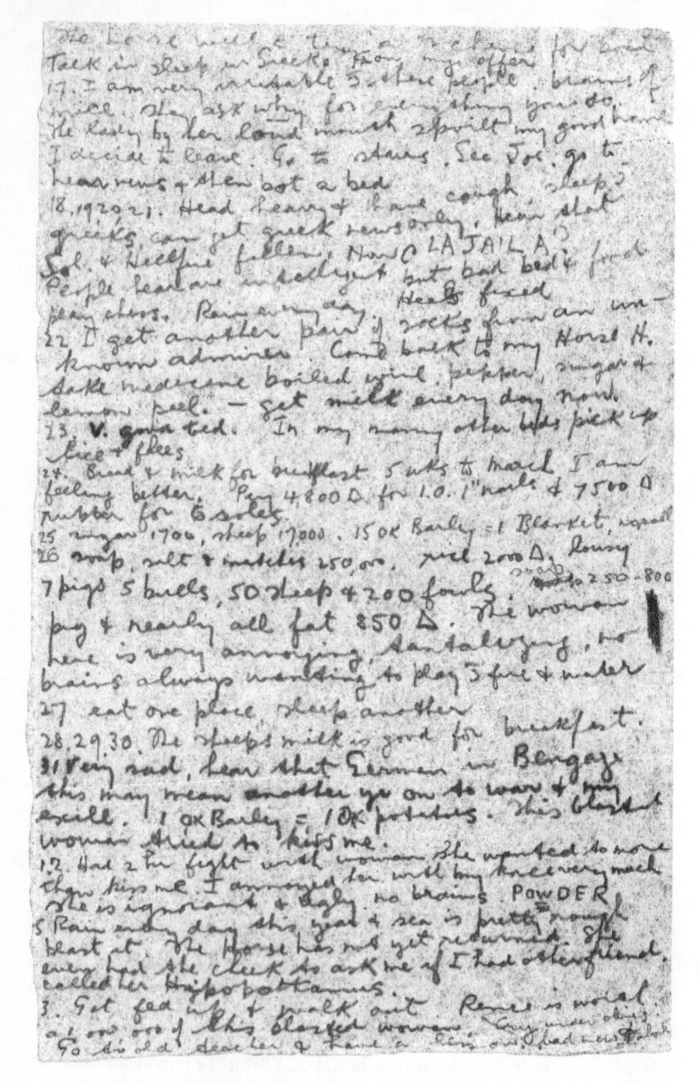
[illegible]
Talk in sleep in Greek [illegible] my offer [illegible]
17. I am very irritable 5 these people . brains of
mice. they ask why for everything you do.
the lady by her loud mouth spoilt my good [illegible]
I decide to leave. Go to [illegible]. See Joe. go to
hear news & then got a bed cough sleep?
18, 19 20 21. Head heavy & have [illegible]. Hear that
Greeks can get Greek news only. [illegible]
Sol. & Hellfire fallen, Now C LA JA'I LA A
People here are intelligent but bad bed & food
[illegible]. Rain every day. Heals fixed
22 I get another pair of socks from an unknown admirer. Come back to my Horse H.
take medicine boiled wine, pepper, sugar &
lemon peel. — get milk every day now.
23. V. [illegible] bed. In my many other [illegible] pick up
lice & flees
24. Bread & milk for breakfast 5 wks to march I am
feeling better. Pay 4,800 D. for 1.0. 1" nails & 7500 D
rubber for 6 soles
25 sugar 1700, sheep 17,000 . 15 OK Barley = 1 Blanket, [illegible]
26 soap, salt & matches 250,000. [illegible] 2000 D, lousy
7 pigs 5 bulls, 50 sheep & 200 fowls. soap 250-800
pig & nearly all fat 850 D. The woman
here is very annoying, [illegible], no
brains always wanting to play 5 fire & water
27 eat one place sleep another
28, 29, 30. The sheeps milk is good for breakfast.
31 Very sad, hear that German in Bengazi
this may mean [illegible] go on to war & [illegible]
[illegible]. 1 OK Barley = 10K potatoes. this blasted
woman tried to kiss me.
1.2. Had 2 [illegible] fight with woman She wanted to more
than kiss me. I annoyed her with my [illegible] very much
She is ignorant & ugly no brains. POWDER
5 Rain every day this year & sea is pretty rough
blast it. The horse has not yet returned. She
even had the cheek to ask me if I had other friend.
called her Hippopottamus.
3. Get fed up & walk out. Renee is [illegible].
[illegible] of this blasted woman. [illegible]
Go [illegible] [illegible]

Excerpt from Len's diary

bad weather and shortage of time had prevented Cougas from finding Len. Nevertheless, Len was instructed to come to Hania to prepare for evacuation. He was to go to a certain hotel, ask for the proprietor, and say, 'My name is Janie [Yianni]; Markos sent me.' Markos decided that it would be best if Len went to Hania by bus, accompanying a local policeman who was making the trip. Len takes up the story:[11]

> The next thing was an identity card. Markos started working on this as well. He was the Mayor and had the authority to issue cards. The only trouble with this was if he was caught issuing a false card, then the penalty was death. The Germans had already invited him to the shooting of a Mayor who had disobeyed this order from the Commandant of Crete. It was then Markos's wife came to the rescue. There was a half-witted man from Gavdos Island who worked on odd jobs for Markos. He was very poor, had never worn boots in his life, had a wife and two children who were half starved. My fair lady arranged it so that he gave me his pass for £1 and a few pounds of dried beans. Besides he always got a good feed when near their place, and a glass of wine. All he had to do was later make a declaration before the garrison commander that he had lost his pass and get issued with another one. This suited me fine. Now I became George Bougaros, labourer, 31 years of Palyochera. If I was caught and questioned about this, then I was to say that I found the card.

It is heartening to note that 'my fair lady', the married woman who had so unsuccessfully set her cap at Len, must have still liked him well enough to dream up the idea of the false identity card! Many of the stragglers who were moving about, as opposed to being based on a cave or other hideout, were supplied with a similar forged or faked identity card by village mayors or policemen. For example, Gunner H. F. James of the Australian 2/3 Field Regiment said:[12]

> With a forged Identity Card under the name Philipos Paschalakis acquired from an inebriated Greek Mayor, I lived for two years in the western end of Crete, in the provinces of Kissamo and Selino in the district of Chania [Canea].

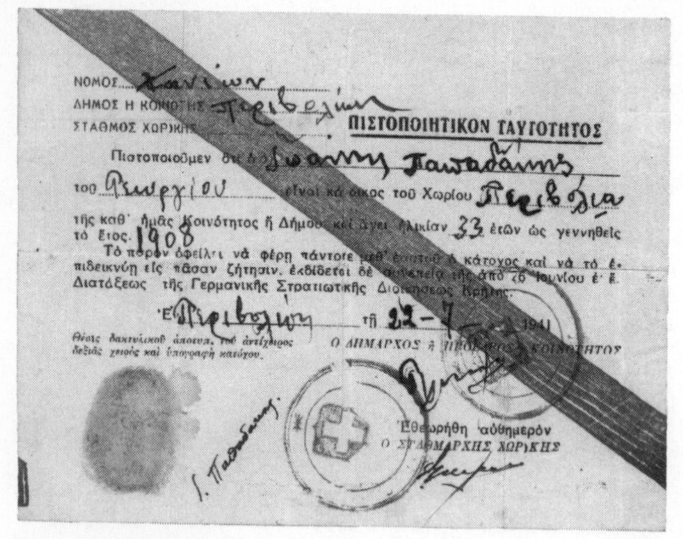

ΝΟΜΟΣ Χανίων

ΔΗΜΟΣ Η ΚΟΙΝΟΤΗΣ [illegible]

ΣΤΑΘΜΟΣ ΧΩΡΙΚΗΣ

ΠΙΣΤΟΠΟΙΗΤΙΚΟΝ ΤΑΥΤΟΤΗΤΟΣ

Πιστοποιοῦμεν ὅτι ὁ [illegible]

τοῦ [illegible] εἶναι κάτοικος τοῦ Χωρίου [illegible]

τῆς καθ' ἡμᾶς Κοινότητος ἢ Δήμου καὶ ἄγει ἡλικίαν 33 ἐτῶν ὡς γεννηθεὶς τὸ ἔτος 1908

Τὸ παρὸν ὀφείλει νὰ φέρῃ πάντοτε μεθ' ἑαυτοῦ ὁ κάτοχος καὶ νὰ τὸ ἐπιδεικνύῃ εἰς πᾶσαν ζήτησιν. ἐκδίδεται δὲ [illegible] τῆς ἀπὸ 26 Ἰουνίου ἐ. ἔ. Διατάξεως τῆς Γερμανικῆς Στρατιωτικῆς Διοικήσεως Κρήτης.

Ἐν [illegible] τῇ 22-7 1941

Θέσις δακτυλικοῦ ἀποτυπ. τοῦ ἀντίχειρος δεξιᾶς χειρὸς καὶ ὑπογραφὴ κατόχου.

Ο ΔΗΜΑΡΧΟΣ ἢ ΠΡΟΕΔΡΟΣ ΚΟΙΝΟΤΗΤΟΣ

Ἐθεωρήθη αὐθημερὸν

Ο ΣΤΑΘΜΑΡΧΗΣ ΧΩΡΙΚΗΣ

Len's forged identity card

And Kiwi Ken Little, who was recovering from his wound in the same region, said:[13]

> Towards the end of September, I was issued with a Cretan identification card or Taftotita. This had my thumb print stamped on the bottom right hand corner and was obtained from the Mayor or President as he was known, of Tsiskiana. My Cretan name was Pavlos Dimitriakis.

The Northerners

Those who chose to base themselves in a cave, like Dick Huston and his mates, suffered from hunger and weight loss during that bad winter of 1941–1942. Huston's group had by now grown to six, with the inclusion of two other Kiwis, Gordon Davis and Milton Knight, both from Divisional Signals, and 'Aussie' Rankin from the 11th Battalion. However, they stuck to their logic, as he explains:[14]

> On the north side of the Island we lived a different type of existence,

> never living near the villages and only associating with one family in the villages. We lived so far from any village that if captured no village could be held responsible for feeding us and could disclaim any knowledge of us. On our side of the island, Germans were in the villages that aided us almost every day and drank at their cafeneions [sic]. It would have been very foolhardy of us to have lived in our villages as I believe many escaped prisoners did on the south coast . . . Varipetro was the village for Colin Ratcliffe and I and the Ledaki family were our family. Jack Symes and Aussie had adopted Fournes as their village and their family friends were Anastasia and her brother Johny [sic] whose Greek name was hard to pronounce, so he was named Johny by us. Gordon Davis and Knightie had adopted Meskla and their family was the Tsamandaki family, Niko Tsamanadaki later being wounded in the skirmish when Dudley Perkins was killed.

They were as versatile as ever, devising ways of repairing the all-important boots:[15]

> Gordon had one other great asset, he invented the 'Lazy Davis Stitch', as we called it. This was a stitch we could use to get at inaccessible parts of the boot, to sew rubber to the welt of the boot with the stitch inside the material so it could not wear. When Gordon and Knightie joined us they had rubber soles on their boots which we thought was an excellent idea for the rubber obtained from car or truck tyres would wear for years. The rubber had been nailed to their boots and this was not a success for the nails would not hold in the leather which was becoming soft or rotten . . . To make the stitch, all you needed was an awl to make a hole, the awl we made from a piece of wire we found, a thin strand of stainless steel wire obtained from the wire on the [parachute] canisters became the needle when doubled over to form an eye. The thread came from ropes off the parachutes being waxed with some stuff the Greeks gave us.

By now, Huston had become 'reasonably fluent' with the Greek language, and helped his family at Varipetro with the spring planting in 1942, although he insisted on sleeping outside the village, curled up in his *kapoti*. Such precautions were sensible, for one never knew when the Germans might appear in an area so close to the important provincial capital and garrison town of Hania. On one occasion, they caught the usually hyper-alert Huston by surprise:[16]

> Manoli and I were hoeing in wheat on the ridge above the house when Manoli whispered in a whisper that could be heard a hundred yards away, 'Mister, Mister, Germans.' I nearly dropped my hoe with fright but slowly straightened up and there were six Germans just a few yards away. They came over to me and said something that sounded like 'wasser', so I put on my 'no understand' act until they made signs of drinking, and I replied, 'Ah, nero' (water), and was going to lead them down to the well. I pretended I had a bad limp and was semi-crippled as I moved and one of them patted his leg in a sympathetic way so I said, 'Boom, Boom, Albania,' and he gave me a friendly pat as Momma came up and led them away to the well. Manoli and I carried on hoeing until they were well out of sight and I quietly got out of sight too.

Shortly afterwards, towards the end of March, 'Jim' from Varipetro brought the cave dwellers the news that escaped prisoners were being taken off the south coast by submarine, but had no further details.[17] It was decided that Jack Symes and Dick Huston would venture south to see if they could establish what was going on. By this time they were so fit that this journey did not represent a major challenge. In a village near the south coast they met an Australian who had been living there for some months, in the sort of situation of which Dick Huston personally disapproved, as we have seen. But the Australian told the Kiwis of rumour and counter-rumour, of having been to two alleged evacuation points fruitlessly, and of German traps. He had decided to stay put until something definite came up.

At this juncture, Dick and Jack were accosted by three heavily armed Cretans, apparently guerrillas, who grilled them about their recent movements. While the Kiwi pair established their own credentials, they refused to name any of their local helpers. The guerrillas told them that they were doing the right thing in staying up north as there were now too many stragglers on the south coast. The guerrillas then said that they would take Jack to the east and Dick to the west, and that they would all meet up again in the same spot in three days' time. The Kiwis had concluded that these men knew something, and agreed to go. Dick Huston was taken off at speed, and passed from guerrilla to guerrilla, to eventually meet two shepherds, who he did not think looked quite right. Their clothes weren't ragged enough, and they spoke Greek with an odd accent. Huston challenged them in the Cretan dialect:[18]

> they both laughed, and the other shorter man answered in English with a definite Oxford or was it Cambridge accent. There could be no doubt about him. While we all smoked English cigarettes, they asked a lot of questions about what was happening on the north side of the Island, in particular, how restricted was movement near Maleme and Suda Bay harbour . . . The Englishman had a double-barrelled name which even today it may not be wise to disclose. The other man was Greek, but I was right, he was not a Cretan.

The Englishman then recruited Huston into a secret organisation. He would become operational in a little while, but in the meantime not even his fellow cave dwellers were to know the nature of his mission. He was assigned what we would now call a 'dead letter box,' and, to his complete astonishment, his contact was the bandit Kiriakos! Further, these two agents had news for Huston:[19]

> They told me that escapees dashing up and down the coast were interfering with their work and that a move was afoot to have all the escapees contacted and told to remain in static positions until required for embarkation. It seemed that too much activity had caused the Germans to create look-out stations along the coast and it was now becoming difficult to find a secure place on the coast to carry out a landing from the sea.

Huston was then led back to meet Jack Symes by the Cretan guerillas. Jack was a day late because he had met a lot of escapees living in south coast villages, and there had been much wine-drinking and talk. These parleys had confirmed that there *were* too many stragglers chasing non-existent boats, and that German watch stations *had* been set up. Jack had not met any agents. As the two Kiwis headed back up north, they agreed to sit tight in their safe area until summoned to the south coast. Huston could not tell his mate about his new, secret work.[20]

Western Crete

Early in 1942, Tom Moir and Dudley Perkins were hiding in Fifi Papantonakis's house because the latter had suffered jaundice over the winter. They were given a sharp reminder of how perilous their situation actually was:[21]

> Tom Moir recalls an occasion when several German officers arrived at Fifi's house [in Sklavopoula] when he and Perkins were supping wine in an upstairs room. The Germans had trekked up the mountains from their camp several kilometres away, and Fifi, always the perfect hostess, ushered the Germans into her ground floor rooms and served them food and drink. Moir and Perkins were concerned as much for the Papantonakis family as for their own safety. The two New Zealanders were in civilian clothing and, if discovered, the Germans would probably have shot them. Tragedy would almost certainly strike the Greeks – they would have their house burned to the ground and lose their own lives. But Fifi carried on regardless, perfectly calm, reassuring Tom and Dudley that she could cope with the situation. She not only saw that food and more wine was provided for them, but she also managed to wheedle cigars from the Germans for her upstairs guests.

This was only one of the many occasions on which this remarkably courageous young woman outwitted the enemy.

As the spring of 1942 dawned, it brought better weather, growing optimism, and increased movement amongst the men who had been hibernating in western Crete. Jim McDevitt put it like this:[22]

> The month of March saw the return of clearer skies, warmer nights and beautiful blossoms on the fruit trees. Ned [Nathan] and I welcomed the opportunity offered to us of going for evening strolls, or 'voltas', with some of the young ladies of the neighbourhood . . . We were

hankering to move about the wide open spaces again. Our confinement indoors had lasted for some ten weeks or so.

So Jim and Ned took off on walkabout in western Crete, gaining intelligence about the progress of the war from the Cretan Greek-language newspaper *Paratiritis*. They noticed in the paper that the Germans were offering large rewards to people who came forward with information about Allied air drops of personnel and supplies.[23] This news excited the pair because it suggested that the stragglers had not been forgotten by MEHQ. McDevitt and Nathan also tried to gain intelligence about the possibility of evacuation from other men on the run.

In this region of south-west Crete, it is important to realise that the various groups of stragglers usually did manage to maintain some kind of contact, either through their own runners, or their Cretan friends. On this occasion, the duo missed Tom Moir and Dudley Perkins by one day, but caught up with some other Kiwis, all with the one thing on their minds: where was Captain George with the promised boat? By this time, Len Frazer had reached Hania successfully, and had been advised to make his way towards south-central Crete, whence an evacuation was more likely. Shortly afterwards, McDevitt also heard this news.[24]

In this same manner, Nathan heard something very interesting from a fellow Kiwi called Arthur Pauling:[25]

> Ned pricked up his ears when Arthur mentioned a member of the Maori Battalion who was living a lonely existence in the territory heavily infested with Nazi troops. He had been severely wounded during the early stages of the airborne invasion. Even to this day, his gaping leg-wound had not properly healed. The unfortunate man had to choose his time very carefully before it was safe enough to steal out from his hiding-place and bathe his wound in the nearest stream. Arthur reckoned the recluse's name was 'Siphi', which is short for 'Joseph' in the local lingo.

Ned Nathan was flabbergasted because this description fitted his beloved cousin, Joe Angell, whom he had given up for dead in the fighting around Maleme. Ned took off to try and find 'Siphi', and establish if it was indeed his long-lost cousin. Joe Angell gives *his* side of the story:[26]

> Months passed. Finally I heard from a Greek there was another Maori on the other side of the island. I asked him to describe this person. I didn't recognize him . . . So I decided to go across to the other side of the island, which took two or three weeks.

Ned tells what happened subsequently in his own words:[27]

> I went back to where Joe was supposed to be hiding. I walked all night and all the next day, and I got there in two days. I cut the journey in half. When I got there I went straight to the person who was supposed to be sheltering him and he refused to tell me anything. I can't blame him really, for whilst I thought he would know me through our own grapevine message, he did not.

By this time, the Cretans were exceptionally cautious about anybody purporting to be an Australian, British or New Zealand soldier, for the Germans used *agents provocateurs* pretending to be one of the men on the run. But Ned had a foolproof way of identifying himself, and his knowledge of Joe:[28]

> Ned described Joe's appearance, described the unusual tattoo of a beautiful Hawaiian girl on his arm. 'Ah, there is a man called John with that tattoo,' Ned was told, 'but only the Mayor knows where he is. 'I will go to see the Mayor,' said Ned, and up the garden path towards the open door he went, quite unaware that the Mayor's two daughters were at that moment entertaining six German officers in the living-room. When Ned was about a chain away he saw them. What should he do? Run? No, continue up to the door and knock, was his decision. The Mayor himself came to the door, a question in his eyes. 'Who are you?' 'Don't panic,' said Ned quietly, 'I'm British.' The Mayor closed his eyes and said, 'Can't you see who's behind me?' 'Yes,' said Ned, 'I'll come back later.' That walk back down the path to the gate was the longest walk Ned had ever taken. Joe, way back in the hills shepherding for the

Mayor's son, could not reach the village until noon the following day but at eleven o'clock Ned saw him coming and in Maori shouted out, 'Hurry up.' 'You're supposed to be dead,' Joe yelled in reply.

Joe picks up the story of the cousins' reunion:[29]

We ran to each other and hugged each other and cried and talked in Maori, and Greek and Pakeha, everything that had happened to us. It was a real get-together. We were so happy and thrilled to see each other after all this time. I told him the last time I'd seen him I thought he was killed, because he fell in front of me when we attacked the aerodrome early in the morning. There had been machine-gun bursts at the corner of this building and Neddy fell in front of me and I just took off over his head and landed in a shell hole, and that was the last time I saw Ned.

Shortly afterwards, Joe Angell became very ill with malaria, and Ned Nathan was not much better. Jim McDevitt describes their condition when he bumped into them again:[30]

Sad to relate, I could tell from the outset that my two companions were in very poor physical shape. They looked completely exhausted from their travels. Worse still, their arms and legs were covered with ugly sores, just like the ones Bruce [Bella] Johnston had suffered the previous year and which were blamed on acute malnutrition. Joe rolled up his trouser-leg to show me his battle-scar. Incredibly enough, his ugly wound had still not properly healed, even after the lapse of nearly a year. On top of these debilitating ailments, Ned and Joe were struggling to suppress a raging fever. Joe was so weak that he found it difficult to trek over the rugged countryside. There were times when Ned had to carry his cousin on his shoulders.

Ned in fact carried his cousin on his back to Sklavopoula to obtain medication. A day or two later, they were captured by the Germans, and after a week or so in filthy conditions in the condemned cell in Paleochora, from which Cretans were taken every day to be shot, they wound up in Ayia Prison near Hania. The Resistance network rolled into action to spring the pair from prison, but the fact of the matter was that Joe was so ill that Ned thought he was dying, and would not leave him, so the escape plan was cancelled.[31] Joe was flown to hospital in Athens, while Ned arranged to have his identity discs smuggled into the prison to prove he was a New Zealand soldier, as they had been arrested in civilian clothes.

Ned was badly beaten up for refusing to divulge the name of the Cretan family which had brought him his discs, and eventually wound up in a POW camp in Germany, where he worked as an English-Greek-German interpreter. In September 1944, Ned Nathan was repatriated to the UK because of his bad eye, and subsequently was Mentioned in Dispatches. Jim McDevitt went back to the comforts of Fifi's house in Sklavopoula.

At about this time, a couple of interesting examples of Kiwi hunting/gathering practices occurred. Ken Little explains:[32]

> All during my time and adventures on Crete I had managed to keep my mosquito net, and to my utter amazement I found and was able to catch with my net, sufficient whitebait for a decent feed. I had never seen whitebait on Crete before.

What Ken had caught was not whitebait as such, but the similar small fish called *atherina* in Greek. The second example is described by Jim McDevitt:[33]

> Not to be outdone, a Maori lad named Bill Hoani took to diving for sea-urchins, and with some success, he claimed.

Meanwhile, Dudley Perkins and Tom Moir had been continuing their peregrinations in the region, frequently with, or near, fellow Kiwis Reg Rolfe and John Kerr. Perkins was still weak from the after-effects of his illness, although he struggled on gamely. On one occasion, Perkins and Kerr hid outside a village beside a tree overlooking a rocky overhang. Kerr went on to look for a friendly Greek. When he returned:[34]

> he was shocked to find Perkins lying sprawled on his back in a clear space well down the rocks. He hurried down to find his companion torn and bloody. Perkins had lost all the skin off one side of his face, his nose

was bleeding freely, one trouser leg was ripped to shreds and the leg itself was torn and bleeding. Later Kerr found that almost all Perkins' body, especially down one side, was bruised where it was not grazed.

Perkins had fainted and rolled down the rock face. This put paid to any attempt at travel until he recovered.

Another local appeal for funds had raised 380,000 drachmae, a very substantial sum, and enough to make a good offer for a boat. This money had been raised by village priests from their congregations, and also, as if their outstanding hospitality were not enough, from Fifi's family, the Papantonakis. Perkins and Kerr still wanted to buy a boat, but in the meantime, Moir had been conducting a reconnaissance of a village near Sfinari on the coast of western Crete, where 14 craft were kept under German guard, with their oars and sails locked in a shed.[35] Moir decided to steal one of these boats, and assembled a party. His strategy was to seize the boat, sail it to a hidden cave near Elafonissos, provision it, and then sail for North Africa when things had quietened down. Perkins and Kerr were to join them in the raid. Bella Johnston, who was in the party, describes the plan:[36]

> Tom had scouted a fishing village which had several serviceable boats. He gathered a party of ten. Unfortunately no others had sailing experience, but as I had sailed and raced yachts from 12'6 Z class to a B class Keeler, I was just what he needed. The plan was to wait for nightfall, break into a shed which we hoped contained fuel. We would gather the fuel and water containers, seize a boat in the hours of darkness, and proceed to a well hidden cove we knew just North of the South Western corner of the Island. Here we would hide the boat, disperse, collect food and wait until the hue and cry died down (about 4 to 5 days we thought).

The actual surveillance of the village was carried by Bert Gill and Reg Rolfe, as the latter explains:[37]

> Learning of another area where there were fishermen, Bert Gill and I went to the overlooking hillside and from concealment in the bushes we observed all movements carefully. 'That's our boat,' I said. It was in

> the water when seen and it seemed likely to be seaworthy. At night, the owner slept in a shed. We had sufficient food with us for several days so Bert kept watch while I went off to find a crew . . . Bella Johnston was especially welcome because of some yachting experience.

On the night in question, 3 or 4 April, 1942, it was dark and moonless. The various members of the party became separated and lost, and the attempt was aborted. They tried again the next night, breaking into a boatshed and taking the 26-foot vessel inside. There they were confronted by the irate Cretan owners:[38]

> there was argument – heated on the Cretans' side and accompanied by loud protestations – but the escapers were quietly determined. Fortunately the Cretans did not carry their objections to the point of betrayal.

They immediately set sail for their prearranged hiding place. The boat was old but in good condition. Reg Rolfe, who had no boots because he had given them to his mate Tom Collins, takes up the tale:[39]

> The breeze was steady all night. I was suffering from my walk without any shoes. I dangled my excruciatingly sore feet over the side of the boat and bathed them. The relief was marvellous. At Ktista, where the coast was rugged, we moved the boat into a cave that had been shown us. It was a perfect place to hide . . . The cave had a narrow opening, about 4 ft. high and 8 ft. wide, leading in to a fair-sized pool. It could not be seen from either air or sea. At the far end of the cave a small opening into thick bush gave us access to the land. This was familiar territory to us.

Tom Moir now made every attempt to find Dudley Perkins and John Kerr, but after two days' unsuccessful hunt, was forced to abandon the search on the third day, when a favourable wind blew up.[40] It later transpired that Kerr had reached the rendevous successfully on the first night, had found no one, and had therefore returned to the cave where the sick Perkins was hiding. Rolfe describes leaving the coastal grotto:[41]

> We knew that our best chance for a successful escape was to have white caps and high waves to hide us. The weather became very rough on the third night. It was time to go. We left the cave in darkness. Huge breakers pounded the entrance. For half an hour it was touch and go as we fought to prevent our boat from being smashed against the rocks. Eventually, with Bella Johnston and me on the oars and Tom Moir at the rudder, we managed to pull out far enough to hoist the sail.

Bella Johnston takes over the story:[42]

> No moon and a good steady breeze on our port beam. Good progress was made during the night. Everyone was in high spirits, although as the wind and seas increased, I alone knew things were getting a bit tough. The seas were breaking across our beam and I was finding it hard to hold her off the wind. Tom realized the problem and with two of us on the tiller we had more control. At dawn things looked good. We had come much further than anticipated, and were well south of Gavdos Island and any likely boat patrol.

The next couple of days were uneventful, apart from a fright from a couple of German ME 110 planes which did not see them. The men both sailed and rowed. Bella Johnston recounts the food and water situation on the voyage:[43]

> We had little food, but as all of us were used to having little to eat, it was no problem. A spice of variety was added by sampling our different flavours of water. We had enough to last about one month. There were varieties to suit everybody's palate, all according to the container it came from. There was: petrol, diesel, olive oil, engine oil, wine and a couple of unidentified flavours. Needless to say we arrived in Africa with our water supply practically intact.

The party reached a beach three miles from Sidi Barrani, on the morning of the fourth day, to the astonishment of the English troops who met them, for the escapers were all heavily bearded and dressed in ragged Cretan civilian clothes. The last word on this remarkable escape must be left to the irrepressible Bella Johnston:[44]

> At our appearance one of these [English] guys paid me my greatest compliment. After explaining that I was an escaped prisoner, he asked, 'From where, Derna?' I said, 'No, Crete.' 'Gee, chum, did you walk all the way?'

Derna is on the coast of North Africa.

This party comprised New Zealanders Staff Sergeant Moir, Lance Bombardier Johnston, Privates Collins and Gill, and Driver Rolfe, three Australians and a Royal Marine. Moir was awarded the DCM, Johnston the MM, and Collins was Mentioned in Dispatches.[45] The New Zealanders' story, as told to a New Zealand Public Relations Service NCO, concludes with these words:[46]

> The five men appeared to be in good health, but their experience had not left them unmarked. There was that in their eyes and in their manner which showed that they had faced life shorn of civilisation.

The interrogation of Moir and the other members of his party ensured that the plight of the men remaining on Crete was registered thoroughly in Middle East Headquarters. Several contemporary SOE documents mention their numbers and location:[47]

> *Situation in Crete mid-May 1942*
> It is estimated that there are still approximately 300 at large, of whom the bulk are in the centre of the island. These have the advantage of being accompanied by 4 officers in addition to a British surgeon and an Australian doctor, besides an Australo-Greek; they have thus better opportunities for getting over local difficulties than they seemed to have some months ago. Conditions are difficult notwithstanding, and it would be a mistake to minimize them. There are another 60 dotted spasmodically over the SELINO and KISSAMO provinces of Canea, who have not suffered any noticeable troubles and have been cut off from the rest by the barrier of the White Mountains, which is all to the good. It is hoped to attempt the rescue of some of these in the near future.

It is interesting to note the attitude being displayed here. The fact that *officers* are present is deemed to have helped the men on the run overcome 'local difficulties'! The Greek Resistance leaders in the Amari area, who had been looking after the stragglers since June 1941, and resourceful and self-reliant soldiers like Jim McDevitt, Dudley Perkins, John Kerr and Murray McLagan in western Crete must have been thrilled to bits by the presence of their 'superiors'.

McDevitt heard the news of Moir's departure from the only Cretan eyewitness. As he said:[48]

> Naturally enough, I was really glad for the sake of the escape party, but I felt like weeping because Ned and I had been left behind.

Shortly afterwards, McDevitt bumped into Perkins and Kerr again:

> I was surprised to see this pair still on Crete. They were both such bosom pals of Tom Moir. Sure enough, they were terribly dejected at having missed out on the escape.

On 2 May, McDevitt celebrated his second birthday on Crete. The escape of Moir's party, and the stranding of McDevitt, Perkins and Kerr, inter alia, demonstrates that an element of luck still played its part in successful evacuation, however good the stragglers' networks.

Shortly afterwards, still in May, Australian Reg Saunders and two mates were told by a friendly shepherd to attend a 'meeting.'[49]

> At the meeting, they found 15 British, New Zealand and Australian troops – and a Greek agent with an American accent and the improbable name of 'Sam'. The same night Sam escorted the 15 escapees to the beach, where they found about 75 other Allied troops – organized in three separate batches. Three agents whose clipped British accents did not match their scruffy peasant garb took charge, and ordered all the troops to strip off on the beach. 'Most of you chaps are thick with lice,' one of them explained. 'We've got a trawler coming in at dawn, and we don't want to take lice on board. You'll be getting fresh equipment and blankets once you get aboard.' While they waited for the trawler, they sat around in naked little circles, handing around tightly-rolled tobacco leaves. Each man would take two draws, then pass the leaf on to the next.

The trawler was HMS *Hedgehog*. Reg Saunders continues the story:[50]

> It turned out to be a British trawler – a North Sea trawler with a little old crude oil motor in it and a bloody great big sail . . . and it was sailing up and down with an Italian flag on it . . . Anyway that was about ten o'clock that night and then they got us all on board – ninety of us – and we sailed off heading for Alexandria or Bardia at the time and [when] we were about three miles off shore the chimney stack caught alight. (laughter) The flames were going about thirty feet into the air. Well we thought here come the bloody U-boats any time now or an aeroplane would come out . . . We must have sailed for half an hour with a bloody thirty foot sheet of flame coming out of the old stack. Suddenly she went out but glowed for another ten minutes – red hot – and eventually we disappeared into the darkness.

Saunders managed to enjoy the trip back to Egypt nevertheless:[51]

> We had a great big thing full of rum there and everyone got stuck into the rum – even I got drunk. We were sort of celebrating getting away from it all.

But once back in Cairo, Reg Saunders's interrogation was very thorough.[52]

> we were put in isolation. No one was allowed to talk to us. We weren't allowed any leave, we could order what we liked, we ate in isolation. The officers and the diggers and the sergeants and everybody all ate together. We weren't allowed to talk to anybody, except amongst ourselves because they suspected there could have been a German spy among us . . . My personal experience was I was three days interrogated in Greek – not a word of English – English officer but he questioned me, he spoke nothing but Greek, and at the end of it all he said to me, 'I know you're telling the truth,' and I said, 'Why, how do you know that?' He said because you speak Greek with the accent of where you said you were for nearly twelve months. It was as simple as that.

None of the men in western Crete – including Perkins, Kerr, McDevitt, and McLagan – were brought out on this particular evacuation. This was probably because, at this particular time, Xan Fielding had his hands full with the Greek Lieutenant-Colonel Papadakis, the self-styled leader of the Cretan Resistance, and was involved in ongoing, delicate and dangerous negotiations.[53]

Len Leaves

During the course of these events, Len Frazer was moving from western to central Crete. He met Xan Fielding on his travels, but appears to have been singularly unimpressed by him. (Fielding's codename was 'Aleko', hence 'A.' in Len's diary.)[54]

> *Sunday – 15 March 1942*
> In the fields. Only rice today. Sleep fully dressed these days. Little water. I stink. A. is a B.B., a liar, a cynic, a deceiver. Will not co-operate one inch. I refuse to go back with him and he leaves me stranded. A prig. Co-operation in the British Army seems to be tell those who should know nothing. Move to better hole.

While the details of their interaction are unknown, and Fielding does not mention him in his memoir, Len's judgement on a resourceful and courageous SOE officer with a thankless task seems unduly harsh. But throughout April and May, Len's morale was steadily declining, as his diary reveals:[55]

> *Wednesday – 1 April 1942*
> IAN'S BIRTHDAY. I hope that my present is that he heard that I am alive. I am the April Fool. Teeth holes being found out through eating so many sultanas. Wet.

> *Thursday – 2 April 1942*
> My birthday, 34 today. My second birthday with no presents and no good wishes. Only worrying where I am going to find a bed. 12 lice and 2 fleas.

> *Sunday – 12 April 1942*
> Up at 5.30 and away to the hills to snow and clouds and only milk and

its products for food. Fresh sour milk is delightful. The business of waiting, waiting, is maddening.

Sometime in early May, Len was hiding near the village of Asi Gonia. Xan Fielding asked George Psychoundakis to guide Len to the Amari, where another local would take him down to the south coast. Psychoundakis describes Len's condition:[56]

he could only walk very slowly, his broken shoes having badly mangled his feet . . . In spite of all my efforts to help him on and cheer him up, we didn't get there. He fell down half an hour from the village and said: '*Okhi kalo, Yorghi. Poly arrostos. Edo ypno!*' ('Not good, George. Very ill. Here sleep!') . . . He had taken his boots off the moment we sat down, and his feet were in such a pitiable state that I confess that, had it been me, I wouldn't have been able to walk at all . . . There was a great sadness in his face and I often tried to make him laugh. 'Never mind, Johnny,' I told him, 'everything will be all right when you get to Egypt,' and laughed, telling him various amusing tales. But all in vain.' All he did was to say, '*Panayia mou! Kako paidi! Ego pethaino kai esy gelas.*' (All Holy Virgin! Bad boy! I die and you laugh.')

Len's own description of this part of the journey is:[57]

Wednesday – 13 May 1942
To thus and thus. Have a swim. Sleep between rocks. Not eat. Feet badly blistered.

Friday – 15 May 1942
What a hike. I am all done in. Tired, hungry for food, in rags. Sleep as a dog, my clothes in rags.

Later in May, the pace of the move towards the south coast accelerated, as a boat was due:

Thursday – 21 May 1942
Move down hill. Left alone. Ravens arrive with food. Later crowd arrives. Sleep. Go like hare. [The 'ravens' are black-clad Cretan women.]

Saturday – 23 May 1942
A mad rush with mad Greek across low hills. Line broken. We stranded. Left. Sleep in gully. Stranger arrives. Another mad rush with *****. Go to ground. Truck. I break up completely. Boys carry me up the hill. Get a donkey but miss by two hours due to windy gorge. Feet very badly blistered. All has not yet ended well.

Kiwi Driver Stove was on this march, and depicts Len's abject state:[58]

> Lying low we gripped our *katsounas* (walking sticks) and resolved that even unarmed, we would put up a fight if we had to. The truck turned around and made off in the opposite direction. We dashed across the road and took to the mountains again. Here the going was tougher than ever. The Australian officer could not take it. Our guide abused him soundly while we looked on in disgusted silence. Dragging him on his feet we moved up to a village where we obtained a drink of milk for him but, within the next few yards, he lay down and cried. Manoli pleaded with us to leave him to his fate. All the abuse we heaped on him made no difference so we had to take turns in dragging him up the mountain. Manoli streaked ahead at this stage and procured a donkey from the next village. However by now we had lost a lot of time and Manoli was not the only one who was afraid that we would never make the distance. We threw the officer on the donkey. He protested while we removed his boots for Percy, a Tommy whose feet were bleeding the most. Somehow we reached the summit. Now the going was straight down to the rugged coastline of Southern Crete. It was too steep even for the donkey and the officer demanded his boots from Percy. In dead silence we got going, hoping against hope that we would be in time. The brave little Manoli went on ahead. When we met him returning we did not need to be told that our band had missed the boat.

They had just missed the fast naval Motor Launch (ML) which arrived on 25 May 1942. It speaks volumes for the loyalty of these soldiers that they did not abandon Len in his wretched condition.

Lieut. Frazer, LT VX15205 2/8 Fd Coy. RAE
Sgt. Barrington HT 4436. 4th R.M.T. Coy NZEF
Marine Mintram P EX4504. R.M (P...)
Pte Allen H 4915370 1st Bn Sth Staffs Regt (Arry)
" Maclean KH. 2982139 A&S. Highlanders
Gnr Cross GL 29220 7 A/T 33rd Bty
Drvr Shaull M T/79518 RASC
Cpl Christie, C.V. 7542 Div Supply Column
Pte Delforce G. NX1523 16th Bde 6th Div (Snow)
L/C Hand WR 4916353 1st South Staffs Regt
Pte Whitfield JW 13155 Div HQ. NZ. (Jack)
" McAnulty P VX10558 2/7 Bn D Coy
Sgn Fleischer JDH. 5636 Div Sigs NZEF (L...)
Pvr. Stove H 2 DSC NZ (Herbert)
Pte Catherwood DM 15227 HQ. 4th Inf Bde NZEF (Dave)
Spr McCauley P 33154, 19th Army Tps Coy NZ (Pat)
Pte Gybson A.M WX 5664. 1st Aust Guard Bn AIF
Spr Dowling M WX 3321 2/2 Fd Pk RAE (Mick)
Sigamos Emmanuel, air force trainee Greece
Pte. Paterakis V.K. S.T.G. 102 No 21.
Cpl Tahir H 1834. No 5 Coy. Cyprus Inf
Sgt Malas EC. S.T.G. 102 No 32...
Papadakis Lefteris, Cretan Civilian.

Len's list of evacuees

Driver Stove picks up the story:[59]

> Realising that we could not stay on the mountainside in the bitter cold with dawn approaching, we got moving until we reached a rocky fissure where we collapsed in a heap, wondering what was to happen to us now. Our kind friend broke the news gently that we might have to live here on the rocks for perhaps a month.

A week later, Len said in his diary:[60]

Monday – 1 June 1942
Cannot get rid of lice. 1 year today. Freedom is only obtained with blood. Clothes in rags.

But one week after that:[61]

Sunday – 7 June 1942
At night move to coast. Mick and I go to sleep and wake up to see big surprise. FREEDOM. ML 354. It hardly seems true. 25 knots. Free at last. 372 days. 372 days at large.

Len had finally got away with a party which included four other Australians, eight New Zealanders, and a couple of British, along with a few Cretans.[62] They were evacuated from a beach called Trofalos, below the village of Krotos, which had been found by Captain Woodhouse.[63] Len eventually returned to Australia, and survived the war.

Shortly after this successful evacuation, all attempts at further rescues by MI9 were temporarily put on hold during what was known as the 'Great Flap', when Rommel advanced on Egypt, with Tobruk falling on 21 June 1942. It was not until the end of the month that the Allied defensive line stabilised at El Alamein.

CHAPTER 8

Shifting Fortunes: June–December 1942

Western Crete

When Tom Moir reached Egypt, he told the authorities that there were *still* Allied men on the run in south-western Crete, not least fellow Kiwis Dudley Perkins and John Kerr. Needless to say, the morale of the latter had taken a nosedive when they learned that their mates had managed to escape – and Perkins was still weak from illness. But they were not the sort of men to give up; they continued their hunt for a boat, with the considerable sum of 380,000 drachmae they had amassed for this purpose. In early June, they encountered the elusive Captain George, this time with a caique he had sailed with his wife from north-western Crete.[1] They joined him, and were soon spotted by an astonished Jim McDevitt, still roaming the area:[2]

> The craft looked most impressive. In the half-light, I could make out the forms of four people on board. Two of the crew appeared to be Dudley Perkins and John Kerr. Could the others be Captain George and his wife? . . . To my horror I noticed that the caique was slowly being manoeuvred away from the shoreline . . . I yelled out to them for all I was worth. But still the caique kept edging away from me. After a while, someone standing upright in the boat shouted back to me not to panic. The boat was only being shifted westwards to a safer

anchorage. Despite this assurance, I felt angry and overcome with acute disappointment. So near and yet so far, I thought to myself!

As the caique disappeared, McDevitt was challenged by the bandit, Yiannis Glabedakis, the escaped convict we came across in Chapter 6. Once he was satisfied that he wasn't a German, the Cretan took Jim with him to locate the caique's new anchorage, shooting, roasting and eating a goat on the way.[3] But when they found the caique beached at Stomiou, near a German coast-watching post, it was wrecked! It had hit a reef in the night, and the four on board had been lucky to escape with their lives.[4] This was yet another severe blow to the morale of Kerr and Perkins, not to mention McDevitt.

Then, also in early June, several parties of SBS commandos were landed on the south coast of Crete from the Greek submarine *Papanikolis* to raid the German aerodromes at Timbaki, Kastelli, Maleme and Heraklion. Eighteen aircraft were destroyed at Heraklion and five, plus 200 tons of petrol, at Kastelli, on 13 June. The next day, 50 Cretan hostages were executed, and an attack of nerves swept the island.[5]

In western Crete, Dudley Perkins and John Kerr had temporarily split up. Other New Zealand stragglers were told by excited Cretans that 'heavily armed Germans in British uniforms' were in the area hunting for them.[6] But the Kiwis soon realised that these men were in fact British commandos, contacted them, and learned of a rendevous with the *Papanikolis* later that very evening. A mad scramble ensued. Kerr was told that 'English John' had come back for him, and realised that this must be Commando Sergeant John Medley, who had been evacuated earlier and who had sworn blind that he would come back for them. Kerr tore around the landscape, desperately trying to find Perkins as they had precisely two hours to make it. This meant that they had no chance of rounding up the other men on the run in the area, including Jim McDevitt. Frantic not to miss this chance of evacuation, they threw caution to the winds and took off overland directly to the rendezvous, a sea cave on the western coast. McDevitt, who was told the story in detail much later, relates their instructions:[7]

There they would find some inflatable rubber rafts hidden under some rocks. They had to be bold enough to row out to sea after deep darkness and then try and meet up with the surfaced Greek submarine. They were ordered to discard all their clothing and footwear before being hauled naked on board their rescue vessel. Presumably, precautions had to be taken to lessen the risk of uninvited guests going on board, such as body-lice!

But their troubles were far from over. A heavy sea was running, and the trip by dinghy out to the waiting submarine hazardous. Murray Elliott takes up the narrative:[8]

> a sudden wave reared up, the dinghy hit a projection and one of the planks at the stern was holed. Water poured in, steadily filling the boat until Perkins took off one of his German knee boots and rammed it into the hole. With the other he baled and gradually made the boat sufficiently buoyant to put off. Kerr and one sailor took the oars while Perkins and the other took turns at baling . . . then they sighted the submarine slowly moving away. The captain had evidently given up for the night. All four yelled, and yelled again. As they watched they saw the long shape slowly start to turn and circle back towards them.

The four naked men dived off the dinghy, grabbed the ropes which were thrown to them and were hauled on board. Kerr and Perkins found another six New Zealand soldiers in the submarine.

The *Papanikolis* moved off to complete its patrol off Gavdos. Two days later, it set off for Alexandria, and all being quiet, the skipper took it to the surface and opened the hatch. It was immediately attacked by an enemy aircraft, and went into an emergency dive. Elliott again:[9]

> It was a steep, fast dive, so precipitate that the vessel was at maximum depth before the forward tanks filled; weighed down by the weight behind she was unable to level off. Instead, she moved from the forward diving angle into a reverse position, almost perpendicular. . . . Gradually, the craft righted itself. By that time, some of the crew had to be freed from the controls, their muscles cramped into rigidity. One degree more, said the captain later, and the ship would have become

unmanageable, tilting further and further and plunging into the depths with machinery tearing loose and crashing through the steel skin.

Jim McDevitt, left behind in Crete, may actually have eye-witnessed this attack without knowing who was involved:[10]

> A couple of miles out to sea, and almost due south of my hill-top position, three Luftwaffe planes were taking turns in some dive-bombing exercises. Every time the depth-charges exploded over their target, tall plumes of agitated spray leaped into the air. Fascinated and curious, I watched this puzzling marine display. The sea was flat calm that day, just as it is all around Crete in summer time. What stumped me most was that I could see no likely target. This made me assume that the object of their serial attacks must lie under the sea, which could only mean one thing – an Allied submarine.

Kerr and Perkins were only too glad to finally reach Alexandria, where they were personally greeted by Admiral Cunningham before being subjected to the rigours of the now well-developed debriefing process by Army, Navy and Air Force Intelligence. Both men rejoined their units in the desert shortly afterwards.

German Counter-intelligence

At this point, it is necessary to diverge briefly from the main story of the men on the run to give an account of the general atmosphere on Crete from May until about the end of August 1942. In a word, it was awful. During the spring, German counter-intelligence had increased its raids on the mountain villages, and expanded its number of agents. In May, the Cretan Resistance shot half a dozen traitors, but the Germans executed 14 hostages in reprisal.[11] This development, taken along with the German successes in North Africa, made the Cretan villagers jittery. Tobruk then fell on 21 June, the news of which was a severe blow to the morale of all the men still at large. However, the Allied defensive line in North Africa stabilised between El Alamein and the Qattara Depression by the end of the month, which was better news.

In Crete, the more irresponsible Resistance bands were champing at the bit, as they favoured a general armed insurrection. As we have seen, the peasantry had armed itself to the teeth with weapons looted during the Battle of Crete. The records of Middle East Headquarters show that it had considered such an uprising, but given the situation in the Western Desert, instructed the SOE officers on the island to tell the Resistance to stay underground. Allied military support, especially in terms of manpower, was simply not available. By the same token, there was a hiatus in the rescue of the stranded men.[12] In other words, given the very limited number of craft then available, SOE had to balance the need to supply the Cretan Resistance, and thus maintain its morale, against the evacuation of these men. All these factors made life on the ground very difficult for SOE officers like Captain Xan Fielding and Major Patrick Leigh Fermor. But it also made life onerous for the stragglers.

Amongst the German counter-intelligence agents, Jim McDevitt describes a German freelance super-sleuth at length, a dedicated Nazi called Hans Wachter, a loner who was very active in western Crete. He kept a particular eye on Sklavopoula, and the redoubtable Fifi Papantonakis, whose work on behalf of the men on the run had never faltered.[13] Wachter had an English mother, and was apparently able to imitate a lot of regional English accents, thus enabling him to pass as an escaper himself, and trap the unwary. But Fifi ran circles round him. By this time, the German officer in overall charge of counter-intelligence operations was Captain Hartmann. As Beevor puts it:[14]

> Hartmann first used amnestied criminals as spies, then in the summer of 1942 he managed to recruit a number of the Tsouliadakis clan in Kroussonas by exploiting a family feud and an inter-village feud.

In a contemporary report, Xan Fielding said:[15]

> COUNTER-ESPIONAGE AND TERRROISM.
> With the issue of the new identity passes, the Germans have started a new reign of terror. Whereas Germans used to raid villages with a body of 24–30, they are now using a force of anything up to 600. Countless arrests have been made both for arms-holding and helping British.

Several men have also been executed in the APOKORONAS district for not being in possession of identity papers. Not a single eparchia [district] in my two Nomoi [counties] has been spared this renewed German activity. Cretan agents in German pay have been operating successfully and, I believe, have been responsible for a large number of the arrests.

The postwar SOE Report on the Cretan Resistance confirms all this intelligence on the ground:[16]

In addition to using GREEK agents, GERMANS of the secret police or counter-espionage service toured the country masquerading as escaped BRITISH prisoners, to find out who would shelter them. This also became dangerous as time went on, and the CRETANS learned to distrust their first naïve confidence that everyone was what he seemed. Probably the most reliable source of GERMAN information was from interrogation of suspects whom they arrested. With all the apparatus of torture, threats of firing-squads, solitary confinement and the trick of stool pigeon or friendly warder, they broke down many men, and having drained them dry shot them.

At this juncture, July–August 1942, SOE estimated that:[17]

there are still approximately 300 British stragglers still at large, the bulk of them in the centre of the island.

Xan Fielding describes meeting them on his travels:[18]

Each time I encountered these cheerful tattered men roaming about the countryside, usually singly or in pairs, I felt conscience-stricken; for I could offer them no immediate hope or assistance. Until arrangements could be made to take them off from one of the nearby beaches I had just reconnoitred, the only advice I could give them was to stay where they were. For now that enemy patrols were more active in the mountains thanks to the better weather and improvements in German counter-espionage, it was impossible to assemble them, as we had done in the earlier stages of the occupation, and send them down in a body to the evacuation points on Monty's [Captain Woodhouse's] part of the coast. Most of them, considering their condition, were in surprisingly high spirits, and would have taken any pity I might have shown them as an insult.

The Northerners

Meanwhile, Dick Huston and his mates had developed a well-organised routine to their cave-based existence near Varipetro. Every now and then, they let off steam by having a 'birthday party' and doing some serious drinking. As Huston puts it:[19]

> If we had not had the odd party we probably would have all become mental. They were to celebrate some distant relation's birthday and I am sure that relation had two or three birthdays in the same year.

His fellow caveman, Kiwi Milton Knight, found a new source of protein – hedgehogs – and even started a snail farm! They also tried to trap hares with a wire snare. Occasional visits were paid to 'their' villages, but always with the greatest circumspection, and they always left before midnight, mindful of German dawn raids. Occasionally, they also raided the gardens in what their Cretan friends told them was a 'Turkish' village – that is, one which had been allegedly deracinated by intermarriage with Turks under the Ottoman Empire. One night they stole some chickens, and this gave rise to an amusing incident:

> because of an error by Aussie. When he wrung the chucks' necks, he placed one in each sakouli and it was not far from the scene of the crime when the fowl in Aussie's bag suddenly came alive and jumped around inside the sakouli on Aussie's back giving him a big scare and Jack and I a good laugh.

Oddly enough, Dick Huston never felt bored while on the run. Foraging for food, mending their boots, yarning away, playing cards – and, of course, his secret mission – seems to have kept him fully focused. This group's great luxury was cigarettes. Huston expresses it like this:[20]

> A cigarette was one of the few pleasures we had left to us and even if

they were scarce, the pleasure we derived from them helped to make our lives worth living. They provided a goal to our lives, not only in achieving the cigarette but the self-discipline we had to impose on ourselves with rationing. We were scrupulously honest in sharing the cigarettes even to the fraction of a cigarette. The soldiers of those days will know what I am talking about.

However, a grim reminder of the reality of the Occupation came shortly afterwards when two of Huston's mates eyewitnessed an execution squad of Germans take 12 apparent civilians, including one woman, from a lorry into a wooded gully. The road was screened carefully by armed troops. They could not see into the gully but heard 12 bizarre, metallic clanks. The Germans came out of the gully and left. Later that night, Huston's party raided the graves to obtain the boots from the corpses, but they had already been removed. Huston believes that the secrecy surrounding this operation may have meant that those executed were Italians – but he never found out for sure.[21]

Huston and his mates had also become friends with the local bandits, a not uncommon feature of contemporary Cretan society, and it appears that this association stood them in good stead. The bandits had no axe to grind with his party, as opposed to villagers, for they were all fugitives together. Huston's remarks about these bandits are insightful:[22]

There can be no doubt that the bandits I met were a hard lot and we were fortunate that they became our friends. If they had decided we were enemies I am sure our fate would have been very uncertain . . . A strange thing about the bandits is that they did not form into bands but operated as individuals and this made them very difficult to approach by Germans or the police. I formed the opinion that they had not formed bands because they did not trust each other . . . The bandits led a very solitary life, living in the open most of the time. For them there could be no wife, no home comforts, no doctor when injured or ill and never knowing when the end might come. They would never know a genuine friend. Perhaps the reason why they liked us was because they could feel a kinship with us, or that we had no reason to betray them, or even that we did not criticize them but accepted them for what they were.

Endurance

Throughout the whole of 1942 thus far, Norm Scott had been holed up in his cave above Samonas, still paralysed, still tended to by the courageous Lagonikakis family, most often Irini, because the Germans were less suspicious of a woman moving about than her husband Dimitris. Sometimes the family even sent the children with food and drink for the fugitive. Quite apart from his crippling illness, hunger, and the cold, loneliness was a terrible problem for Norm. So when they could, Irini and/or Dimitris would spend the day with him, bringing him up to date with what news of the war they could glean from clandestine radios.[23] At about this time, Xan Fielding was taken to see him:[24]

> It was here that I first saw him – lying on a bed of twigs, from where he greeted us and apologized for not getting up and shaking hands. He then explained why he could not move: from the neck down he was completely paralysed. Rheumatic fever had reduced him to this state. The villagers told me that they remembered him as a giant of a man, immensely strong. Now he was incapable even of feeding himself. I did not know which to admire more – the fortitude with which he bore the discomfort and humiliation of total immobility, or the steadfast courage with which his protectors attended to his needs.

As the weather improved around Easter 1942, Norm regained some mobility in his upper body, and could feed himself. Shortly afterwards, it was his birthday, and Irini and other village women baked him a cake, making the long journey to the cave to share it with him. But this was risky business:[25]

> The Germans became suspicious of Irini's regular trips to the mountains. Irini and Dimitri Lagonikakis were arrested. The couple were put in jail but continued to deny any knowledge of the Australians. Then after ten days they were released. Their verdict, insufficient evidence. This

> was the most dangerous time for Irini Lagonikakis. Now she knew the Germans would be watching her every move. For a few weeks she couldn't leave her home but she knew if she did not get supplies to Norman he would die. She devised a scheme. On the pretext that she was taking food to her little girl at school, she kept making her trips into the mountains.

Norm Scott was to remain in that particular cave for some considerable time, as we shall see.

Central Crete

While these dramatic events were unfolding in western Crete, Arthur Lambert and his mate Ted Goodall had made their way back to central Crete from the Lassithi, around March 1942.[26] By this time, they had both gone barefooted for several months. They headed for the village of Lambini where Arthur had been sheltered earlier on his travels by a friendly family. There they were confronted by the brutal reality of the Occupation:[27]

> On reaching Lambini I led the way to Vassoleki's house. When she saw me Vasso broke down screaming, 'Thanassi [Arthur's Greek name], they have shot him! They have killed my brother!' and she wailed her lament for the dead. Never before or since have I heard such an unrehearsed outpouring of grief. Her wails wrenched my heart, and Ted, who had never met her, was shattered. We couldn't console her, but her grief eventually ran its course. I decided right then that I must leave as soon as possible; the sight of me had brought back such terrible memories, and I couldn't bear to see such grief again.

So Lambert and Goodall took off on their travels yet again, this time striking out for the Messara Plain, as they figured the coast near there might be a good spot for an evacuation by sea. Here they encountered an 'Australian intelligence officer' who had been landed on Crete a short while before, and who had just called for a bombing raid on the Messara aerodrome (Timbaki); Lambert and Goodall eyewitnessed the subsequent raid.[28]

Shortly afterwards, still in the same area, the two men encountered some Cretans who were:[29]

> talking of attacking the Germans by ambush, and [we] counselled against this, because these men were untrained, undisciplined, and not well equipped. While they might achieve some initial success with an ambush, once the enemy regrouped the Greeks wouldn't have stood a chance. Also the retribution the Germans would wreak on the nearest village didn't bear thinking about. We advised them to wait until they had sufficient numbers and leaders to attack simultaneously in many places, to wait for the arrival of more arms, and their own or British officers to lead, train and organise them.

Lambert and Goodall then made for the village of Zaros, but discovered that they were not welcome there, so continued on to a cave they knew. There they were confronted by three local men armed with pick-handles, who took them down to their village, where they were surrounded by an angry mob.[30] It was plain to the two soldiers that all it required was someone to strike the first blow and they were goners. So they decided to tough it out.[31]

> We both made speeches telling them what rats we thought they were, and concluded by saying that when the British recaptured Crete we would come back here with police, and the villagers would pay dearly for the way they had treated us. Ted and I then turned and shoulder to shoulder marched slowly out of the village. We wanted to run, but we knew that our British act must continue until we were well away from the village.

The two soldiers had no clue as to why the Cretans should have treated them in this manner. Lambert said:[32]

> I can only guess that it was due to some act perpetrated by three drunks, a Kiwi, an Aussie, and a Britisher, who were loose on the island.

Shortly after this incident, towards the end of April 1942, Lambert and Goodall were hiding in another cave when they were betrayed by the *Agrofilachas* of the nearby village.[33] The cave was surrounded by a platoon of police. A uniformed captain of police then informed the two Kiwis it was his job to arrest them as escaped prisoners of war. Lambert tried to bluff it out:[34]

> Ted and I heard him out, then in my best Greek I said, 'Captain, you are a traitor to the Allied and Greek fight for freedom. We came here to fight for and or die for Greece! Now you are arresting us for the enemy, and you intend to hand us over to the Germans. You are a traitor, sir, and one day soon you will have to answer for this crime.' When I had finished, I saw tears running down his cheeks. He replied, 'I have a wife and three little girls. If I let you go I could be executed and my family might be shot, whereas you will only become prisoners of war, so I must do what I do not want to do.'

Lambert and Goodall were duly arrested and put in a cell for the night. The next morning, a couple of armed policemen were moving the two Kiwis down the road to a point where the Germans would pick them up, when Lambert saw the *Agrofilichas* who had betrayed them:[35]

> I turned to one of the policemen and said in Greek, 'Could I borrow your rifle and one round, if you please?' The policeman turned and saw the Agrofelicus [sic], patted my back, and said in Greek, 'Do not worry about him, he is mine. The day the British land on Crete, I personally will cut his throat from ear to ear.' I have no reason to doubt that this threat was carried out.

Lambert and Goodall were subsequently interrogated by German Intelligence officers. Lambert describes what happened:[36]

> We were interviewed separately, and when my turn came I was questioned closely about Capt. Monty [Woodhouse]. I told a few lies, that I'd never met him, and that though I'd heard Greeks talk about him, I believed that he was a myth. The intelligence officers did not agree, saying that men who had been taken off Crete by Capt. Monty got drunk on leave in Cairo and were telling the world about their adventures. They concluded, 'We know men are getting off Crete, and

> we suspect that some are coming back, but we don't know where this is taking place. One day we'll find out, and then no more will get off or come back to Crete.'

This startling observation demonstrates both the efficiency of the German Intelligence service within Cairo, and that the extreme security measures taken by Allied Intelligence when debriefing evacuees were more than justified.

Lambert and Goodall were transported to Germany and spent the rest of the war in a series of POW Camps. Both survived. Goodall died in 1975, and Arthur Lambert is still alive and lives in Whangarei. We believe that he, and Gil Cross who lives in Christchurch, and was evacuated on the same boat as Len Frazer, are now the only Kiwi survivors of the men on the run.[37]

El Alamein and Its Consequences

On 23 October 1942, the pivotal Battle of El Alamein commenced. As the Allies subsequently broke out eastwards, the consequences were clear, as the Official SOE Report on the Cretan Resistance makes clear:[38]

> Clear signs of a fall in GERMAN morale were visible from the time that the GERMANS realized that EGYPT and AFRICA were lost to them. Occasional suicides and desertions began. Capt. LEIGH FERMOR spent a number of evenings eavesdropping on GERMANS in their billets, or listening to their conversations wrapped in a shepherd's cloak. He also began a direct attack on morale with a chalk-scrawling campaign for scribbling short slogans in public places. This was the first GERMAN language propaganda to be carried out in CRETE, and was taken up by HQ which supplied excellent black propaganda throughout 1943. This was distributed widely and enthusiastically and for a long time completely fooled the enemy who made many arrests of GERMAN soldiers, searches of billets and of parcels arriving from Germany.

From his vantage point in western Crete, Murray McLagan could observe the results of the fierce fighting:[39]

we daily watched hundreds of trimotored troop carriers conveying troops from Maleme and Debache aerodromes on Crete to North Africa and returning with the wounded. What wounds these men had – blind from the glare of the desert, septic wounds, paralysed throats from lack of water – some of these men would never again be able to talk – where were the young arrogant soldiers who had gone to North Africa but a few months earlier – these were men lined of face, haggard in countenance and with nerves shattered by the terrific bombarding from the British . . . These returning wounded had an adverse affect [sic] on the garrison troops and they became more determined than ever to get us dead or alive.

German morale may have taken a knock, but they were still proactive. In the Amari Valley in central Crete, most of the men on the run had now been evacuated, but both the Resistance and SOE were still active. Locals knew practically all of the German agents, and fed them disinformation, or shot them. But in November, the Germans launched a big raid on the villages of Vafes, Kouroutes, Nithavris, Apodolou and Platanos, and netted several prominent Resistance leaders, including Andreas Polentas, who were subsequently tortured and executed.[40] This was the work of a traitor called, variously, Komnas or Komninas. Xan Fielding describes what happened to him:[41]

[He] met an unpleasant death in broad daylight, even though he had taken the precaution of moving into a house [in Hania] surrounded by German billets. His body was discovered still bleeding from seventeen knife-wounds, under a table- cloth on which the blood his assailants had wiped from their hands had not yet had time to congeal.

Dick Huston expands on the role of these turncoats, and their fate:[42]

The latter half of 1942 and the beginning of 1943 was a hard time for us and also the Cretan people. Many became 'prothodetes' (traitors), because of the hopelessness of the war situation and many men and women were betrayed to be interrogated and executed. In some cases, in fact most, the traitor was known and I know for sure in some cases

> only suspected, but it seemed to make little difference, in all cases it was a death sentence to the betrayer and this was carried out as soon as possible, not only by their own people but by special squads set up for this specific purpose. The policy was simple, no traitor must be allowed to live and I believe very few did survive. It could be said that a traitor only had a short time to live after a betrayal and the policy did have the desired effect, in time betrayals became very rare . . . Men and women were treated the same, there was no preferential treatment and I know of two cases where women died horrible deaths.

Autumn and Winter in the North and West

Dick Huston and his mates managed to experience a modicum of Christmas cheer that winter.[43]

> One of the more pleasant memories I have of that last cave must have happened near the Xmas period of 1942. Anastasia and Johnny [from Varipetro] had brought a girl with them on this occasion and she brought a Greek string musical instrument with her. This girl had a wonderful voice, such a lovely singer, that the first time I heard Nana Mouskouri singing, I thought it was our girl. The difference was that the girl Anastasia brought with her had ginger hair, this being the first and only time I have seen a fiery haired Greek. She came up the cave several times and sang for us.

However, the unhealthy and insanitary reality of their situation was never far away. The men were afflicted by a plague of boils.[44]

> I had to attend to Gordon Davis who had three monstrous boils in a cluster in his armpit. They must have caused him considerable pain because he had determined they would not be touched until they were completely ripe. When they were ready he lifted his arm and I had barely touched the affected area which was terribly swollen, when they erupted right in my face. Not a pleasant thing to have happen. Gordon, of course, was very upset about it but it was just one of those things and certainly not his fault. I washed my face, even sponged it with that disinfecting spirit called 'tskikouthia' [raki], but the damage had been

done and from that time on I had boils, mostly on my face, my neck and on my arms. So with boils throbbing on my neck and head and two teeth doing their best to be competitive, it was not the happiest of periods.

In the remote and isolated corner of Ktista in south-west Crete, Jim McDevitt and Des Reynolds continued what the former called 'another period of abject loneliness and acute starvation.'[45] They encountered two men on the run in the area, Australian Joe Salmon and Kiwi Jim Quinn, who became very ill, the former with appendicitis, the latter with malaria. However, nursed faithfully by their mates, these two men survived. Shortly afterwards, McDevitt and Reynolds had a brush with the armed bandit Yiannis Glabedakis again, who relieved them of their boots while they were sleeping, leaving only his own rundown, smelly pair behind![46] McDevitt and Reynolds shamed the incorrigible bandit into returning one pair of their own boots, and were yet again helped out by Alex Makrakis, the loyal miller. He gave the men some money and they managed to find another pair of boots on the black market.

The pair headed east, and joined a well-established community of stragglers at the Kakodiki Stream which follows the Paleochora road down to the sea, near the village of Vlithia, at a location nicknamed 'Waterview'. This was probably the last group of men on the run in western Crete, and comprised mainly Australians, with a few British and New Zealanders. Life there was a well-organised routine of foraging for food – dock, dandelions, fennel, *horta*, mulberries, snails, eels, and freshwater crabs.[47] Local villagers would bring them what they could, when they could. Yet again, a 'Returned Yank', Chimon, the local kafeneion owner, took the initiative in looking after this group. They played backgammon and cards, had singsongs, and 'what-we-did-before-the-war' storytelling sessions.

But Jim McDevitt became close to a local girl, Electra, incurred the wrath of the leader of the Australians, and '. . .took off in a huff until things cooled down again'.[48] This proved to be a very lucky move. Shortly afterwards, Jim bumped into a few other Aussies and Kiwis he had not met before, and was shocked to learn that 'Waterview' had been raided, with 11 of his mates arrested. They had been betrayed by a conscripted worker who thought they were commandos about to raid the German base at Paleochora. But the arrested men maintained resolutely that they had been living off the land, refused to name any villager who had helped them, and were shipped off to a POW camp in Germany.

The days of large, happy, carousing, Robin Hood-type bands – anything between 20 and 50 strong – such as those living near Therisso, Meskla and Agia Irini, were long over. The German Intelligence machinery was by now far too sophisticated for any larger gathering of men to survive undetected. This effectively meant that the remaining men on the run were now surviving either on their own, or in small groups of two to five, and were permanently on the move. And their second winter in the mountains was fast approaching.

CHAPTER 9

Last Round-up: Christmas 1942—May 1943

For the second year running, Jim McDevitt managed to make it to Fifi's house at Sklavopoula a few days before Christmas.[1] There, he learned some exciting news: an SOE mission had recently been landed, and one of its tasks was apparently to round up the last of the Anzacs on the run. McDevitt, mindful of previous missed evacuations, immediately set off eastwards, although now warned to steer clear of Souyia, where a permanent German listening post had been established. He was in the village of Moni for Christmas Day, and shortly afterwards headed on up to Koustoyerako. There he found Australians Charlie Hunter, John Simcoe and Frank Ezzy, plus 'Jim the Pom', living in the *Nerospili*, the 'water-cave', so-called because fresh water trickled down its rock face. McDevitt was apprised of what had actually happened with the SOE landing.

In actual fact, this was a joint ISLD / SOE mission, and for complicated reasons was a blind landing off the Greek submarine *Papanikolis* at a small cove called Tripiti, 5 km east of Souyia. When the submarine surfaced offshore, a near gale was blowing. Xan Fielding and ISLD agents Arthur Reade and Stelios Papaderos, a local, loaded their gear into the sub's dinghy, climbed in, and made for shore in Stygian darkness and rough seas. The dinghy was soon swamped, and the occupants had no clue where they were. Fielding takes up the story:[2]

> Further reconnaissance was out of the question; our main concern now was to keep afloat and get ashore as quickly as we could. We therefore made for the nearest point where the foam seemed to splash less fiercely. Out of control, and with our speed alarmingly increasing, we were caught in the breakers and driven straight towards a solid block of cliff; and as I tensed my muscles in anticipation of a head-on crash, we were brought prematurely and unexpectedly to a standstill as the boat abruptly fell to pieces round us, spilling us out on to the rock we had struck. We clung to it as another wave dashed over us, bombarding us with bits of wreckage and bundles of equipment, which a second later were swept away and vanished out to sea.

Fielding and his two companions found themselves in a gully where some sheep were sheltering, thus suggesting the absence of Germans. Soaking wet and freezing, they promptly lit a fire and tried to dry out, aware of sinister rustling noises in the dark beyond the loom of the fire. Dawn revealed that a group of heavily armed local partisans had had them under observation all night. They immediately recognised their fellow villager Papaderos and there was a joyful reunion. Shortly afterwards, they were joined by the three Australians from Koustoyerako. Fielding describes their appearance:[3]

> Though we had lost practically everything except the clothes we stood up in, our shirts were at least unpatched and our boots intact; while these men were barefoot and in rags. Even so, their morale was high, which said as much for their own natural resilience as for the friendliness of their village hosts, and their cheerful banter soon dispelled our sense of gloom and foreboding. Like most of their compatriots, they were all three expert swimmers, and when they heard of the loss of our kit they at once volunteered to see how much of it they could recover . . . They spent the rest of the morning plunging in and out, and only rarely came up empty-handed; until almost all the kit, which I thought we had lost for ever, was miraculously landed high and, if not dry, at least undamaged since the more fragile items had been mercifully wrapped in waterproof material.

What Fielding does not mention, but which the Aussies told Jim McDevitt in their cave, was that they had also salvaged a small fortune in banknotes:[4]

> Egyptian, Turkish and British sterling as well as franc notes from Switzerland and France.

Then John Simcoe had dived deep and retrieved not only Fielding's party's personal weapons, but also bags of gold sovereigns! All of this money was both to buy provisions for the Resistance on the black market and to bribe officials.

Not long after his stop at the *Nerospili*, McDevitt went walkabout westwards again, as no evacuation was on the cards in the immediate future. Indeed, in the first couple of months of 1943, McDevitt must have completed a circle round the interior of western Crete. In February, he arrived back in Koustoyerako, to hear from Frank Ezzy that there seemed to be major German troop movements in the area, and that the male villagers, who were practically all partisans anyway, were heading for the hills. The two men decided to make off north-west over the mountains, down to the Omalos Plateau, and on to the village of Lakkoi – about 16 kilometres as the crow flies.

But these two fugitives were no crows. First of all, they had to climb up steeply from Koustoyerako over tough terrain onto the east–west Psilafi Ridge, then descend steeply at the pass of Strifomadi – with a sheer drop on their right down to the start of the Samaria Gorge – to the Omalos Plateau, cross the plateau, and drop down to Lakkoi. This was in mid-winter, with inadequate boots, when the whole of their route was covered with snow! Seán, a very experienced mountain walker, has done this route from Koustoyerako to the Omalos several times in both directions, but always in spring or summer. Even then, he regards it as a testing walk, which requires physical fitness, route-finding ability, and a good head. His friend Loraine Wilson, also an experienced mountain walker, who has written the definitive walking guide to the White Mountains, reckons that there is a height gain of 1442 metres, and a height loss of 692 metres, on this route, that it is

14 map-kilometres long, and requires nine hours – and that's just to reach the entrance to the Omalos at Xyloskalo.[5]

Nothing daunted, McDevitt recounts the trip:[6]

> The entire region was completely silent, with no sign of other travellers, nor of animals such as roaming deer. As we climbed higher and higher, we heard flocks of puzzled, curious pigeons whirring above our heads. Trees, such as spruce, cypress and pine abounded on the snowy mountain slopes. All the usual tracks were buried under deep snow-falls and there were no signposts pointing the way to the Omalos. Frank proved to be a reliable guide, pointing out the piles of flat stones placed high up in the boughs of trees . . . Our walking sticks came in mighty handy on this trip. Time and time again, we saved ourselves from falling into deceptive crevasses as we probed our way forwards. All this time our feet felt like frozen lead. Our boots began to change into a gangrenous-green colour, and our limbs looked purple under the strange daylight.

Note the manner in which the local shepherds indicated the route, and the fact that Australian Frank Ezzy had picked up on this ingenious signposting.

After a few days in Lakkoi, McDevitt and Ezzy moved on again, this time to the north-west, as the Germans visited the village on a regular basis to pick up and return their conscripted labour. At the village of Kalathenes they encountered Australians Flap Jones, John 'Papastratos' Duncan and Sergeant Corbould. ('Papastratos' was and is the name of a cheap Greek cigarette.) The group decided to return over the mountains to Koustoyerako, as Charlie Hunter and John Simcoe were old mates of the three Aussies. They arrived back in the village some time in the first half of March, to find that a small group of men on the run had now congregated there.

On 29 March 1943 an event of great significance occurred for this group. A sentry spotted two strangers approaching from the north – an unusual direction – so all the men took cover immediately. One of the strangers was identified as a local, Petros Georgiakis, but McDevitt wasn't sure of the second man's identity.[7]

> Those square-set shoulders and that Turkey distinctive beard looked familiar enough. You can well imagine the extent of my surprise and pleasure when I finally recognized Tom Moir, my fellow countryman, and one of my former pals. How come? Had he not been reported as having sailed away to the Middle East on a stolen caique, and later rumoured to be kaput by the Jerries at Paleochora?

Moir brought exciting news. After his successful escape he had been recruited by MI9, and had volunteered to come back and arrange for the last round-up of the men on the run. But Moir had been landed at the extreme *east* end of Crete on 14 February for some unfathomable reason, and had taken six whole weeks to walk to the west end. The proposed evacuation date of 1 April, only 48 hours away, was plainly impossible, as word had to be circulated to all the small pockets of men in their various hidey-holes.

While Moir set about arranging a new departure date, he also organised the purchase of provisions with the considerable amount of money he had brought with him, and the standard of living of the men in the 'water-cave' above Koustoyerako improved considerably, as did their morale. Several other men – Jim Quinn, 'Papastratos' Duncan, and the hugely bearded Wally Allen joined the muster, and for security reasons, it was now broken up into two parties.

Tom Moir asked Jim McDevitt to join the small team which he needed to organise this final big evacuation, and after a moment's hesitation remembering his previous narrowly missed escapes, Jim agreed.[8] Charlie Hunter was put in charge of this local team. It was likely that the evacuation would take place from a coastal cave called Tripiti, south of Koustoyerako, but Moir ordered Hunter and McDevitt to keep this information secret. This evacuation operation was going to be planned with maximum security in mind, on a 'need-to-know' basis, for some time after Easter. Tension was mounting.

SOE Major Tom Dunbabin's Report from Crete of February 1943 summarises the contemporary situation as regards 'British Stragglers' as follows:[9]

> There are known to me 16 British stragglers in LASITHI, 6 in PEDIADA,

8 (Cypriots) in AMARI, and about 30–40 in the west of Crete. The Cypriots are a source of constant uneasiness as their hosts fear they may betray them. The British are fairly well looked after and are not endangered except by their own incaution.

The Northeners

In late March of 1943, Dick Huston and his fellow 'troglodytes' noticed an increase in German patrol activity up on their Kastelos plateau and deduced that, somehow or another, the enemy must have become aware of their existence, if not their exact location.[10] Nevertheless, in late April, the men decided that they would have an Anzac Day party to celebrate the fact that they had been on Crete for two whole years. Jim and Sofia were due to come up from Varipetro the next day with food and drink for this shindig. On the night of 23 April, 1943, Dick Huston, Colin Ratcliffe and Gordon Davis were in their cave while the other three were in another nearby cave, at Demonyaris. Huston woke up on the morning of 24 April, as Davis went out of the cave for a look around. Suddenly:[11]

> When Gordon came bursting through the mouth of the cave with, 'Come on chaps, there's Jerries outside,' he imprinted these words in my memory forever. I only had to put my boots on, but even so, Colin Ratcliffe was going out the entrance before me and as I came out he was standing outside with his hands above his head with a German pointing a machine-gun at him and shouting in German. What he was saying I have no idea, but it would be a safe bet that he was calling up his mates. In fact, he never stopped shouting until the others arrived . . . There was no doubt we had been betrayed.

Huston knew this because the German sergeant who was the patrol commander spoke English, and demanded to know where the other three men were. Huston had to act quickly, because not only were Jack Symes, Aussie Rankin and Milton Knight likely to wander up from *their* cave at any moment, but also the Cretan villagers Jim and Sofia were due with supplies. Quick as a flash, Huston started an argument with the sergeant about the relative merits of his sub-machine gun and the

British equivalent. The Kiwi pointed to a rock and said the German weapon would never hit it. The sergeant fell for it, and fired three bursts, and as Huston says:[12]

> You had to give him credit, he hit it. We knew now everyone would be warned.

Milton Knight records his reaction:[13]

> Aussie Rankin and I were sleeping in another cave situated on the other side of the gully from the one Dick was hiding in. The noise of the tommy guns, which Dick had tricked the Germans into firing, woke us up with a hell of a start and immediately warned us of the danger. Crawling along the floor to the mouth of the cave, we were confronted with the sight of the boys with their hands up in front of a German patrol. Realising that sooner or later the chances of them searching further afield and finding our cave was a distinct possibility, as it was only about 200 yards away (though on a higher level), we elected to try and get out without being seen. Above the cave was a 30 or 40 ft stretch of big jumbled rocks, so, although in full view of the Germans we made our way as quickly and as quietly as possible up the rocks, expecting at any minute to be challenged. Miraculously they never saw us.

Huston was now satisfied, as he had hidden his pistol and secret papers in a safe place outside the cave. But he noticed that Gordon Davis seemed agitated as the Germans searched the cave. Later, on the way to Hania in a truck, Huston asked him why he had been uneasy. Davis replied that he had kept a diary, and had run back into the cave when he saw the Germans, and dropped it down a deep crack in the cave floor near his bed. Huston said:[14]

> I shuddered to think of what might have happened if the Germans had found that diary, for keeping diaries was strictly taboo, especially if they had names in them.

In Hania, the three men were interrogated thoroughly and at length, but not ill treated. Huston did the speaking for the trio, and quickly adopted an effective strategy:[15]

> I made sure that I only answered questions and never volunteered sentences and kept the replies as short as possible . . . It was obvious their main purpose was to get the names of the people who had been feeding us. We were equally determined that they would never find this out from us.

The three soldiers maintained stoutly that they had survived by stealing food and clothes, and living off snails and *horta*. Although the Germans did not believe them, and kept them on their feet for hours, they could not break their resolve. Huston recalls:[16]

> It was dark when they gave up and the officer said he was sorry we had not cooperated with them for it left them no other option than to shoot us in the morning. We were then taken out to a truck where the patrol who had caught us were waiting and they all shook hands with us and the interpreter said they were pleased they had met us. It sounded very strange to us.

The three men were taken to Ayia Jail, but they were not shot in the morning. Instead, they were interrogated further on a daily basis by German Military Police. But they stuck to their story that they were simple soldiers and knew no Greeks. They continued only answering questions and made no statements of any kind; their dialogue more or less limited to merely saying 'No' or 'I don't know'. After two weeks of this grilling, Dick Huston was eventually told that if he did not give his interrogator the name of one Greek, he would be handed over to the Gestapo. He was given 10 minutes to make up his mind. As Huston says:[17]

> Well, I did have a good think about it and decided I would never be able to live with myself if I betrayed my Cretan friends and in any case sooner or later the Gestapo would take us over, so really there could only be one answer.

When his interrogator returned, Huston told him he knew no Greeks. As he escorted the Kiwi back to his cell, the German said, 'As a man I admire you and am pleased you told me nothing.' Davis and Ratcliffe had made the same decision, and, so far as we can determine, so did every other single Allied soldier who was captured on Crete in similar circumstances. These three men were to be in Ayia Jail for a total of two months, overhearing executions on a daily basis. But from Day One, they started planning to escape, sawing through their third-floor cell bars with the aid of a hacksaw blade smuggled to them by Cretan women imprisoned on the ground floor. We will return to these staunchest of soldiers shortly.

Endurance

Meanwhile, in his cave near Samonas, Norm Scott was finally regaining some power of locomotion. The paralysis had left both his hands and feet twisted, and his leg muscles wasted. But he wrapped bags round his hands and knees, and was able to crawl on all fours. A Northern Victoria newspaper article relates his efforts at foraging:[18]

> Sometimes he had to crawl up to two miles over the mountains to get food for himself and had to eat grass [*horta*] and snails. To get water he had to carry a two gallon water tin in a bag on his back to a well. Going out was not so hard but returning to the cave was very awkward.

And Irini Lagonikakis still hiked up the mountain from her village faithfully, as often as she could, transporting Norm food, drink, company and news.

Back to the West

Throughout March and April, Tom Moir travelled extensively around western Crete, alerting the remaining stragglers that their evacuation was impending, and to stand by to move to the coast at short notice; he contacted a total of 51 men. Moir also conducted a reconnaissance of both Maleme airfield and the port at Souda Bay for a series of commando raids scheduled for July.[19] But it seems that the Germans knew he was on the island. Moir himself left no memoir or record of his time in Crete, but Murray Elliott tells the following story, confirmed by Tom's son Dudley (named for Dudley Perkins), about what he saw through a crack when concealed in a Cretan house:[20]

> The Germans had called at the house, seeking 'the Englishman, Tom'. They demanded to know where he was and threatened to shoot every member until they revealed his whereabouts. Fortunately, most of the members of the family had managed to get away earlier; only about three remained. The Germans first shot one and again demanded an answer and, when it was not forthcoming, shot another and later a third.

Then further disaster struck. Early in May, Moir, returning from his recce with his interpreter, RAF man Harry Masters, entered the village of Moni. They encountered a mixed patrol of four Germans and two Greeks; one of the Greeks was a traitor called Christos, from Souyia. Moir's Greek could have fooled the Germans, but not Christos. Moir and Masters were arrested, the former managing to slip some confidential papers and gold sovereigns to the other Greek policeman, a patriot. The two men were transported to Ayia Jail, and news of their capture swept around the men on the run like wildfire. But Xan Fielding took over the organisation of the evacuation, and after a false alarm caused by a glitch with his secret radio transmitter, the departure date was fixed for 2200 on 8 May 1943.

As Jim McDevitt went about his rounds ordering his mates to stand by, they heard very exciting news on one of the clandestine radios: the fighting in North Africa had ended, and '. . . over 200,000 Axis troops had been forced to put down their arms'.[21] The news of the impending evacuation could not have come soon enough for Murray McLagan, for he had been learning at first hand the back-breaking nature of the work of local shepherds:[22]

> During the last six weeks of my sojourn on Crete I was tending and milking 150 sheep with two Greeks. During that period I was working approximately 20 hours a day rising at 5 a.m. and tending the sheep until 11 when we did the morning milking which took three of us an hour. The sheep were driven into a rectangular pen which narrowed down at one end; a large container was set into the ground at the narrow end of the pen and the milking commenced. We three gathered round the container with our legs well spread waiting for the ewes which were sufficiently well trained to know what was required of

them. As each ewe halted between our straddled legs we leaned over them and milked them from behind. Only the thumbs and forefingers were used in the process. After a feed of fresh milk and junket I spent the afternoon grazing the sheep on the hills, bringing them in again at 8 p.m. for the evening milking. Milking finished, we had tea and set about the job of making the cheese.

At about this time, Xan Fielding passed on news of Norm Scott's plight to Charlie Hunter, who was in charge of the waiting evacuees, to see if anything could be done for him. Jim McDevitt records their reaction:[23]

> Well, after having had this pathetic problem tossed into our laps, and with the time of our evacuation fast approaching, we sat down in a huddle to discuss things. We wondered how we could jack up guides, escorts and a pack animal at such short notice. The helpless victim would need a constant escort to keep him from falling off his beast's saddle. Besides that, his procession would tend to attract suspicious attention as it passed along the main highway and up into the foothills villages. We devoted quite a lot of time to discussing this serious matter. In the end, Charlie decided to advise Xan that, all things considered, it would be impossible for us to fetch the afflicted Aussie to our assembly point with such a short time at our disposal.

The men were also told that a mysterious 'Lady X' would be joining their party, escorted by Xan Fielding, and that she had absolute priority for evacuation. They were completely puzzled by this order, for if there was one thing about which they were all in agreement, it was that there wasn't a *woman* amongst the men on the run! 'Lady X' was in fact Katina Beirakis, the daughter of a merchant in Hania, who had been a key agent for SOE, but who had now been compromised.[24] Fielding was extremely embarrassed by his filthy, unshaven appearance when he went to pick up the elegantly dressed and attractive young woman at the family's country home. He was also worried about the journey to the coast:[25]

> My one concern was how she would put up with the rigours of a long march over the mountains, but this was dispelled as soon as we started.

. . . Effortlessly, she kept up with us all the way, even at the breakneck pace which Stelio habitually set, and without a murmur settled into our nest in the carob tree, sleeping, as we did, fully dressed, making a pillow of her small knapsack whose meagre contents differed from those of our own only in one item – a modest object, unknown to the peasants on whom we modelled our disguise, and one which we had therefore learnt to do without – a toothbrush.

As Evacuation-Day (E-Day) approached, and the arrival of a naval craft was confirmed by an ISLD wireless operator hidden in a cave high above Koustoyerako, runners were dispatched to round up the waiting men. Absolute secrecy was the name of the game. Only the small 'committee' knew from where the evacuation would take place, and they would only congregate the men there at the last possible minute. Murray McLagan describes how he was summoned:[26]

On the morning of May 7th 1943 a Greek runner came to the village where I was working and took me aside for a discussion. He told me that arrangements had been made for us to be picked up on the night of May 8th and that I was to locate all the troops in my area, and take those who did not know the way to our headquarters. Could it be the real thing, were we really going to be taken off? I picked up as many as I could find, and headed for our headquarters where we were joined up with many more of our boys.

The rendevous point was a small wooded valley near Koustoyerako called Koukonara. Xan Fielding depicts it as he arrived with 'Lady X':[27]

The little dell in which they were assembled looked like a brigands' lair. The sight of it and the sounds from it reminded me of a similar scene I had witnessed just after my first landing in Crete: the coffee-shop of Akendria, which had likewise been thronged by a crowd of potential evacuees. But these men, though more desperate and destitute after a year and a half longer in the hills, did not fill me with the same apprehension as their former counterparts, not only because I was now more inured to the violence and lawlessness which I felt they represented, but also because they themselves were in a more

NATHAN FAMILY ARCHIVE

Ned Nathan, 1940.

WINTER FAMILY ARCHIVE

Peter Winter.

MCLAGAN FAMILY ARCHIVE

Murray McLagan.

MOIR FAMILY ARCHIVE

Tom Moir, darning.

JOHNSTON FAMILY ARCHIVE

'Bella' Johnston.

IMPERIAL WAR MUSEUM

Typical Greek caiques (*Imperial War Museum Negative Number A23311*).

Dudley Perkins.

PERKINS FAMILY ARCHIVE

MARITIME MUSEUM OF GREECE

The submarine RHNS *Papanikolis* in Alexandria, Egypt. There are the signatures of the officers at the top part of photograph.

AUTHOR FAMILY ARCHIVE

Church of Agios Ioannis, Ktista.

LITTLE FAMILY ARCHIVE

Ken Little.

AUTHOR FAMILY ARCHIVE

Paleochora War Memorial listing of villagers executed in September 1941.

AUTHOR FAMILY ARCHIVE

Azoyires cave where Len Frazer slept.

SCOTT FAMILY ARCHIVE

Norm Scott.

AUSTRALIAN WAR MEMORIAL MUSEUM

The Lagonikakis family at Neo Horio on 11 June 1945 (Irini – centre, Dimitris – right) (*Australian War Memorial Negative Number 131012*).

SUBJECT'S FAMILY ARCHIVE

Milton Knight and Dick Huston.

LAMBERT FAMILY ARCHIVES

Arthur Lambert.

AUSTRALIAN WAR MEMORIAL MUSEUM

Lt Reg Saunders (left) exchanges congratulations with Lt Tom Derrick after their commissioning parade (*Australian War Memoral Negative Number 083166*).

Village of Koustoyerako.

MCDEVITT FAMILY ARCHIVE

Jim McDevitt.

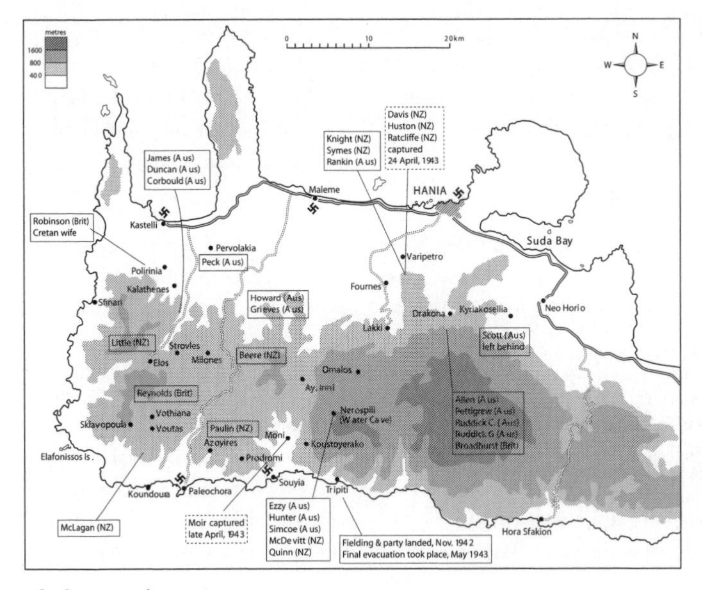

The last round-up

co-operative frame of mind. Their high morale was naturally due to the prospect of freedom. For their unusual discipline, however, I had to thank the trio of Australians who had first helped us by recovering the kit we had lost in our shipwreck the previous winter. As soon as the New Zealander responsible for organizing the evacuation had been captured [Tom Moir], these three had spontaneously taken over his duties. Not only had they helped to assemble their comrades from other areas; having done so, they had themselves reconnoitred a suitable landing-beach, notified its position to Headquarters through the I.S.L.D. station and arranged for the boat to come on and fetch them that very night. All we had to do now was wait till it was dark before moving down to the coast.

Before they moved off, Jim McDevitt was delighted to meet 'Lady X', Katina Beirakis, whom he already knew from his travels as a cousin of Fifi Papantonakis. He noted her choice of footwear:[28]

Strange as it may seem, the female traveller was not kitted out in a suitable pair of stout boots as one would expect. No, she wore her usual pair of high-heeled shoes instead. Just think of it! Had she traipsed out of her village wearing boots, then all her neighbours would have become alerted about her present secret travel plans – something the S.O.E. tried hard to avoid.

But there was another young Cretan woman in the evacuation party, Elevtheria, along with her husband, a British soldier on the run called Sid Robinson. An Australian newspaper subsequently told Sid's story:[29]

Soon she and I were in love. We met secretly, dodging Germans and Fifth-columnists. She risked her life to help me and my comrades. Last January we decided to marry. We and two Australians went to the village at two o'clock one morning and knocked up the village priest. He at first refused to perform the ceremony, but the Australians waved their revolvers. We were married in three minutes. We obtained the mayor's signature to the wedding certificate in the same way.

SOE had already transmitted a radio message that it might be possible to evacuate only 20 people on this run. 'Lady X' was to be given top priority, followed by two SOE agents who were being rotated. Charlie Hunter made the rest of the men put their names in a saucepan, and lots were drawn for the remaining seventeen spots. Jim McDevitt drew Number 20.

The word to descend to the beach arrived on the afternoon of 8 May. Murray McLagan describes the scene:[30]

The track led us along razorback ridges where again a false step would have resulted in death. One had an impression of the Grand Canyon of America as one gazed down into creek beds thousands of feet below where sheep and goats appeared as no more than moving specks. The descent safely accomplished, we had tea and made our way down to the sea as soon as it was dark.

Geoff Ruddick of the 2/7th Australian Battalion takes up the story:[31]

The boat was due to arrive at 9.40 p.m. As darkness settled in, the tension and excitement began to build up. Then there was a deep rumbling out to sea. Twenty minutes or so later, the vague outline of a boat could be seen. What it was, no one knew. Then the engines stopped. It was 9.40 p.m.

Xan Fielding continues:[32]

We had been signalling for less than an hour, when we heard the sound of an engine out to sea – a deep purr, much louder than I expected, which quickly increased to a full-throated roar utterly unlike the noise made by a submarine or John Campbell's *Hedgehog* . . . Alec [Tarves] had instinctively stopped signalling as soon as the boat appeared, and the ensuing darkness and silence increased our tension to such an extent that for several seconds we remained as though dazed before breaking into nervous laughter and cheers at the sound of unmistakably English invective directed at us across the water: 'Put the bloody light on; we can't see where we're going!'

Jim McDevitt relates what happened next:[33]

The next highlight of our unfolding drama took place when Big John Simcoe, the expert Australian diver and hero of the 1942 salvage operation, proudly announced that he was about to 'take off'. Those closest to him cheered him on his way as he dived into the starlit sea. Charlie Hunter had earlier given the swimmer his blessing to do his act. He wanted to be the very first to reach our dream-boat, and to assure the skipper that all was in readiness for the big show.

Shortly afterwards, the first rubber dinghy appeared, disgorged two SOE agents, and embarked Katina and Nikos Souris, another SOE agent. All the remaining men were steadily ferried out to the motor-launch; the limit of 20 had proved to be a false alarm. McDevitt describes the departure:[34]

At last, our M.L.'s turbo-charged engines were now revving up from a pulsating throb to a shattering din, then she shuddered from stem to stern. Instinctively we grabbed hold of our seats with a firmer grip.

> Some of the steel-helmeted gun crews swivelled their guns so as to face the westerly direction, whence our feared enemy trouble might come. Orders were bellowed. There was a ringing of bells, and a hissing of steam. With a powerful lurch forwards, we felt we were well on our way to freedom.

The next morning, the 14 New Zealand and 15 Australian soldiers were landed at Tobruk. Ruddick tells what followed:[35]

> After being issued with British army uniforms at Tobruk, we were taken to Alexandria for interrogation. After the debriefing, we were required to sign an undertaking not to divulge any details of our escape. The security for the entire Cretan rescue operations was pretty tight; so much so, in fact, that the drivers of the British transport unit which met and later moved us were told only to pick up some cave men from Tobruk.

For these 29 Anzac soldiers, their life on the run in Crete was finally over.

An anomaly now appears in accounts of the number of men left behind on Crete. The end-of-the-war summary of MI9's activities in the Eastern Mediterranean states:[36]

> 1 July 1943 – 31 December 1943:
> Escapers and evaders evacuated from Crete: 54.

We do not understand where this figure could come from. The May evacuation left only four known Anzacs on the island. These were Kiwis Driver Wally Swinburne and Sergeant D. Nicholls, and Australians Tom Spriggs, and, of course, Norm Scott. Swinburne and Spriggs made their way to eastern Crete and joined a band of partisans in the Lassithi area around May 1943. They were evacuated by Motor Torpedo Boat (MTB) on 8 September 1943, along with a West Indian pilot, a New Zealand pilot, and 14 Cretans, in Operation HORHAM VI.[37] The fate of Nicholls is unknown. In his book on Crete, Beevor mentions the failed attempt to evacuate Norm Scott, and says: 'He died soon afterwards.'[38]

However, Beevor is spectacularly wrong. Norm Scott in fact survived right throughout 1943. After 34 months in his cave in the mountains – that is, *two years and ten months* later – he was ultimately betrayed and captured on 11 April 1944, the day before his birthday. The Australian newspaper takes up the story:[39]

> He was put in the big prison of Ayia. He was there for one month during which the Gestapo questioned him two or three times a day to find out who had been feeding him. He told them that the rebels had been feeding him. The Gestapo informed him that he was a spy. They said no man could stay three years behind German lines in military uniform and not be caught. He fully expected to be shot. The Gestapo told him that if he revealed who fed him he would be treated as a prisoner-of-war and put in hospital, and that if he did not tell them who had helped him he would be treated as a spy and shot. He told them nothing except to say that he had been helped by the rebels.

Nor was Beevor the only one to get the fate of Norm Scott wrong. His own regimental history has him marked as KIA (Killed In Action)![40]

After a month of interrogation in Crete, Scott was sent to the Luftwaffe hospital in Athens where it was determined that his condition was caused by rheumatism. He was then transported to a POW camp in Germany, where he impressed his fellow prisoners with his amazing courage. The Commanding Officer of his camp said:[41]

> This man is at present in Reserve Lazarette XIII.D. His story is that on the seventh escape in Crete after capture he fell very ill and suffered unbelievable privation for three years until his final capture by the Germans about the April of this year [1944]. He has come through these trials with a twisted body but a sane and wonderful mind, and he has been an inspiration to those of his fellow prisoners who have seen him since his capture. I consider that he is worth specially interrogating as an example of fortitude on his return.

In late 1944, Norm Scott was passed for repatriation by the Red Cross. He arrived in Britain in February 1945 where subsequently, in the Glasgow Western Infirmary, his condition was correctly diagnosed as being caused by beriberi, due to poor diet and severe vitamin deficency. Norm arrived home in Mildura, Australia, in June 1945, managed to walk again, initially with callipers, then without, although his legs were never the same again and he had to wear surgical boots to correct the differences in their length.[42] A local newspaper, the *Argus*, printed a humorous story about him in October 1947, eating a few dozen snails for his lunch![43]

Norm Scott eventually died in 1985, without ever seeing the regimental history which had him posted KIA. Although he always wanted to go back to Crete, he never made it as he was not strong enough, and latterly, too ill. However, Irini Lagonikakis's son John emigrated to Australia in 1966 and visited Norm shortly afterwards.

The situation in Crete at the end of 1943 as regards MI9 was summarised as follows:[44]

> Crete was by now clear of the original Escapers and Evaders; but a most comprehensive system existed throughout the island to ensure that any forced-landed aircrew personnel were contacted, hidden, and subsequently evacuated.

The same source notes that seven Cypriots were evacuated in January 1944.

There are two footnotes to the story of the men on the run. Back in Ayia Prison, Dick Huston and his mates were most surprised when two newcomers were shoved into their cell: Tom Moir and Harry Masters![45] While their interrogation by the Gestapo continued, they maintained their say-nothing routine, until they were all marched to the execution wall in the yard and blindfolded. But it was a dummy execution which their guards found very amusing. The officer who arranged all this flicked Huston continuously under the nose in a subsequent interrogation, to his intense discomfort. Huston says:[46]

> I hit him a beauty in the face. There was a guard on either side of me but I had caught them by surprise and I got that one blow in.

Needless to say, he was badly beaten up and thrown into solitary. The prison commandant came to visit him, and asked why he had struck an officer. Huston retorted that, in the New Zealand Army, officers do not hit their men, and he was provoked. Rather to his surprise, he was not shot. When he was returned to the big cell with the others, they continued working on their escape plan, sawing gradually through the bars on the window. But the day before they were going to go for it, they were shifted to mainland Greece.

Perhaps the strangest feature of the whole process since their arrest was that Huston managed to retain his gold sovereigns, even though one of the German soldiers who had apprehended the party at the cave had discovered them. This group of men was to survive the war, although they were forced to eyewitness the horrors of Mauthausen Concentration Camp in Austria before eventually arriving in a prisoner-of-war camp in Germany. But that is another story.

The postscript to our account of men on the run concerns Dudley Perkins. After his evacuation, and following an unsuccessful posting to officer school in the Middle East, he volunteered for SOE about which he had been told by his friend Tom Moir. He passed the training course with flying colours and was landed back in Crete on the night of 29/30 July 1943, now a Staff Sergeant. He became Captain Xan Fielding's right-hand man, and a legendary leader of the band of guerrillas – including the Paterakis brothers – operating in the White Mountains above Koustoyerako. Tragically, he was killed in action on 27 February 1944; he had only been back in Crete for seven months, and was just 29 years old. All who knew him – Australians, British, Cretans, New Zealanders – mourned the death of an exemplary man and soldier. Fortunately for posterity, his whole story is told in detail in Murray Elliott's fine biography.[47]

CHAPTER 10

Discussion

The Numbers Game

It is impossible to give an *absolutely* accurate figure for the total number of Australian, British and New Zealand servicemen who removed themselves from Crete, or who were subsequently evacuated, following the surrender on 1 June, 1941. While several 'Nominal Rolls' of evacuees have been unearthed in the Public Record Office in London, there do not appear to be any separate Australian or New Zealand equivalents. Indeed, the Appendix on 'Escapes' to the volume on Crete in the New Zealand *Official History* of war states:[1]

> This Appendix does not give the names of all soldiers who were free in Crete. So many escaped prisoners moved round the island and so much happened to them that it is practically impossible to trace all of them or relate all their adventures. Lack of records and passage of time are yet further bars.

We have compiled the most complete lists to date in the Appendices, using these Rolls and a variety of other sources, which are footnoted. Our total is 878 men who escaped, or were evacuated, from Crete. An analysis of these lists provides the following figures.

(i) Original Evaders

The original evaders comprised 317 troops in total. Of these 84 (26%)

were Australian, 15 (5%) were New Zealanders, 208 (66%) were British, and 10 (3%) were Miscellaneous (Palestinians, Greek Cypriots.) Thus at 99 men (31%), Anzacs were in a minority of the original successful evaders, those who got off Crete under their own steam.

However, a large, but unknowable, number of the 67 men evacuated on HMS *Thrasher* must also have been evaders. Some of these men would have been in the original British/Australian garrison at Heraklion, and some from those landed belatedly at Timbaki. Hence the actual figure for successful evaders must be considerably higher than 317. The final figure, it appears, will never be known.

(ii) Escapers

The official British history of the Cretan Resistance says, talking of the Tripiti evacuation on 7/8 May 1943:[2]

> This ended a chapter of the history of the [SOE] Mission in CRETE, in which about 450 men were rescued.

How accurate is this figure? An initial problem is that we do not know how SOE categorized the 'rescued'. Then, if we subtract the 317 known evaders from the total of 878 men who reached safety, we are left with 561, much more than 'about 450'. But for the reasons stated above, this figure of 561 contains an unknown number of evaders. Our best guess is that the balance between evaders and escapers is probably about 50/50.

If we exclude the early escapes by barge, along with the very small Buchecker/Carter group, 561 men were subsequently evacuated, of whom 330 (59%) were Anzacs, 124 (22%) were British, and 107 (19%) were Miscellaneous (but the majority were Greek Cypriot.) In other words, at 59%, Anzacs were in the clear majority of the men on the run in the Cretan mountains.

Of the total of 878 men who got off Crete one way or another, 253 (29%) were Australian, 176 (20%) were New Zealanders, 332 (38%) were British, while 60 (7%) were Miscellaneous. In other words, 429 (49%) were Anzacs.

By any criteria, a total of 878 troops who escaped from Crete one way or another is an impressive total. It has to be remembered that Crete was occupied in its entirety by the enemy, that enemy had total air superiority, and the Mediterranean Fleet had suffered severe losses during the evacuation from mainland Greece, the Battle of Crete and the Malta convoys. In other words, the number of naval vessels available to MEHQ for evacuation purposes was *always* strictly limited during this period, and limited further by the exigencies of the campaign in North Africa. It is greatly to the credit of the Royal Navy – and the Royal Hellenic Navy – that they achieved as many evacuations as they did.

The total number of *all* personnel evacuated from Crete is of course much higher. This number included Cretan patriots evacuated to the Middle East either for SOE or ISLD training, or to join the regular Greek armed forces; SOE agents who, like 'Lady X', were compromised; guerrilla leaders who were badly wanted, with a price on their head; a large number of Greek Cypriot Pioneer troops; professional pests like Colonel Papadakis; a few cowards and imposters; a number of German and Italian deserters; the Italian General Carta, who commanded the Siena Division; and the unfortunate General Kreipe, kidnapped by Patrick Leigh Fermor and Billy Moss. One SOE Report puts the total number of 'Personnel Evacuated' from Crete at 913.[3] Our lists suggest that this figure must be a substantial underestimate.

If 429 Anzac troops made it back to the Middle East, then probably between 100 and 200 were captured by the Germans during their various sweeps, while perhaps a few dozen gave themselves up. A few, probably not more than a dozen at most, were executed. For example, the New Zealand *Official History* of the Battle of Crete and aftermath, recounts the summary shooting of three soldiers, including two Kiwis, during German round-ups.[4] And we have already quoted a German account of summary executions on the Omalos.[5] A few also met their death by misadventure. In July 1941, Kiwi Private C. C. Nicholl (19 Bn.) and an Australian, Private Gilby, saw a boat out to sea off the south coast, and swam out thinking it might be evaders like themselves. But it contained two Cretans who attacked them with the oars. The two soldiers made it back to shore, but Nicholl collapsed. Gilby carried him eight miles to a German post, but Nicholl died two days later.[6] And in a well-known story, after the War, Manolis Paterakis of Koustoyerako found the skeleton of a soldier, identifiable only by his buttons and brasses, stuck up a cliff at the head of a gorge inland from Hora Sfakion.[7] There would have been a few others who similarly perished in the trackless and waterless wastelands in this region.[8]

While all credit is due to the Navy for doing what it did, when it could, an evaluation of the activities of the secret services involved is also in order.

MI9 & SOE

We have already suggested that the standard history of MI9, particularly as regards Crete, suffers from a severe dose of self-congratulation. We have shown that right up until 1942, at the earliest, the staff of MI9 in the Middle East was comprised of derisory numbers. When it eventually got its act together, its main efforts were in preventive training, and its active agents in Crete and elsewhere in Greece, were recruited from the actual Anzac (and a few British) escapers and evaders. Further, the infiltration of these agents, and the evacuation of the men on the run, was actually organized by SOE. To all intents and purposes, MI9 and SOE on Crete were one and the same organization up until the last main evacuations of 1943, and both worked closely with ISLD. But it is imperative to stress that from the moment of surrender, the *initiative* in looking after the men on the run was taken by Cretans, not by Cairo. As a Greek SOE officer put it:[9]

> The British reports all suggest that hiding/evacuation arrangements were only made as a result of MI9/SOE intervention. But Cretan villagers and Greek officers organized both the hiding and guiding of Escapers and Evaders from early on after the Battle of Crete.

This officer was quite correct, and we have already demonstrated that the sophisticated Resistance network in the Amari valley, led by Cretan Lieutenant-Colonel Christos Tsifakis, was caring for large numbers of men well before the first SOE British officer was landed on the south coast.

We retain an abiding impression that the rescue of the men on the run was given a very low priority in the Greek section of SOE in Cairo, and given the ruthless and unpleasant personality of its head, Brigadier Keble, this is not surprising.[10] By all accounts, he was not interested in Crete, but concentrated his energies on mainland Greece, where the rapidly growing scale of SOE operations would guarantee his own promotion. Jack Smith-Hughes, a highly capable officer, was in fact in charge of the Cretan desk. Be that as it may, the organization of the evacuations could have been more efficient, and certainly faster. For example, there seems to have been no effort to employ the Levant Schooner Flotilla in the rescue of the men on the run, and this unit of Greek caiques under naval command, on the face of it, would have been ideally suited to exfiltrating men from Crete, albeit in small numbers.[11] Further, there was an absence of imaginative action, like commandeering fast private craft owned by wealthy Egyptians for the same purpose. At the very least, it seems regrettable that so many soldiers, particularly in western Crete, had to wait for two whole years before evacuation when the Allied-held coast of North Africa was only some 200 miles away. Arthur Lambert, who was stranded by the failed Treis Ekklessies mission, is in no doubt whatsoever about his feelings:[12]

> Those of us left behind in Crete feel nothing but disgust with the British High Command in Alexandria for their failure to come to our aid, especially in December 1941 when more than one hundred of us were waiting at Tris Eklises [sic] under the command of their agent, Capt. Monty Woodhouse. We were expected to die for them, yet they would not lift a finger to help us; we could have been taken off Crete without any danger to anyone.

There is actually some evidence to suggest that on occasion SOE could evacuate selected personnel from Crete at will. Quite apart from the fact that from time to time, especially in 1943, SOE could and did land or evacuate its own and/or ISLD personnel without reference to the escapers and evaders, Jim McDevitt tells a curious story. He had teamed up with fellow Kiwi Ken Little, who in turn had been on the run for a year with an English Commando Sergeant called John

Medley, who had been in Randolph Churchill's 'Layforce' unit assisting in covering the retreat to Hora Sfakion in 1941. One night, Ken Little heard Medley sobbing quietly to himself in the cave where they were hiding. The next day, he had simply vanished. McDevitt asks:[13]

> Could it be that the Tommy was smouldering inwardly at not being able to tell Ken of his secret and imminent departure, let alone include him in the evacuation party?

The fact of the matter is that Medley *was* evacuated secretly, to return as an SBS Sergeant-Major in the raiding-party landed by the Greek submarine *Papanikolis*, and spent a considerable amount of time looking unsuccessfully for his mate, Ken Little.

There is another, unpleasant, question which also has to be raised. Had the majority of the troops on the run in Crete been *British* – as opposed to Anzac – would they have been rescued sooner? We suspect that they would. Churchill had already shown in the fighting on mainland Greece as well as on Crete that he was prepared to ride roughshod over agreements with the governments of both Australia and New Zealand when it came to committing their troops.[14] As he demonstrated on many occasions, such as on the Dieppe Raid, he welcomed the fighting capabilities of Dominion troops, but was not over-concerned about either casualties, or prisoners-of-war, amongst them. We think it fair to say, therefore, that neither the British government nor the British High Command in the Middle East displayed any great energy, imagination or enthusiasm for evacuating the thousand or so Anzac troops stranded on Crete. As we said in Chapter 1, these men were left to their own devices.

Cretans and Anzacs

To the extent that the record of escapes from Crete is impressive, we believe that it owes a lot more to the dialectical relationship which developed rapidly between the Cretans and the men on the run, than to the efforts of Middle East Headquarters. This relationship was based on overwhelming Cretan support, on the one hand, and formidable Anzac initiative, on the other. We will consider the Cretan villagers first.

The Cretan support for our men was based on a combination of factors. The first was the simple fact that the Australians and New Zealanders were Allies against a common enemy, the Germans.[15] The fact that these men had come from the other ends of the earth, from two countries about which the Cretans knew very little, impressed them mightily. And they had been even more impressed when they fought alongside the Anzacs in many actions in western and central Crete. The Cretans admired the Aussies and the Kiwis as *pallikáres*, as warriors, as exemplars of young manhood. The feeling was mutual. And for many Cretan women whose own sons were far away, trying to return from the Albanian Front, these young foreign men became surrogate sons.

A second factor was the overwhelming *filoxenía*, or hospitality, which was, and is, a key element of Cretan culture. This custom *requires* Cretans to look after all travellers generously under normal circumstances, but under the circumstances of war and invasion, it became an absolute cultural imperative. Food and drink, clothes and money – a very great deal of money, overall – were pressed upon the men on the run. Not only that, but the Cretans spontaneously began to equip the Anzacs with false IDs, medical assistance, hiding-places, work, and all the other services which gave the men on the run a chance of survival. For many of the men, this hospitality was generosity beyond reason, and they were embarrassed by it, for they could see that their hosts possessed little.

A third factor is a more subtle one. The Cretans *liked* the Anzacs. Not only did the latter display great *pallikariá* (bravery, courage), but also they were possessed of *levendiá*. This is a difficult concept to translate into English; it resembles, but is not identical to, *pallakariá*. Patrick Leigh Fermor provides a seminal discussion of its meaning:[16]

> This attribute embraces a range of characteristics: youth, health, nerve, high spirits, humour, quickness of mind and action, skill with weapons, the knack of pleasing girls, love for singing and drinking, generosity, capacity to improvise *mantinades* . . . it is universal zest for life, the love of living dangerously and a readiness for anything.

In other words, the Cretans liked the informal, carefree, humorous *style* of these men.

For their part, the troops greatly admired and respected the Cretan villagers. In the first place, the vast majority of the Anzacs were country boys, used to a life of hard graft and little luxury as stockmen, shepherds, shearers, and roustabouts in the remote stations of the Australian and New Zealand bush. They were versatile men who made things, or adapted them, rather than buy them, for there was little money about in the pre-war depression years. Hence they could empathize with the hard life of the Cretan mountain villagers. This explains their embarrassment at the generosity of their hosts because they could see that only too often, they were literally taking the bread from the local children's mouths, not to mention the adults'. And this explains why many, like Dick Huston and Jim McDevitt, tried to live off the land as much as possible. It also explains why quite a few of these men provide accurate and detailed observations about Cretan agricultural and domestic implements, work, customs and daily life, in their memoirs. For example, Len Frazer has a detailed sketch of a handloom in his diary, inter alia, and the words of a well-known Cretan war-song noted down in near-perfect Greek. And Murray McLagan's memoir contains a concise description of the whole process of shepherding and cheese-making in the mountains, which is not only remarkably accurate, but also insightful, and predates Seán's own professional ethnography of this pastoral work by fully forty years!

A fourth factor was that the Anzacs reciprocated the Cretans' affection. The soldiers were taken by the formidable charm and passionate spirit of the mountain peasantry – and more than a few were smitten by the formidable beauty of their young women! The charm of the Cretans is difficult to explain if it has not been encountered; they press food, drink and friendship upon one with warmth and elegance, and a simple and heart-warming dignity.

Fifthly, the Anzacs also admired the Cretans' courage. Quite a few of the men on the run eye-witnessed executions, and *all* of them knew the consequences for the Cretans of sheltering them. Yet very, very few of the mountain villagers did betray any of these men, the majority of the Greek traitors being mainlanders and/or jailbirds recruited for the purpose. It is hardly surprising that men like Jim McDevitt, Tom Moir and Dudley Perkins were staggered by the calm courage of Fifi Papantonakis, or that Norm Scott was kept alive by the dogged courage of Irini Lagonokakis – both young women at the time.

Many of the troops also eye-witnessed their reckless courage when the Cretans did attack the enemy, a courage that applied to men, women and children, irrespective of age. Further, the soldiers admired the sheer ingenuity of the locals at outwitting the Germans, and the efficiency of the 'Cretan wireless' at spreading news of an impending raid. It is important to note that the Cretans mobilized their dense, extended family networks spreading as they did from town to country, to pass the men on the run up to safety in the mountains. In Crete, kinship is *the* fundamental form of social organization, and many of our men were impressed by the closeness of cousin relationships, for example, which would not always be thought of as significant in their own culture.

Other aspects of local culture played their part as well. Many of the Anzacs who were wounded or ill were treated by the methods of traditional medicine, such as cupping, bleeding, and the use of *tsikoudia* (raki) for cleaning wounds, and applied both externally and internally for a wide range of ailments. Many of the men were hidden in caves known only to locals, often where previous generations had hidden from the depredations of the Turks. Others met and became friendly with, or at least cooperated with, Cretan bandits, well-known figures in local culture and history. This relationship worked precisely because both the soldiers and the bandits were fugitives. And we have already seen how in many cases, specific Anzac fugitives were looked after by, and indeed became honorary members of, specific local extended families. Some of the men on the run developed relationships with Cretan women; a few were actually married, and more were married after the War. And if you believe the kind of story you are likely to hear on Crete, a few of the Anzacs did not bother to go home at all! The dense and warm relationships which were created on Crete were of course cemented by the willingness of so many of the Anzacs to work on the land with the locals – men like Dick Huston, Murray McLagan, Jim McDevitt and Len Beere. And this was even further reinforced by the willingness of so many of the latter to try and learn Greek, and their consequent ability to 'pass' amongst the Germans as Cretan villagers, with a panache which the locals loved. It is small wonder that they responded by knitting the soldiers socks and jerseys, weaving *kapotis*, and mending or making boots and shoes for them.

Some of these Anzac exploits were almost unbelievable, as we have shown – the cases of Joe Angell and Murray McLagan, for example. But there were many more. A document in the New Zealand Archives tells a story about Kiwi Driver S. D. Tisdall, who escaped twice from the POW Camp:[17]

> An Australian secured clothes for him and he escaped again. Befriended by girl from brothel in Canea who sent him to her cousin in Potamida where he was given food and shelter for five months. Later lived in cave where fed with food and cigarettes.

Tisdall was subsequently safely evacuated; we see no reason to enquire any further into his friendships with working girls!

Murray McLagan also tells a characteristic story:[18]

> A few encounters with Hun soldiers are worth mentioning. Two friends of mine were indulging in some heavy drinking in a town on Crete when in walked a German soldier, also a little under the weather. He asked if he might join the two 'Greeks', Aussies in reality, and sat down with them. As the party became merrier so the Aussies became bolder and soon were singing 'Roll Out the Barrel', 'There'll always be an England', 'Tipperary' and other soldiers' songs. Jerry highly approved and suggested that Greek songs were similar to German and English ones.
>
> They agreed and the German declared them the best Greeks he had ever met. At 10 p.m. the German patrol came round collecting the soldiers but this particular one refused to go back to barracks unless his two 'Greek' friends agreed to meet him the following night. The two parties separated and within half an hour the Huns were searching the

town and its outskirts for two British Secret Service agents; apparently their friend had sobered sufficiently to be suspicious of his erstwhile friends.

There are also repeated stories of an escaper who actually worked in Hania for many months as a barber, cutting Germans' hair, but unfortunately, we have been unable to validate this story – although it would not surprise us if it were true.

Escape, Evasion, and Frame-of-mind

All of this, of course, says nothing about the *mental* attributes necessary to successful escape and evasion in the first place. The MI9 history quoted earlier states:[19]

> Among prisoners, again, Mr. Faintheart was as common a type as Mr. Valiant. Enthusiasm for, even interest in, escape varied widely between different times, places and personalities.

This was as true of evasion as it was of escape. But what caused these wide variations in individual behaviour? The MI9 history again:[20]

> A particular frame of mind was needed to make men abandon the ignoble safety of captivity for the changes and chances of men on the run. Men who were contrary, enterprising, adventurous, quick-witted by nature usually did better than the plodders, though they almost always needed plodders to help them in the meticulous tasks of fabricating disguises, forging passes and copying maps.

What, then, were the *components* of this frame of mind? The MI9 history lists physical strength, acting ability, cold-blooded courage, adaptability, and not least, luck. Luck apart, perhaps the most important of these attributes is adaptability. To take the decision to evade capture rather than surrender, or to decide to escape after capture, and survive until the opportunity for evacuation (or what was called a 'home-run' in mainland Europe) presents itself, requires a certain flexibility of mind, an ability to improvise, a physical and mental versatility which also incorporates sheer bloody-mindedness. Once the initial decision to either evade or escape had been taken by the Anzacs, we believe that their subsequent experience demonstrates that these men possessed both physical and mental versatility to a quite remarkable degree. And we would also argue that this versatility derives directly from the tough living and working cultures of pre-war Australia and New Zealand. These men were brought up to be self-reliant, and that self-reliance proved itself when they were on the run, in very difficult terrain. As Lew Lind observed:[21]

> Opportunity is where you find it and it seldom comes to the escaper.

Local Difficulties

The Cretan terrain was a factor which also united the Cretans and the Anzacs, ironically. The Cretan shepherds by-and-large believe that only they are capable of surviving in the stony wastelands of the high peaks, as Seán found out when he went walking there on his own while living in a Sfakiot mountain village. The interior of the White Mountains, or the Dikti range in eastern Crete, for example, contain areas which are best described as 'badlands', which resemble nothing so much as a lunar landscape, and where you need a good head to survive. But many Australian and New Zealand soldiers like Jim McDevitt, Frank Ezzy, Arthur Lambert and Ted Goodall proved that they *could* survive up there, thus earning the respect of the locals. Even Len Frazer, no superman, did some marathon walks over the mountains. The terrain protected the men on the run, as it had protected the Cretans for centuries. The remotest areas of the White Mountains, between the Gorge of Aradena and the Gorge of Samaria, or between the latter and the village of Koustoyerako, for example, were seldom if ever penetrated by the Germans. It was, quite literally, a guerrilla's paradise.

But as has been demonstrated, life on the run in the mountains was no paradise. A first problem the fugitives faced was with boots and clothes. Army boots were simply inadequate to withstand the battering they received from long journeys in harsh terrain. We have seen how often problems with mangled boots affected the men on the run, Len

Frazer, for example. And some of the men, such as Arthur Lambert and Ted Goodall, had *no* boots for weeks at a time. How men could walk barefoot in the rocky terrain of the Cretan mountains is beyond our comprehension – yet some of them did it when the mountains were covered with snow! By the same token, the battledress blouses and trousers worn by the soldiers soon disintegrated as their wearers traveled through scrub, thorn and rock, and the limestone landform of the Cretan mountains means that the rock is very sharp-edged, and can slice easily though material, and flesh.

Then there were problems with diet and health, both inextricably inter-related. The record shows how common serious diseases like jaundice, rheumatic fever and malaria were, not to mention other afflictions connected with starvation and vitamin deficiency – sores and boils. Many of the men were also afflicted with severe colds and influenza. And as the U.K. diagnosis shows, Norm Scott was suffering from beri-beri. Severe weight-loss was endemic. Another factor was the mental wear-and-tear suffered by the men on the run, the sheer emotional pressure of being on the *qui vive* for week after week, month after month, the stress suffered by having to continuously protect their hosts, and the trauma induced by eye-witnessing executions. It is hardly surprising that more than a few of the men who survived suffered problems with both physical and mental health for the rest of their lives, and that some of them could never bring themselves to talk about their experiences. For reasons of confidentiality, we do not intend to discuss individual cases; indeed, several families have specifically asked us to protect their confidences.

In spite of all their privations, we cannot help but be impressed by the sheer good humour, tenacious morale, formidable versatility and dogged courage of these men on the run. That they managed to maintain such good spirits for so long is, as Xan Fielding remarked, a testament to their 'natural resilience', and inner strengths – qualities for which the Anzacs have come to be justly famous. We take our hats off to these brave men.

A final point is this. If one reads the Appendix on 'Escapes' in the New Zealand *Official History* of the Battle of Crete, one could be forgiven for gaining the impression that only Kiwis were involved in escape and evasion.[22] Indeed, when film-maker John Irwin was making his documentary 'In Rich Regard' about Dick Huston and Milton Knight, he advertised in *Crete News*, the paper of the NZ–Crete Association, for memoirs. Arthur Lambert, who has already featured prominently in our story, wrote to John with details of his own saga. He included the following observation:[23]

> the [NZ] War History Editor did not want any mention of the Aussies, he insisted on their exclusion. Crete was an Anzac action. One has only to look at the graves in Suda Cemetery, there are as many or more Aussies buried there as New Zealanders.

Arthur Lambert is quite correct. Crete *was* an Anzac action, and the subsequent escape and evasion *was* equally a joint effort. This book has demonstrated conclusively that Aussies and New Zealanders teamed up on the run, and were very effective partners. One has only to think of Australian Reg Saunders' refusal to abandon Arthur Lambert when he was extremely ill. Nearly all the escape groups between 1941 and 1943 were mixed Anzac parties.

CHAPTER 11

Conclusion

After the war, both Australian and New Zealand veterans founded Cretan Associations, and did everything within their power to aid the reconstruction of the war-ravaged island, including sponsoring assisted immigration from Crete. Special war memorials commemorating the Battle of Crete exist in both New Zealand and Australia, and parallel memorials to the Anzacs exist in Crete. Every single Anzac soldier who was on the run in Crete and left a memoir, either published or unpublished, paid generous tribute to the staunch courage of the Cretans who looked after them. There can be no doubting the sincerity, spontaneity and warmth of these tributes. Considerations of space do not permit us to quote every single one, but here is a selection:

Bella Johnston: Before closing, I would like to make some comments on the Cretan people.

As I have stated, they would go to any lengths to protect us with complete disregard for their own personal safety . . . Although the years have dimmed the memories of names, people and places, I will never forget the debt I owe to the people of Crete, and it is with this in mind that I close this Cretan Interlude.

(*Cretan Interlude*)

Ken Little: In 1946, three years after returning to New Zealand, I received through the mail, an envelope addressed thus:

Ken
New Zealand Soldier
New Zealand

and it enclosed a photograph of my mother that I had hidden, because of the English print on it, in a rock cleft near Spinarion.

In actual fact, Crete has never ended for me. I remember these people with deep affection and gratitude. We exchange cards, letters and photographs. As a people they gave so willingly and without thought of themselves.

Forty years may have passed but my regard for the Cretan people is something that will live with me forever.

(*Story of Crete: 1939–1945*)

Lew Lind: When the war ended I initiated through my regimental association a Clothing for Crete Appeal. Hundreds of garments for all ages and an equal number of shoes and accessories were collected, dry-cleaned and packed carefully into a large crate. Funds were raised by raffles and donations to meet the cost of shipment and distribution . . .

I maintained a close relationship with the Cretan people over the years which followed and have returned to the island on five occasions to renew the bond. In Australia I have also been closely associated with the Cretans who migrated in the years after World War II . . .

I, and others who shared similar experiences, know there is no escape from Crete for those who have fallen under the spell of the mountain heart of the island

and the hearts of the people who live there. Like Lord Byron and Patrick Leigh Fermor, I know Cretan bonds are forever.
(*Flowers of Rethimnon*)

Charles Jager: My father continued to send food parcels to friends in Skines and St Nicolas. Manoli Dimirakis, the older son of Yiorgo, the late Mayor of Skines, wrote and asked me to sponsor him to Australia. Aided by Jo Gullet of 2/6th Battalion, then a member of Menzies' team, he eventually arrived, studied hard and became a civil engineer.
(*Escape from Crete*)

Jim Rolfe: Reg returned to Crete 15 times to visit those wonderful people who befriended him. 'Vassili', they greet him . . . As part of their continuing appreciation of the Cretans' help in 1941, Reg and Estelle in 1994 sponsored a visit of four of those heroes to New Zealand for the 53rd anniversary of the Battle of Crete. This visit became a Rolfe family celebration as Jack and I and our wives were able to thank Reg and Estelle's four visitors for their part in helping him survive.
(*Brothers at War*)

Arthur Lambert: I, and all the Allied troops who were abandoned in Greece and Crete, and who roamed the mountains of both countries, owe our lives to the friendliness and compassion of the Greek people; without their help, many of us would have perished. Consequently none of us would have been prepared to carry out any action that could have caused a German reprisal on the Greek people.
(*Greece to Crete: Before and After: A Kiwi War Story*)

Reg Saunders: They were magnificent people.
(*Sound Archive of Australia*)

We are happy to report that the bonds between both Australia and New Zealand, and Crete, are still as strong as ever. As we have seen, Geoffrey Edwards, of the Australian 2/11th (City of Perth) Battalion, had been evacuated from Limni Beach, near Preveli, on HMS *Thrasher* in 1941. After the war, he took the initiative in having a Greek Orthodox Chapel designed and built at Prevelly in Western Australia, named after the Preveli Monastery in Crete. The chapel was formally opened in 1979, and in 1985 a plaque with the following inscription was added:

> This tablet commemorates the deep gratitude of the British, New Zealand and Australian servicemen befriended by the monks of Preveli Monastery and Cretans from surrounding villages, who at great personal risk helped them to escape by British submarines during the dark days of 1941.

Edwards and his committee also raised the money for an annual scholarship for a Cretan student to come to Australia.

Completely independently, Bella Johnston's son Peter also created a similar scholarship in memory of his father, in 2005, at Mahurangi College, Warkworth, New Zealand, where he is Director of International Students. Unfortunately, Bella Johnston never made it back to Crete before he died in 1983. As Peter says:

> The 'Bruce Johnston Memorial Scholarship to Mahurangi College' is, in a small way, an acknowledgement of the debt he owed to the Cretan villagers and a chance to strengthen the bonds forged by war between the people of Crete and New Zealand.

This year (2005), the first Cretan student, Alexandra Artsidakis, from Hania, attended Mahurangi College.

At both the 50th and 60th Anniversaries of the Battle of Crete, in 1991 and 2001 respectively, substantial parties of both Australian and New Zealand veterans were present. And even although there will be very few veterans left alive for the 65th anniversary in 2006, plans are afoot to have the survivors attend memorial services in Crete. Further, friendship networks connecting Australia, New Zealand and Crete still flourish, and many sons and daughters of wartime Anzacs are now part of extended Cretan families, and regular visitors to the island, and vice versa. John Irwin made a documentary film, 'In Rich Regard', in 1991 about Dick Huston and Milton Knight's return to Crete, and there are plans to make another based on aspects of this book. Ian is already working on publishing Len Frazer's diary, while Seán is writing a novel called 'The Cretan Connection', about the links between the island and New Zealand. It is our belief, therefore, that the bonds of friendship, forged out of mutual esteem during a bitter war and occupation in Crete, will never die, and it is our hope that this book will contribute in some small way to keeping them alive.

CHAPTER 12

Epilogue

Len Frazer's diary was the catalyst for this book. It is important, therefore, to finish his story, and offer some judgement on the man and his diary.

Len Frazer returned to Australia soon after he escaped from Crete and was finally reunited with his family after more than two years away from home. He served out the rest of the war in Australia, Papua New Guinea and Borneo, before returning to his old job at the Melbourne City Council. Of the four men from his own unit who accompanied him on the bolt from Hora Sfakion on 1 June 1941, one of them (Corporal Con Curtain) arrived back before him, having reached Preveli in time to catch the *Torbay* in August 1941. Two others (Lance Sergeant Norm Wiseman and Sapper Ron Day) gave themselves up when Wiseman became seriously ill in September 1941.[1] Wiseman died two months later in a prison camp at Salonika, while Day spent the rest of the war as a POW. The fourth man, Sapper Doug Lyons, was captured and also spent the rest of the war in a prison camp.[2]

For a short time after he got back to Australia at the end of the war, the Crete experience was a big part of Len's life – more so than for most other members of his unit. He gave talks for different service organisations around Melbourne, exchanged letters with his friends on the island, sent gifts, and did his best to follow events in post-war Greece. It wasn't long though, before his family and his career as a civil engineer took priority, and there was less time for the Cretan connection. He always intended to write up his wartime experiences, but made little progress before he died in 1968.

With regard to these experiences, it is to Len's credit that he refused to surrender following the Battle of Crete, took to the hills, evaded capture, and was eventually evacuated successfully after just over a year on the run. As an officer, Len was demonstrably neither decisive, nor the stuff of which heroes are made. However, both Len's behaviour and his diary entries have to be interpreted in the light of two considerations. Firstly, Len did not have the tough country background possessed by most of the men on the run. He was a city boy, a white-collar worker, and was physically and psychologically ill-equipped for a life of basic survival in extremely demanding terrain. Nor was he a regular army officer who had chosen a military career. Secondly, the harsh judgement passed on him by Driver Stove has to be interpreted through the prism of contemporary events. That particular party of men was involved in a desperate burst for the coast in the hope of evacuation, after a whole year on the run. Their nerves must have been jangling, the stress must have been unbearable, and Len's pitiful state and behaviour would have only ratcheted up the tension. It is instructive that another witness to Len's state, his guide George Psychoundakis, felt nothing but pity for him. Stove's anathema, to coin a Greek term, was singularly lacking in empathy for an older man at the end of his tether.

Further, Len's account of his mental state, as provided in his diary, was *contemporary*, and reflected his mental state and his mood at the time. In this sense, his diary is brutally honest, warts and all. Len was going through hell, and his diary reveals it.

Len used his diary to vent his feelings from day to day, recording his mood swings, frustrations and disappointments. He complains a lot, is frequently depressed, and often attacks the people who were doing their best to assist him. However, it contains much else besides this, including detailed observations of local technology and practices, numerous insights into Cretan family life, close attention to the birthdays, anniversaries and holidays that he was missing, references to Greek history and culture, information about the inflation in prices and onset of the winter famine in 1941–1942, and much other news about the war and critical events during that period. All the other memoirs from which we quote were written long after the event – in most cases, decades later – and it is noteworthy that personal feelings are expunged in all of them. There can be little doubt that all of these writers would have felt something like Len, at least for some of their time on the run.

Of course, it has to be admitted that it was irresponsible of Len to keep the diary in the first place, but the irony is that if he had not, this book would not exist. The diary clearly demonstrates that Len was an intelligent observer of the culture through which he passed, and in this sense, is a valuable document in its own right. We are happy to report that Ian is preparing his father's diary for publication, in an annotated form. To conclude, we feel that, all in all, it is reasonable to be generous to a man singularly unprepared for the demanding year of survival, in harsh terrain, into which he was plunged by the exigencies of war.

On a more personal note, in 2002, Ian, on his third trip to Crete, after much painstaking research and numerous enquiries around the villages of Selino, found one of the places in which Len took refuge in the autumn and winter of 1941. This was the Makrakis homestead at Vothiana. It is a secluded location, well inland, between two ravines and steep hills covered in olive trees. The family church, dedicated to *Agios Ioannis Prodhromos* (St John the Baptist) is close by, as are the ruins of the old flour mill, 'Makris Mill', where there were numerous clandestine meetings among the Anzacs in 1941–1942. The mill, which was also an olive-crushing plant, was destroyed by a flood in 2000. The Makrakis family still live in the family homestead and farm the olives, and Alexander's son and daughter-in-law, Spiro and Marika Makrakis, greeted Ian warmly when he unexpectedly appeared on their doorstep, and announced that he was the son of the Australian officer who had been sheltered there during the war. The following extract describes one among many days that Len spent there:

Monday – 24 November 1941

Tired today. Breakfast tomato, olives & bread & gin. Lunch boiled fish,

> onions and greens mixed. ½ fish 15" long was obtained for 2 oka [oka = Greek measure] of flour. Climb hill and admire scenery. Go below [to the mill] and come back with A. for tea. Crushed wheat & rice with raisins boiled and oil added. Not unlike a white pudding. 2 glasses of wine. We sit around the fire, eat some orange. Bed on couch.

Today the house remains much the same as it was in 1941 (including the couch), so there was much pleasure in experiencing a similar kind of unstinted hospitality, just over 60 years later. It showed Ian quite vividly that the bonds that were established during those life-threatening days of the occupation are still as strong as they were, reinforced more generally by intermarriage and migration, and the sort of visits that he (and later his wife and himself) have been able to make a generation later.

Bibliography

Articles and Books

Allbaugh, Leland G. (1953): *Crete: A Case Study of an Underdeveloped Area*, Princeton, NJ, Princeton University Press.

Barter, Margaret (1994): *Far Above Battle: The Experience and Memory of Australian Soldiers in War, 1939–1945*, Allen & Unwin.

Bentley, Arthur (1984): *The Second Eighth: A History of the 2/8th Australian Infantry Battalion*, Melbourne, 2/8th Battalion Association.

Beevor, Antony (1991): *Crete: The Battle and the Resistance*, John Murray.

Bishop, Les (1998): *The Thunder of the Guns! A History of the 2/3rd Australian Field Regiment*, Sydney, 2/3rd Field Regiment Association.

Campbell, Alistair Te Ariki (2001): *Maori Battalion: A Poetic Sequence*, Victoria University of Wellington, Wai-te-ata Press.

Clark, Alan (1981): *The Fall of Crete*, Athens, Efstathiadis Group.

Cooper, Artemis (1989): *Cairo in the War*, Hamish Hamilton.

Crawford, John (ed.) (2000): *Kia Kaha: New Zealanders in the Second World War*, Auckland, Oxford University Press.

Cunningham, Admiral-of-the-Fleet Sir A. B. (1952): *A Sailor's Odyssey*, Hutchinson.

Damer, Seán (1988): 'Legless in Sfakia: Drinking and Social Practice in Western Crete', *Journal of Modern Greek Studies*, Vol. 6, No. 2.

Damer, Seán (1989): 'Cretan "Highlanders": The Making of the

Sphakiot Legend', *University of Glasgow Centre for Urban & Regional Research Discussion Paper No. 37.*

Damer, Seán (2004a): 'Requiem For a Kiwi', *Listener*, 24 April 2004.

Damer, Seán (2004b): 'Divine Intervention? The Origins of Tourism on Symi', *South European Society & Politics*, Vol. 9, No. 3.

Damer, Seán (2004c): 'Signifying Symi: Setting and Performance on a Greek Island', *Ethnography*, Vol. 5, No. 2.

Davidson, Reginald (1964): *With Courage High: The History of the 2/8th Field Company Royal Australian Engineers 1940–1946*, Melbourne, R.A.E. Association.

Davie, Michael (ed.) (1976): *The Diaries of Evelyn Waugh*, Weidenfeld & Nicolson.

Davin, Dan (1953): *Crete, Official History of New Zealand in the Second World War* 1939–1945, Wellington, New Zealand, War History Branch, Department of Internal Affairs.

Detorakis, Theocharis (1994): *History of Crete*, Iraklio, Detorakis.

Edwards, Geoffrey (1989): *The Road to Prevelly*, WA, Armadale, E. G. Edwards.

Elliott, Murray (1987): *Vasili: The Lion of Crete*, Century Hutchinson.

Fermor, Patrick Leigh (1983): *Roumeli: Travels in Northern Greece*, Penguin.

Fielding, Xan (1954): *Hide and Seek: The Story of a Wartime Agent*, Secker & Warburg.

Folkand, F. C. (ed.) (1983): *The Fiery Phoenix: The Story of the 2/7 Australian Infantry Battalion, 1939–1946*, Parkdale, Victoria, 47 Fifth Street, 2/7 Battalion Association.

Foot, M. R. D. & Langley, J. M. (1979): *MI9: The British Secret Service That Fostered Escape and Evasion 1939–1945 and its American Counterpart*, The Bodley Head.

Forty, George (2001): *Battle of Crete*, Hersham, Surrey, Ian Allan Publishing.

Freyberg, Paul (1991): *Bernard Freyberg, V.C.: Soldier of Two Nations*, Hodder & Stoughton.

Gordon, Harry (1962): *The Embarrassing Australian: The Story of an Aboriginal Warrior*, Melbourne, Lansdowne.

Gorter, Sandra (2002): 'Escape From Crete', *New Zealand Weekend Herald*, April 21–22.

Harokopos, George (1993): *The Fortress Crete 1941–1944*, Athens, B. Giannikos.

Heckstall-Smith, A. & Baillie-Grohman, H. T. (1961): *Greek Tragedy*, Anthony Blond.

Helm, A. S. (1943): *Fights and Furloughs in the Middle East*, Auckland, Whitcombe & Tombs.

Hetherington, John (1944): *Air-Borne Invasion: The Story of the Battle of Crete*, Auckland, New Zealand, Oswald-Sealey.

Heydte, Baron von der (1958): *Daedalus Returned: Crete 1941*, Hutchinson.

Hutching, Megan (ed.) (2001): *'A Unique Sort of Battle': New Zealanders Remember Crete*, Auckland, New Zealand, HarperCollins.

Irving, Fred (1996): *Escape From Crete: Island of the Gods*, Otautau: Fred C. Irving.

Jager, Charles (2004): *Escape From Crete*, Australia, Floradale.

Johnson, K. T. (2000): *The History of the 2/11 (City of Perth) Australian Infantry Battalion, 1939–1945*, WA, Swanbourne, John Burridge Military Antiques.

Kenna, Margaret (1993): 'Return Migrants and Tourism Development: An Example from the Cyclades', *Journal of Modern Greek Studies*, Vol. 11.

Kiriakopoulos, G. C. (1985): *Ten Days to Destiny: The Battle for Crete, 1941*, New York, Franklin Watts.

Kiriakopoulis, G. C. (1995): *The Nazi Occupation of Crete 1941–1945*, Westport, CT, Praeger.

Kokonas, N. A. (1991): *The Cretan Resistance 1941–1945*, Rethymnon, Crete, Kokonas, with a foreword by Patrick Leigh Fermor & others.

Lambert, Arthur (2001): *Greece to Crete: Before and After*, Whangarei: Arthur H Lambert.

Leaf, Joan (1983): *Sons of Te Ramaroa*, Rawene: Joan M. Leaf.

Le Souef, Leslie (1980): *To War Without a Gun*, WA, Artlook.

Lind, Lew (1991): *Flowers of Rethymnon: Escape From Crete*, Kenthurst, NSW, Kangaroo Press.

Lind, Lew (1994): *The Battle of the Wine Dark Sea: The Aegean Campaign 1940–45*, Kenthurst, N.S.W, Kangaroo Press.

London, Paul R. (2004): *When the War is Over – Let the Battle Begin*, Wellington, Paul R. London.

Long, Gavin (1953): *Greece, Crete and Syria*, Series 1 (Army), Vol. 11, Australia in the War of 1939–1945, Canberra, Australian War Memorial.

McAra, Jill (2004): *Stand For New Zealand: Voices From the Battle of Crete*, Christchurch, New Zealand, Willson-Scott Publishing.

Macartney, Lieutenant Roy (1941): 'An Epic of the Escape From Crete', *Argus Supplement*, August 9.

McDevitt, Jim (2002): *My Escape From Crete*, Auckland.

MacDonald, Callum (1995): *The Lost Battle: Crete, 1941*, Papermac.

McGill, David (1987): *P.O.W: The Untold Stories of New Zealanders as Prisoners of War*, Lower Hutt, Mills Publications.

Malethakis, E. (1981): *Vrosta sto Ektelistiko Aposama*, Hania. In Greek.

Mason, W. Wynne (1954): *Prisoners of War, Official History of New Zealand in the Second World War*, 1939–1945, Wellington, War History Branch, Department of Internal Affairs.

Mazower, Mark (2001): *Inside Hitler's Greece: The Experience of Occupation 1941–1944*, New Haven & London, Yale University Press.

Mitchell, D. & Mitchell, J. (1978): *Homage to Crete: A New Zealand Tribute*, Mitchell.

Moss, W. Stanley (1950): *Ill Met by Moonlight*, George Harrap.

Pack, S. W. C. (1973): *The Battle for Crete*, Ian Allan.

Parish, Michael Woodbine (1993): *Aegean Adventures 1940–1943, and the End of Churchill's Dream*, Sussex, The Book Guild.

Phillips, C. E. Lucas (1965): *Cockleshell Heroes*, Pan.

Playfair, I. S. O. (1956): *The Mediterranean and the Middle East, Vol. II: "The Germans Come to the Aid of Their Allies"*, History of the Second World War, H.M.S.O.

Pyrolovakis, N. (1998): *Paleochora: A Look Back Into the Past.*

Psychoundakis, George (1978): *The Cretan Runner: His Story of the German Occupation*, John Murray. Translation and Introduction by Patrick Leigh Fermor.

Reid, Richard (2001): *A Great Risk in a Good Cause: Australians in Greece and Crete April–May 1941*, Commonwealth of Australia, Department of Veterans' Affairs.

Rendel, A. M. (1953): *Appointment in Crete: The Story of a British Agent*, Allan Wingate.

Robinson, Charles (1991): *Journey to Captivity*, Canberra, Australian War Memorial.

Rolfe, Jim (with his brothers Reg and Jack) (1995): *Brothers at War*, Manukau. Republished by Penguin, 2004.

Seligman, Adrian (1997): *War in the Islands: Undercover Operations in the Aegean 1942–1944*, Stroud, Sutton Publishing.

Simpson, Tony (1981): *Operation Mercury: The Battle for Crete, 1941*, Hodder & Stoughton.

Smith, Harold (1996): *Memories of World War Two*, Thames, Hauraki Publishers.

Smith, Michael Llewellyn (1973): *The Great Island: A Study of Crete*, Allen Lane.

Spencer, John Hall (1962): *Battle for Crete*, Heinemann.

Stephanides, Theodore (1946): *Climax in Crete*, Faber.

Stewart, Ian McD. G. (1991): *The Struggle for Crete: A Story of Lost Opportunity, 20 May –1 June 1941*, Oxford University Press.

Sweet-Escott, Bickham (1965): *Baker Street Irregular*, Methuen.

Thomas, David (1972): *Crete 1941: The Battle at Sea*, Andre Deutsch.

Thomas, W. B. (2001): *Dare To Be Free*, Hororata, Dryden Press.

Thompson, Julian (2001): *The Royal Marines: From Sea Soldiers to a Special Force*, Pan.

War Office & Ministry of Information, The (1942): *The Campaign in Greece and Crete*, H.M.S.O.

Waugh, Evelyn (1964): *Officers and Gentlemen*, Penguin.

West, Nigel (1993): *Secret War: The Story of S.O.E., Britain's Wartime Sabotage Organisation*, Coronet Books.

Wick, Stan (1977): *Purple Over Green: The History of the Australian 2/2nd Infantry Battalion.*

Williams, Tony (2000): *Anzacs: Stories From New Zealanders at War*, Auckland, Hodder Moa Beckett.

Wilson, Loraine (2000): *Crete: The White Mountains*, Milnthorpe, Cumbria, The Cicerone Press.

Winter, Peter (1993): *Free Lodgings: The True Story of a Kiwi Soldier's Amazing Bid for Freedom*, Auckland, Reed Publishing.

Wright, Matthew (2000): *A Near-Run Affair: New Zealanders in the Battle for Crete*, 1941, Auckland, Reed.

Newspapers

Argus

Crete News

Kellog Newsletter

New Zealand Herald

Sunraysia Daily

Sydney Morning Herald

Unpublished Sources

Len Frazer's diary

Dick Huston's mss

Bruce 'Bella' Johnston, *Cretan Interlude*, mss

Milton Knight typescript

Murray McLagan's mss

Arthur Lambert letter

Ken Little's mss

W. G. Hughes' diary

Australian War Memorial

Report of Captain F. J. Embrey, 2/1 Australian Infantry Battalion, S4 781/6/2

Lance-Corporal Ian Walker and Lieutenant Keith Walker, PRO 0178 PRO 0723

Keith Murdoch Sound Archive of Australia in the War of 1939–1945: Interview S520: Reg Saunders, 2/7 Battalion, January 1989

Kippenberger Military Archive, NZ Army Museum, Waiouru

Private Earnshaw, 2001: 670

Private Charles Moorman, 2002: 130
Private Sonny Sewell, 2002: 322
Sergeant Tarrant, 1992: 1076

Archives New Zealand/Te Rua Mahaa o te Kāwanantanga, Wellington Office

Driver J. H. Thompson, DA 447 22/28
Driver Kerr, WAII I DA541 22/29
DA447 22/2; DA 73/15/8; DA447 22/14; DA 447 22/28; DA541 22/8; DA541 22/9; DA541 22/13; DA541 22/14; DA541 22/15; DA541 22/16; DA541 22/17; DA541 22/22; DA541 22/30; DA447 22/41

Public Record Office, Kew, London

ADM 236/30
ADM 236/32
AIR 20/2330
AIR 23/8631
HS 3/678
HS 5/418
HS 5/618
HS 5/670
HS 5/678
HS 5/681
HS 5/723
HS 5/725
HS 5/727
HS 5/728
HS 7/150
HS 7/151
HS 7/152
HS 7/154
HS 7/172
HS 7/173
HS 7/266
HS 7/267
HS 7/629
WO 169/24879
WO 208/3253
WO 311/368
WO 311/372
WO 311/613

Radio New Zealand Archives

UCDR 25/1; UCDR 235/2; TX 992

Notes

1 Manuscript diary of Lieutenant Len Frazer, 2/8 Field Company, Royal Australian Engineers, in the possession of Ian Frazer. Hereafter: 'Frazer Diary'.

2 See, for example, E. Malethakis (1981): *Vrosta sto Ektelistiko Aposama* ['In Front of the Firing Squad'], Hania. (In Greek.)

3 Arthur Lambert (2001): *Greece to Crete: Before and After*, Whangarei; Jim McDevitt (2002): *My Escape From Crete*, Auckland; and Jim Rolfe (with his brothers Reg and Jack) (1995): *Brothers at War*, Manukau. (The latter has recently been republished by Penguin, New Zealand: 2004.)

4 Harold Smith (1996): *Memories of World War Two*, Thames, Hauraki Publishers; Peter Winter (1993): *Free Lodgings: The True Story of a Kiwi Soldier's Amazing Bid for Freedom*, Auckland, Reed Books.

5 N. A. Kokonas (1991): *The Cretan Resistance 1941–1945*, Rethimnon, Crete, Kokonas. With a foreword by Patrick Leigh Fermor & Others.

6 George Psychoundakis (1978): *The Cretan Runner: His Story of the German Occupation*, John Murray. Translation and introduction by Patrick Leigh Fermor.

7 Xan Fielding (1954): *Hide and Seek: The Story of a War-time Agent*, Secker & Warburg; W. Stanley Moss (1950): *Ill Met by Moonlight*, George Harrap; A. M. Rendel (1953): *Appointment in Crete: The Story of a British Agent*, Allan Wingate.

8 Murray Elliott (1987): *Vasili: Lion of Crete*, Auckland, NZ, Century Hutchinson.

9 Dan Davin (1953): *Crete*, Official History of New Zealand in the Second World War 1939–1945, Wellington, New Zealand, War History Branch, Department of Internal Affairs; Gavin Long (1953): *Greece, Crete and Syria*, Series 1 (Army), Vol. 11, Australia in the War of 1939–1945, Canberra, Australian War Memorial.

10 The sources include: in New Zealand, the Army Museum, Waiouru; Archives New Zealand/Te Rua Mahara o te Kāwanatanga and the Alexander Turnbull Library, Wellington; the Hocken Library,

Dunedin. In Australia, the Australian Army War Memorial. In the United Kingdom, the Public Record Office of the National Archives, Kew, and the Imperial War Museum, Lambeth.

CHAPTER 1

1 Kinder Diary, Manuscript Papers 1622, Alexander Turnbull Library, Wellington; quoted in Matthew Wright (2000): *A Near-Run Affair: New Zealanders in the Battle for Crete, 1941*, Auckland, Reed Publishing, p. 103.
2 Major-General R. F. K. Belchem, quoted in Tony Simpson (1981): *Operation Mercury: The Battle for Crete, 1941*, Hodder & Stoughton, p. 49. The somewhat Byzantine politics of this aid and intervention are discussed in detail in Ian Wards: The Balkan dilemma, in John Crawford (ed.) (2000): *Kia Kaha: New Zealanders in the Second World War*, Auckland, NZ, Oxford University Press, pp. 20–35.
3 Simpson, op. cit., pp. 69ff.
4 ibid., p. 111.
5 A. Heckstall-Smith & H. T. Baillie-Grohman (1961): *Greek Tragedy*, Anthony Blond, p. 224.
6 Harold Smith (1996): *Memories of World War Two*, Thames, Hauraki Publishers, p. 57.
7 Antony Beevor (1991): *Crete: The Battle and the Resistance*, John Murray; Alan Clark (1981): *The Fall of Crete*, Athens, Efstathiadis Group; Dan Davin (1953): *Crete*, Official History of New Zealand in the Second World War, 1939–1945, Wellington, New Zealand, War History Branch, Department of Internal Affairs; George Forty (2001): *Battle of Crete*, Hersham, Surrey, Ian Allan Publishing; John Hetherington (1944): *Air-Borne Invasion: The Story of the Battle of Crete*, Auckland, New Zealand, Oswald-Sealey; Baron von der Heydte (1958): *Daedalus Returned: Crete 1941*, Hutchinson; Megan Hutching (ed.) (2001): *'A Unique Sort of Battle': New Zealanders Remember Crete*, Auckland, New Zealand, HarperCollins; Charles Jager (2004): *Escape From Crete*, Australia, Floradale; G. C. Kiriakopoulos (1985): *Ten Days to Destiny: The Battle for Crete, 1941*, New York, Franklin Watts; Lew Lind (1991): *The Flowers of Rethimnon*, Athens, Efstathiadis Group; Gavin Long (1953): *Greece, Crete and Syria*, Series 1 (Army), Vol. 11, Australia in the War of 1939–1945, Canberra, Australian War Memorial; Jill McAra (2004): *Stand For New Zealand: Voices From the Battle of Crete*, Christchurch, New Zealand, Willson-Scott Publishing; Callum MacDonald (1995): *The Lost Battle: Crete, 1941*, Papermac; S. W. C. Pack (1973): *The Battle for Crete*, Ian Allan; Richard Reid (2001): *A Great Risk in a Good Cause: Australians in Greece and Crete April–May 1941*, Commonwealth of Australia, Department of Veterans' Affairs; John Hall Spencer (1962): *Battle for Crete*, Heinemann; Theodore Stephanides (1946): *Climax in Crete*, Faber; I. McD. G. Stewart (1991): *The Struggle for Crete: A Story of Lost Opportunity, 20 May –1 June 1941*, Oxford University Press; The War Office & Ministry of Information (1942): *The Campaign in Greece and Crete*, H.M.S.O.; Matthew Wright (2000): *A Near-Run Affair: New Zealanders in the Battle for Crete, 1941*, Auckland, Reed.
8 Paul Freyberg (1991): *Bernard Freyberg, V.C.: Soldier of Two Nations*, Hodder & Stoughton, p. 268.
9 A. S. Helm (1943): *Fights and*

Furloughs in the Middle East, Auckland: Whitcombe & Tombs, p. 141.
10 cf. Beevor, op. cit., p. 230; Davin, op. cit., pp. 486–87; Reid, op. cit., p. 151; Stewart, op. cit., pp. 317–18; 374–75, 476.
11 Jager, op. cit., pp. 14ff.
12 Stephanides, op. cit. p. 113.
13 Alistair Te Ariki Campbell (n.d.): *Maori Battalion: A Poetic Sequence*, Victoria University of Wellington, Wai-te-ata Press.
14 Davin, op. cit., p. 415.
15 Stan Wick (1977): *Purple Over Green: The History of the Australian 2/2 Infantry Battalion*, p. 134.
16 Michael Davie (ed.) (1976): *The Diaries of Evelyn Waugh*, Weidenfeld & Nicolson, p. 506.
17 MacDonald, op. cit., p. 279.
18 Davin, op. cit., pp. 427ff.
19 Kippenberger Military Archive, Army Museum, Waiouru, New Zealand: 1992: 1076. Hereafter, KMA.
20 Private Rangitepuru 'Sonny' Sewell. KMA: 2002. 322.
21 Hetherington, op. cit., p. 137.
22 Harry Gordon (1962): *The Embarrassing Australian: The Story of an Aboriginal Warrior*, Melbourne, Lansdowne, pp. 86–7.
23 Evelyn Waugh (1964): *Officers and Gentlemen*, Penguin, p. 222.
24 David Thomas (1972): *Crete 1941: The Battle at Sea*, Andre Deutsch: Appendix: Principal Characteristics of Ships Engaged in the Battle for Crete and Losses Suffered, pp. 210–213. See also, I. S. O. Playfair (1956): *The Mediterranean and the Middle East, Vol. II: 'The Germans Come to the Aid of Their Ally'*, History of the Second World War, H.M.S.O., p. 147.
25 Admiral A. B. Cunningham (1952): *A Sailor's Odyssey*, Hutchinson, p. 376.
26 Winter, op. cit., p. 5.
27 Leslie Le Souef (1980): *To War Without a Gun*, W.A, Artlook, p. 146.
28 Quoted in Davin, op. cit., p. 454.
29 Lambert, op. cit., pp. 52–3.
30 Quoted in Margaret Barter (1994): *Far Above Battle: The Experience and Memory of Australian Soldiers in War, 1939–1945*, Allen & Unwin, p. 115.
31 Jager, op. cit., p. 27.
32 Davin, op. cit., p. 455.
33 Long, op. cit., p. 307.
34 Personal communication, Major-General W. B. Thomas.

CHAPTER 2

1 M. R. D. Foot & L. M. Langley (1979): *MI9: The British Secret Service That Fostered Escape and Evasion 1939-1945 and its American Counterpart*, The Bodley Head, p. 13.
2 Lieutenant Roy Macartney (1941): *An Epic of the Escape From Crete*, Supplement to the *Argus*, Saturday, August 9th, p. 3.
3 Australian War Memorial PR00178, typescript by Lance-Corporal Ian Walker, 1941. Hereafter: AWM.
4 ibid.
5 Macartney, op. cit.
6 ibid.
7 Davin, op. cit. p. 491.
8 AWM PR00178, op. cit., typescript of Lieut. Keith Walker. He was the brother of L.-Cpl. Ian Walker quoted above in the same reference.
9 Macartney, op. cit.
10 ibid.
11 F. C. Fokand ed. (1983): *The Fiery Phoenix: The Story of the 2/7 Australian Infantry Battalion, 1939–1946*, Parkdale, Victoria, 47 Fifth Street, 2/7 Battalion Association, p. 119.
12 Les Bishop (1998): *The Thunder of the*

Guns! A History of the 2/3 Australian Field Regiment, Sydney, 2/3 Field Regiment Association, p. 421.

13 AWM PR00178, op. cit.

14 Davin, op. cit. p. 490. There are many accounts of these two escapes by barge. For example, see also, Julian Thompson (2001): *The Royal Marines: From Sea Soldiers to a Special Force*, Pan, pp. 259–62.

15 Harry Gordon, op. cit., p. 88.

16 Margaret Barter (1994): *Far Above Battle: The Experience and Memory of Australian Soldiers in War, 1939–1945*, St. Leonards, NSW, Allen & Unwin, p. 134.

17 Frazer Diary, p. 1. Hereafter, FD. In his actual diary, Len noted the name of the month, and then gave a figure for the date, e.g.: 'June. 6.' For the sake of clarity, and the chronology of the narrative, we have provided the day and date for each extract.

18 Stan Wick (1977): *Purple Over Green: The History of the Australian 2/2 Battalion*, p. 143.

19 Beevor, op. cit., p. 209.

20 ibid., p. 212.

21 K. T. Johnson (2000): *The History of the 2/11 (City of Perth) Infantry Battalion*, 1939–1945, p. 97.

22 ibid., p. 115.

23 ibid., p. 116.

24 Bishop, op. cit., p. 353.

25 ibid.

26 Johnson, op. cit., p. 116.

27 Bishop, op. cit., p. 419.

28 AWM 54: 7816/6.

29 Johnson, op. cit., p. 110.

30 ibid., p. 112.

31 ibid., pp. 112–3.

32 ibid., p. 114.

33 Nathan in Hutching, op. cit., p. 232.

34 See Beevor, op. cit., and Davin, op. cit., inter alia, for descriptions of this action.

35 Ken Little (n.d.): *Story of Crete: 1941–1943*, mss, not paginated.

36 ibid.

CHAPTER 3

1 Winter, op. cit., p. 7.

2 Long, op. cit., p. 307.

3 Jager, op. cit., p. 30.

4 Winter, op. cit., p. 9.

5 Private Charles H. Moorman, 22 Battalion. KMA: 2002: 130.

6 Fred Irving (1996): *Escape From Crete: Island of the Gods*, Otautau, Fred Irving, p. 7.

7 Stove in McAra, op. cit., p. 118.

8 Cosgrave in Hutching, op. cit., p. 202.

9 Lind, op. cit., p. 38.

10 Spencer, op. cit., p. 246.

11 *Report by Sergeant F. Davis, 18 Battalion 2 NZEF*, Appendix III to H.M.S. *Thrasher*'s Report of 2nd War Patrol, PRO ADM 236/30, p. 1.

12 Charles Robinson (1991): *Journey to Captivity*, Canberra, Australian War Memorial, p. 95.

13 *Report by Sergeant F. Davis*, op. cit., p. 5.

14 Lind, op. cit., p. 43.

15 Irving, op. cit., p. 10.

16 Rolfe, op. cit., p. 53.

17 KMA: 2001: 670.

18 Driver J. H. Thompson, Pro Coy/LRDG/4 RMT: CAPTURE AT SPHAKIA AND ESCAPE FROM CRETE, Archives New Zealand, [12], DA 447 22/28, p. 1. Hereafter ANZ. It is unclear from this document whether it was actually written by Dvr. Thompson, or is the transcription of the Intelligence interview conducted after his successful escape from Crete. The highly articulate, at times almost poetic, prose suggest that it is more likely to be the latter.

19 Winter, op. cit., p. 11.

20 ibid., p. 13.

21 Thompson, op. cit., p. 2.
22 PRO WO 311/368, pp. 10–11. This officer wound up in the same POW Camp in Thessaloniki as 2nd Lieut. 'Sandy' Thomas, who soon proved to be a master escaper. See W. B. Thomas (2001): *Dare To Be Free*, Hororata, Dryden Press, p. 84.
23 Leslie Le Souef (1980): *To War Without a Gun*, W.A, Artlook, p. 157.
24 PRO WO 311/368.
25 PRO WO 311/372, p. 2. These incidents are also discussed in Le Souef (1980), op. cit., pp. 154–155.
26 W. Wynne Mason (1954): *Prisoners of War*, Official History of New Zealand in the Second World War, 1939–1945, Wellington, New Zealand, War History Branch, Department of Internal Affairs, p. 67, footnote 3. (At the end of the war, Generaloberst Kurt Student was court-martialled for these killings, and Boileau's testimony, and that of his adjutant, New Zealand Lieutenant L. S. Baigent, were vital to the prosecution. See PRO WO 311/368.)
27 Forty, op. cit., p. 150.
28 Mason, op. cit., pp. 65–66.
29 Thompson, op. cit., pp. 1–2.
30 Corporal Earnshaw, Radio New Zealand Archives, UCDR 235/1, track 23, & UCDR 235/2, tracks 1, 2, and 3. Transcribed by Seán Damer. Several of these accounts have also been transcribed and published in: David McGill (1987): *P.O.W: The Untold Stories of New Zealanders as Prisoners of War*, Lower Hutt, Mills Publications. Seán did these transcriptions before he knew of the existence of this book. There are differences in detail between these two sets of transcriptions; Seán stands by his version.
31 Winter, op. cit., pp. 12–13.
32 Thompson, op. cit., p. 2.
33 ibid., p. 13.
34 Irving, op. cit., p. 10.
35 ibid., p. 11.
36 Thompson, op. cit., p. 2.
37 Athol Cook, Radio New Zealand Archives, TX 992. Transcribed by Seán Damer.
38 Arthur Lambert, personal communication.
39 Arthur Lambert (2001): *Greece to Crete: Before and After*, Whangerei, A. Lambert, p. 53.
40 ibid., p. 54.
41 ibid.
42 Geoffrey Edwards (1989): *The Road to Prevelly*, Armadale, E. G. Edwards, p. 38.
43 Rolfe, op. cit., p. 53.
44 B. W. Johnston (date unknown): *Cretan Interlude*, (mss), p. 1.
45 Murray Elliott (1987): *Vasili: Lion of Crete*, London & Auckland, Century Hutchinson, p. 35.
46 Lind, op. cit., p. 47.
47 ibid., p. 48.
48 Winter, op. cit., p. 14.
49 McDevitt, op. cit., p. 6.
50 Jager, op. cit., pp. 57–8.
51 Hutching, op. cit., p. 189.
52 Lambert, op. cit., p. 54.
53 ibid., op. cit., p. 55.
54 Tony Williams (2000): *Anzacs: Stories From New Zealanders at War*, Auckland, Hodder Moa Beckett, p. 94.
55 Rolfe, op. cit., p. 53.
56 Elliott, op. cit., pp. 35–6.
57 Winter, op. cit., p. 16.
58 McDevitt, op. cit., p. 16.
59 Michael Woodbine Parish (1993): *Aegean Adventures and the End of Churchill's Dream*, Sussex, England, The Book Guild, p. 111.

60 These *kalderimi* are constructed of flattish rocks cunningly interlaid without mortar, and are works of considerable sophistication, beauty and engineering ingenuity. A network of these paths criss-crosses the White Mountains, and although the soldiers on the run did not know the word, they were in fact using them. Unfortunately, with the post-war advent of roads to all mountain villages, many of these *kalderimi* were destroyed or had sections obliterated, and many are now overgrown and invisible. [An interesting footnote to history: the original Greek name for these bridle-paths was *kalos dromos* – 'good road'. Under the Ottoman Empire, these two words were rendered into Turkish as *kalderimi*, and returned to the Greek language, in a bizarre example of loan words going two ways.]

61 cf. Theocharis Detorakis (1994): *History of Crete*, Iraklio, Detorakis, pp. 411ff. Also see Michael Llewellyn Smith (1973): *The Great Island: A Study of Crete*, Allen Lane, pp. 97–100, for the short version.

62 McDevitt, op, cit., p. 23.

63 FD, p. 8.

64 ibid., p. 9.

65 ibid., p. 10.

66 *Misithra*: a soft cheese made from goat's or sheep's milk.

67 FD, p. 16.

68 ibid., p. 14.

69 ibid., p. 15.

70 ibid., p. 19.

71 ibid., p. 20.

72 ibid., p. 24.

73 'Apon' is the village of Epanohori, near Agia Irini, on the road to Sougia, west of the Omalos Plateau, where Len spent some time on the run. Len has shortened the name in his diary, and written it down as he heard it. The 'Capt' mentioned here is Greek merchant marine Captain Emilios Vernikos, of whom more anon. Where asterisks (★★★★★) appear in Len's diary, it is where he blanked out the names of villages where he had received shelter, and the names of villagers, with an indelible pencil, at some point later in 1941, probably September, when there was a very real chance of capture by the Germans.

74 FD, p. 25.

75 ibid., pp. 26–27.

76 Little, op. cit.

CHAPTER 4

1 PRO WO 208/3253.

2 Foot & Langley (1979), op. cit., p. 14.

3 PRO HS7/172.

4 PRO WO 208/3253, loc. cit.

5 ibid.

6 ibid., p. 89.

7 ibid.

8 ibid.

9 Foot & Langley, op. cit., p. 92.

10 Davin, op. cit., p. 495.

11 PRO WO 208/3253, op. cit.

12 PRO WO 169/24879, op. cit.

13 Kiriakopoulos, op. cit., p. 359.

14 Kokonas, op. cit., pp. 27 and 32.

15 Long , op. cit., p. 312.

16 Report of Captain F. J. Embrey, 2/1 Australian Infantry Battalion: *Experiences During the Campaign in Crete, the Conditions in his P.O.W. Camp. And his Escape*, A.W.M. S4 781/6/2, p. 12.

17 Nathan, in Hutching, op. cit., p. 240.

18 PRO HS 7/152, p. 12.

19 Keith Murdock: *Sound Archive of Australia in the War of 1939–45*, Interview S520, Reg Saunders, 2/7

Battalion, January 1989.

20 Fielding, op. cit., p. 24. This refers to the winter of 1941–1942.

21 Leland G. Allbaugh (1953): *Crete: A Case Study of an Underdeveloped Area*, Princeton, N.J., Princeton University Press.

22 Greek Census, 1940.

23 Allbaugh, op. cit., p. 4.

24 ibid., p. 17.

25 See Seán Damer (1988): 'Legless in Sfakia: Drinking and Social Practice in Western Crete', *Journal of Modern Greek Studies*, Vol. 6, No. 2, for a discussion of *filoxenia*.

26 See Seán Damer (1989): 'Cretan "Highlanders": The Making of the Sphakiot Legend', University of Glasgow, *Centre for Urban & Regional Research Discussion Paper No. 37*, for a detailed discussion of this rising.

27 Allbaugh, loc. cit., p. 15.

28 ibid., p. 18.

29 ibid., p. 16.

30 ibid., p. 18.

31 Johnston, *Cretan Interlude*, op. cit., p. 2.

32 Lind, op. cit., footnote 4, p. 127.

33 Jager, op. cit., p. 94.

34 Allbaugh, op. cit., p. 20.

35 ibid., p. 21.

36 Winter, op. cit., p. 21.

37 Allbaugh, op. cit., p. 20.

38 See Margaret Kenna (1993): 'Return Migrants and Tourism Development: An Example From the Cyclades', *Journal of Modern Greek Studies*, 11; & Seán Damer (2004): 'Divine Intervention? The Origins of Tourism on Symi', *South European Society & Politics*, Vol. 9, No. 3, for a discussion of these issues.

39 Winter, op. cit., pp. 16–7.

40 Foot & Langley, op. cit., p. 93.

CHAPTER 5

1 Winter, op. cit., pp. 24–25.

2 Fielding, op. cit., p. 49.

3 Fielding, op. cit., p. 48. See also PRO HS 5/728, where the codename for Crete in general was *Never-Never Land*, Asi Gonia was *Stubborn Corner*, the White Mountains was *Lost Horizon*, and Askyfou was *Lhasa*.

4 Margaret Barter (1994): *Far Above Battle: The Experience and Memory of Australian Soldiers in War 1939–1945*, St Leonards, NSW, Allen and Unwin, p. 139.

5 George Harokopos (1993): *The Fortress Crete 1941–1944*, Athens, B. Giannikos & Co., p. 42. In early June, many of these evaders believed the Navy was going to come back for them, and flashed messages out to sea at night. Reg Saunders did the same on the Sfakia coast after the surrender, until his torch batteries ran out. Cf. Gordon (1962), p. 88.

6 ibid.

7 Stan Wick (1977): *Purple Over Green: The History of the 2/2 Australian Infantry Battalion, 1939–1945*, p. 144.

8 ibid., p. 145.

9 Elafonissos is a small, flat, sand-covered island, located at the south-west tip of Crete, accessible from the mainland on foot at low tide.

10 Len would not have known it, but Private Buchecker and his party did the trip from Souyia to Sidi Barrani (considerably longer than 200 miles) in just under four days (90 hours).

11 Described by Driver J. F. Kerr (HQ Comd ASC), ANZ WAII I DA541 22/29. Another crew member was Gnr K. J. Payne, 5 Fld Regt.

12 F. C. Folkand, op. cit., p. 110. See also: Davin, op. cit., pp. 491–92; Long, op. cit., p. 312; ANZ WAII 1 DA447 22/2: Escape from Crete by B. B. Carter; AWM, PRO O723.

13 Davin, op. cit., p. 492.

14 FD, 25 July 1941.
15 Lind, op. cit., p. 53.
16 Jim McDevitt (2002): *My Escape from Crete*, Auckland: J. T. McDevitt, p. 46.
17 Jager, op. cit., p. 96.
18 Huston Manuscript (n.d.), Chapter 8 (3), pp. 5–6. Hereafter, HM. A note on this manuscript book. This manuscript contains 13 chapters, and is a complete account of Dick Huston's military service, from recruit days at Trentham to POW days in Germany and the end of the war. Chapters 6 to 10 are concerned with his time on Crete, and confusingly are also numbered 1 to 5. The pages are not numbered sequentially from beginning to end of this manuscript. Consequently, we are providing both the original chapter number, the additional Cretan chapter numbers in brackets, and the page numbers as given in the manuscript itself. At the time of going to press, this manuscript is in the hands of Dick Huston's daughters. We are grateful to film-maker John Irwin, who made the documentary 'In Rich Regard' about these men, for drawing our attention to this manuscript in the first place.
19 HM, op. cit., Chapter 8 (3), pp. 8–9.
20 ibid., p. 10.
21 ibid., pp. 17–18.
22 Harokopos, op. cit., p. 46.
23 Beevor, op. cit., p. 241; Kokonas, op. cit., p. 153; Lind, op. cit., pp. 125–26.
24 PRO WO 208/3253.
25 Cunningham, op. cit., p. 393.
26 PRO ADM 236/30.
27 A 'folboat' was a two-man collapsible canoe constructed of plywood and canvas or rubberised fabric. It was notoriously unwieldy, and required considerable physical strength and stamina to paddle and manoeuvre. Details of this craft are contained in C. E. Lucas Phillips (1965): *Cockleshell Heroes*, Pan, Chapter 4, pp. 57ff.
28 Edwards, op. cit., p. 49.
29 Barter, op. cit., p. 141.
30 Beevor, op. cit., p. 242.
31 Johnson, op. cit., p. 98.
32 George Psychoundakis (1955): *The Cretan Runner*, London, John Murray, p. 56–57.
33 Cited in Barter, op. cit., p. 137.
34 Lind (1991), op. cit.
35 Reginald Davidson (1964): *With Courage High: The History of the 2/8th Field Company Royal Australian Engineers 1940–1946*, Melbourne, 2/8th Field Company, R.A.E. Association, p. 172; unpublished diary of Sapper W. G. Hughes, 2/8th Field Company.
36 Lind, op. cit. p. 87.
37 Davin, op. cit., p. 498.
38 ANZ WAII I DA 73/15/8; DA447 22/28; DA541 22/8; DA541 22/9; DA541 22/13; DA541 22/14; DA541 22/15; DA541 22/16; DA541 22/17; DA541 22/22; DA541 22/30.
39 ANZ WAII DA541 22/30.
40 Beevor, op. cit., p. 242.
41 Earnshaw, Radio New Zealand Archives, op. cit.
42 Lind, op, cit., p. 92.
43 Harokopos, op. cit., p. 60.
44 ibid.
45 PRO WO 208/3253. See also Embrey, op. cit., p. 13.
46 Parish, op. cit.
47 ibid.
48 Parish, op. cit., p. 105.
49 Barter, op. cit., p. 138.
50 Irving, op. cit., p. 26.
51 Beevor, op. cit., p. 240; Parish, op. cit., p. 123. In his book, Parish recounts

how both he and Vernikos joined MI9 once they arrived back in Cairo, and were subsequently involved in efforts to rescue British escapees stranded on other Greek islands.

52 Lind, op. cit., p. 121.
53 ANZ WAII I DA447 22/41; Davin, op. cit., pp. 493–494; Long, op. cit., p. 313; Jager, op. cit.
54 G. C. Kiriakopoulos (1995): *The Nazi Occupation of Crete 1941–1945*, Westport, CT, pp. 19–20.
55 Beevor, op. cit., p. 236.
56 Kiriakopoulos, op. cit., p. 11.
57 Beevor, op. cit., p. 237.
58 ibid., pp. 185, 237.
59 ibid., pp. 117, 237.
60 ibid., p. 236.
61 Kiriakopoulos, op. cit., p. 368. This figure is almost certainly a gross exaggeration.
62 Beevor, op. cit., p. 237.
63 Winter, op. cit., p. 30.
64 Stan Wick (1977): *Purple Over Green: The History of the Australian 2/2 Infantry Battalion*, p. 146.

CHAPTER 6

1 The account of this incident is taken from McDevitt (2002), pp. 50ff, and notes made by Len Frazer after the war (his diary has no entries at all for this period).
2 McDevitt, op. cit., p. 59.
3 ibid., p. 60.
4 PRO HS 5/681 (SOE Greece 781, December 1942 – February 1945). When the Germans say 'British' here, they mean Australian, British and New Zealand troops.
5 Nicolaos Pyrovolakis (1998): *Paleochora (A Look Back into the Past)*, pp. 42–43. Other estimates put the number of deaths a lot higher than this; cf. McDevitt, op. cit., p. 59.
6 Mark Mazower (2001) *Inside Hitler's Greece. The Experience of Occupation 1941-44*, New Haven: Yale University Press, p. 173.
7 ibid.
8 There are many different accounts of this episode with varying estimates of the numbers involved. See Elliott, op. cit., pp. 47–49; McLagan, op. cit. p.16; Rolfe, op. cit., pp. 91–92; McDevitt, op. cit., pp. 74ff; FD, 23 September.
9 It is common on Crete to refer to all owners of caiques as Kapetan – 'Captain'.
10 FD, 23 September. The proposal was that there would be two caiques, one, motorised, capable of taking 40 passengers, the second a sailing boat, capable of holding 30. The larger one would take stragglers, generically described as 'English', the smaller boat Cretans.
11 Elliott, op. cit., p. 47; McLagan, op. cit., p. 16.
12 Little, op. cit.
13 Elliott, op. cit., p. 48.
14 McDevitt, 2002 op. cit., p. 80; Elliott, 1987 op. cit., p. 60.
15 McLagan, op. cit., p. 17.
16 FD 1–4 October 1941.
17 Chapel of Ayios Ioannis.
18 A reference to Bert Gill arriving back at Vothiana with lots of friends. Described by McDevitt, 2002 op. cit., pp. 87–88.
19 Rolfe says 'many did surrender' after the pamphlet drop; Rolfe, 2004 op. cit. p. 93.
20 McLagan, op. cit., p. 18.
21 D. Mitchell and J. Mitchell (1978): *Homage to Crete. A New Zealand Tribute*, pp. 7–9.
22 ibid.
23 McLagan, op. cit.
24 Rolfe, op. cit., p. 87.
25 ibid.

26 Nathan in Hutching, op. cit., pp. 237–8.
27 McDevitt, op. cit., pp. 88–89.
28 Elliott, op. cit., p. 167.
29 ibid., p. 50.
30 ibid., p. 52.
31 ibid., pp. 61–62.
32 Johnston, op. cit., p. 3.
33 ibid., p. 4.
34 ibid., p. 6.
35 Kokonas, op. cit., p. 157. Smith-Hughes's *General Survey of Crete* was written in March 1945, but was first published in this 1991 book.
36 ibid.
37 ibid., p. 153.
38 ibid.
39 Ibid, p. 152.
40 ibid., p. 153.
41 ibid.
42 Inter Services Liaison Department (ISLD), cover name for MI6 (Beevor, p. 243; Kokonas, p. 33).
43 Fielding, op. cit., pp. 25–26; Kokonas, op. cit., p 37. *Hedgehog* is described as an iron fishing craft of 5 knots, and *Escampador*, the smaller boat, as being only 20 foot.
44 Beevor, op. cit., p. 244.
45 PRO AIR 20/2330.
46 Lambert, op, cit., p. 57.
47 ibid.
48 ibid., p. 60.
49 Described in Fielding, 1954 op. cit., pp. 31–33.
50 Lambert, op. cit., p. 61.
51 ibid., p. 62.
52 Fielding, op. cit., p. 43.
53 Kokonas, op. cit., p. 39.
54 ibid.
55 Psychoundakis, op. cit., p. 60.
56 Lambert, op. cit., p. 62.
57 Kokonas, op. cit., p. 41.
58 McLagan, op. cit., p. 13.
59 Huston mss., Chapter 3, p. 5.
60 ibid.
61 ibid., p. 6.
62 ibid., p. 10.
63 While *horta* would of course have looked just like a weed to Dick Huston, it is in fact an edible wild green, with many varieties, tasting not unlike spinach when cooked, and equally full of iron. Seán's Kiwi wife Helen picked a lot of *horta* with local women during their two years in Askyfou and became quite expert at identifying the more nutritious varieties, like *stamenagafi*.
64 Huston, op. cit., p. 11.
65 The following information is derived from (i) an article about Scott's experiences on Crete in the *Sunraysia Daily* newspaper (Mildura, N. Victoria), June 1945; (ii) an article about the Lagonikakis family in *Kellog Newsletter* (the newspaper of the Australian branch of the Kellog Company), Vol. 5, Number 10, March 1966; (iii) another article about Scott's experiences in the *Argus* newspaper, 31 October, 1947; and (iv) an extended interview with Mrs Phyllis Scott (Norm's widow), and their three children, Sandra, Douglas and Robyn, by Ian Frazer on 19 June 2005 in Melbourne.
66 Lambert, op. cit., p. 62.
67 McDevitt, op. cit., p. 112.
68 FD, p. 48.
69 McDevitt, op. cit., p. 117.

CHAPTER 7

1 Kokonas, op. cit., p. 38.
2 ibid., p. 39.
3 PRO HS 3/678: 'Review of Situation in Crete in Light of Capt. Woodhouse's Report', p. 1.
4 ibid., p. 2.
5 Kokonas, op. cit., p. 42.
6 PRO HS7/172: 'M.I.9 Activities in the Easter Mediterranean 1941–1945'.
7 PRO WO 208/3253, p. 15.

8 Appendix 3 to HMS *Thrasher's* Report of Second War Patrol, op. cit.
9 McLagan, op. cit., p. 16.
10 FD, pp. 50–54.
11 ibid., pp. 55–56.
12 Bishop, op. cit., p. 427.
13 Little, op. cit., p. 5.
14 Huston mss., Chap. 5, p. 2.
15 ibid., Chap. 4, p. 14.
16 ibid., p. 17.
17 Huston mss., Chap. 5. pp. 4ff.
18 ibid., p. 5.
19 ibid., p. 6.
20 A mystery surrounds the organisation into which Huston was recruited, and what his specific mission was. Security-conscious to the end, Huston went to his grave in 1991 without ever revealing who recruited him. There were two English officers with 'double-barrelled' names on Crete: the first was Major Jack Smith-Hughes, and the second was Major Patrick Leigh Fermor, both of whom worked for SOE. But a careful review of the data shows that neither of these officers was on Crete when Huston was recruited. The only SOE officer present on the island at that particular time was Captain 'Monty' Woodhouse. It may be that Huston heard Woodhouse as 'double-barrelled', and he certainly had an RP accent. But there is no mention of Huston's recruitment in any of Woodhouse's books, any of the other books about the Occupation and Resistance in Crete, or in the SOE files in the Public Record Office. (The second 'shepherd' was almost certainly Greek-Cypriot SOE agent Nikos Souris). For the moment, then, Dick Huston's secret work remains a secret.
21 Elliott, op. cit., pp. 57–8.
22 McDevitt, p. 118.
23 ibid., p. 126.
24 ibid., p. 123.
25 ibid., pp. 128ff.
26 David McGill (1987): *P.O.W: The Untold Stories of New Zealanders as Prisoners of War*, Lower Hutt, L Mills Publications, p. 103.
27 Hutching, op. cit., pp. 243ff.
28 Joan Leaf (1983): *Sons of Te Ramaroa*, p. 88.
29 McGill, op. cit.
30 McDevitt, op. cit., pp. 139–40.
31 ibid., p. 247.
32 Little, op. cit.
33 McDevitt, op. cit., p. 78.
34 The next few paragraphs are based on Elliott, op. cit., pp. 59ff.
35 Davin, op. cit., p. 494. Both Davin and Elliott say this escape was made from Mesara Bay. But this is incorrect, as Mesara Bay is in south-central Crete, and Moir, Perkins et al. were all in south-western Crete. McDevitt, who was in the area at the time, says that Moir & co. 'had sailed away from Ktista', which is in south-west Crete, near Elafonissos. And Reg Rolfe, who was *in* the boat, says they took it from a boatshed near Sfinari (p. 96).
36 *Cretan Interlude*, p. 8.
37 Jim Rolfe (with his brothers Reg and Jack) (1995): *Brothers at War*, Rolfe, Manukau City, p. 63.
38 Elliott, op. cit., pp. 61–2.
39 Rolfe, op. cit., p. 63.
40 Elliott, op. cit., p. 62.
41 Rolfe, op. cit., p. 64.
42 Johnston, op. cit., p. 9.
43 ibid., p. 10.
44 ibid., p. 11.
45 It is unclear why the other men were not also decorated. It should also be noted that there is some disagreement about who was

actually the skipper of this boat. Both Rolfe and Gill give the impression of being in charge, and in an article on this escape in the *New Zealand Herald* (20–21 April, 2002), experienced journalist Sandra Gorter, who interviewed Bella Johnston, says explicitly that he was the skipper.

46 Archives New Zealand, DA 447 22/14, p. 4.
47 PRO HS 5/678, para. 4.
48 McDevitt, op. cit., p. 129.
49 Gordon, op. cit., pp. 98–9.
50 Keith Murdoch Sound Archive of Australia in the War of 1939–1945: Interview S520: Reg Saunders, 2/7 Battalion, January 1989, pp. 98–9.
51 ibid., p. 100.
52 ibid., p. 101. Note that there is a discrepancy between Saunders's estimate of about 75 men on the beach, and the Evacuation Roll which shows a total of 31 leaving on this occasion. This discrepancy may well be accounted for by the fact that the *Hedgehog* did not have room for all of the men.
53 See Fielding, op. cit., Chapters 4–7 for a discussion of this little local difficulty.
54 FD, p. 62.
55 FD, pp. 65–67.
56 Psychoundakis, op. cit., pp. 66–7.
57 FD, pp. 71–72.
58 Stove in McAra (ed.), op. cit., pp. 128–9.
59 ibid., p. 129.
60 FD, p. 73.
61 FD, p. 74.
62 Elliot, op. cit., p. 63; PRO AIR 20/2330.
63 Kokonas, op. cit., p. 41.

CHAPTER 8

1 Elliott, op. cit., p. 63.
2 McDevitt, op. cit., pp. 153–54.
3 ibid., p. 155.
4 Elliott, op. cit., p. 63.
5 ibid., pp. 44–45; Beevor, op. cit., p. 285.
6 Elliott, op., cit., p. 63. The following account of the evacuation of Perkins and Kerr derives substantially from Elliott, pp. 63ff.
7 McDevitt, op. cit., p. 160.
8 Elliot, op. cit., pp. 65–66.
9 ibid., p. 67–68.
10 McDevitt, op. cit., pp. 158-159.
11 Kokonas, op. cit., p. 44.
12 PRO HS 5/678: M.E. Joint Planning Staff paper No. 99: CRETE: 22 June 1942.
13 McDevitt, op. cit., p. 152.
14 Beevor, op. cit., pp. 263–64.
15 PRO HS5/725, p. 2.
16 Kokonas, op. cit., p. 54.
17 PRO HS 7/266: SOE War Diary: Middle East and Balkans, p. 123 [Crete].
18 Fielding, op. cit., pp. 65–6.
19 Huston mss., Chap. 5, p. 8. The following paragraph also derives from this source.
20 ibid., p. 14.
21 ibid., pp. 14-16.
22 ibid., pp. 17–8. And as we have shown, one of these bandits – Kiriakos –was in fact his go-between with whichever secret organisation employed him.
23 'The Lagonikakis Family: A Study in Courage', *Kellog (Australia & New Zealand Newsletter)*, Vol. 5, No. 10, March 1966, p. 2.
24 Fielding, op. cit., p. 66.
25 Kellog, op. cit., p. 2.
26 Lambert, op. cit., p. 78. Corporal Edward 'Ted' Goodall was an Australian who had moved to New Zealand before the war, and joined RMT (4th Reserve Mechanical Transport Company) on its outbreak. The two men met on the retreat to Sfakia and became firm friends.

27 Lambert, op. cit., p. 65.
28 ibid., p. 66. This was possibly Captain Embrey, who escaped northwards from Crete with the English officers Hildyard and Parish, and had successfully made it back to the Middle East via Turkey. He had subsequently volunteered for special service.
29 ibid.
30 ibid., p. 67, for a description of this incident.
31 ibid.
32 ibid.
33 ibid. An *Agrofilichas* is a form of rural Greek policeman whose job is to attend to field-boundary disputes, grazing and water rights, and similar agricultural matters which are of considerable importance in rural and mountain villages. In Crete, they were regarded as much less trustworthy than the Gendarmerie, who although working under German tutelage, were usually patriots.
34 ibid., p. 68.
35 ibid.
36 ibid., p. 71.
37 Cross in McAra, op. cit., pp. 43–45.
38 Kokonas, op. cit., p. 55.
39 McLagan, op. cit., p. 16.
40 Kokonas, op. cit., pp. 52–3.
41 Fielding, op. cit., p. 140. Beevor calls this traitor 'Komnas', Fielding calls him Comninas, while Psychoundakis calls him 'Komninas' (*The Cretan Runner*, p. 91). The latter is correct.
42 Huston mss., op. cit., Chap. 5, p. 20.
43 ibid., p. 19.
44 ibid., pp. 19–20.
45 McDevitt, op. cit., p. 163.
46 ibid., pp. 166ff.
47 ibid., pp. 169ff.
48 ibid., p. 174.

CHAPTER 9

1 McDevitt, op. cit., p. 192. McDevitt (Chaps. XXV–XXX) is the main source for the activities outlined in this chapter, unless specifically footnoted otherwise.
2 Fielding, op. cit., p. 111.
3 ibid., p. 115.
4 McDevitt, op. cit., p. 197. McDevitt consistently says John 'Simpkin', but there is nobody of that name on the escape lists at the AWM or on the nominal rolls from the PRO. There is, however, NX5610 Private John Simcoe, 16 Bde HQ AIF, and we think Jim McDevitt simply misheard the name. We are using the latter spelling in all subsequent quotations.
5 Loraine Wilson (2000): *Crete: The White Mountains*, Milnthorpe, Cumbria, The Cicerone Press, pp. 62–3.
6 McDevitt, op. cit., p. 201. Jim was not to know, but there are no deer on Crete, and the 'pigeons' he heard were in fact chukkar, or rock partridges (*perdika* in Greek).
7 ibid., pp. 218ff.
8 ibid. p. 230.
9 PRO HS 5/723, para. 17.
10 Huston mss., Chapter 5, p. 24.
11 ibid., Chapter 6, p. 1.
12 ibid., p. 2.
13 *M. F. Knight's Account*, p. 1. This is a two-page typescript written by Milton Knight for John Irwin, who made the documentary film *In Rich Regard* about Huston's and Knight's return to their cave, and Varipetro, in Crete. From John Irwin's personal collection.
14 ibid., p. 4.
15 ibid., p. 6.
16 ibid.
17 ibid., p. 9.
18 *Sunraysia Daily*, June 1945, op. cit., p. 2.

19 Elliott, op. cit., pp. 74–5; McDevitt, op. cit., p. 231.

20 Elliott, p. 74.

21 McDevitt, op. cit., p. 263.

22 McLagan mss., p. 8. Having done this work himself, Seán can vouch for both the accuracy of Murray McLagan's description of the process and its back-breaking nature!

23 McDevitt, op. cit., p. 253.

24 Fielding, op. cit., p. 159.

25 ibid., p. 160.

26 McLagan mss., op. cit., p. 16.

27 Fielding, op. cit., pp. 162–3.

28 McDevitt, op. cit., pp. 272–3.

29 *Sydney Morning Herald*, 12 November 1943. Another version of the same wedding is in McDevitt, pp. 242–43.

30 McLagan mss., p. 16.

31 F. C. Folkand (ed.), op. cit., p. 130.

32 Fielding, op. cit., p. 164.

33 McDevitt, op. cit., p. 275.

34 ibid., p. 279.

35 Folkand, op. cit., p. 131.

36 PRO WO 208/3253, 1945, p. 18.

37 Davin, op. cit., p. 501; Long, op. cit., p. 71; PRO HS 7/267 (SOE War Diary 44), p. 903.

38 Beevor, op. cit., p. 281.

39 *Sunraysia Daily*, op. cit., p. 3.

40 Arthur Bentley (1984): *The Second Eighth: A History of the 2/8th Australian Infantry Battalion*, Melbourne, 2/8th Battalion Association, p. 388.

41 AWM 1/9: A112, p. 1.

42 Interview with Mrs Phyllis Scott, Norman's widow, and her three grown-up children, by Ian Frazer on 19 June, 2005.

43 *Argus*, 31.10.1947, 'Five Dozen Snails His Ideal Lunch'.

44 PRO HS 7/173. (SOE History 122/B: MI9 Activities in Eastern Mediterranean December 1943–June 1945. Written: 10.7.45).

45 Huston mss., op. cit., Chapter 6, pp. 10–11.

46 ibid., p. 14.

47 Elliott, op. cit. See also Seán Damer: 'Requiem For a Kiwi', *Listener*, April 24, 2004.

CHAPTER 10

1 Davin, op. cit., p. 519.

2 Kokonas, op. cit., p. 60.

3 PRO HS 7/152, Appendix IV (E): 'Results Achieved on Sea Military Missions,' p. 4. No breakdown of the composition of this figure is provided.

4 Davin, op. cit., p. 516.

5 Loc. cit., p. 114.

6 Davin, op. cit., pp. 515/6.

7 Beevor, op. cit., p. 225.

8 There was so much equipment abandoned in this region, particularly on the route of the retreat over the mountains, that over the years, a local has collected it, and displays it in an amateur 'War Museum' in the village of Askyfou.

9 PRO HS 5/727 (S.O.E. Greece 859): Report by 2/Lieut. Emmanuel Kampakes, 7.3.43.

10 There are many accounts of the unscrupulous personality of this unlovable officer. See Beevor (1991); Cooper (1989); Fielding (1954); Sweet-Escott (1965); and West (1993), inter alia.

11 See Seligman (1997) for a discussion of this unit.

12 Lambert, op. cit., p. 75.

13 McDevitt (op. cit.), p. 160. This incident is also discussed in Ken Little (op. cit.) The implication of McDevitt's question is that somehow or another, Randolph Churchill persuaded S.O.E. to arrange a special evacuation of this Commando

Sergeant, and that the secret organization agreed because Medley would have valuable intelligence about potential targets for raiders. But this has to remain at the level of speculation.

14 See Tony Simpson, op, cit., for a detailed discussion of these considerations.

15 A word of explanation is necessary here. The Italians took no part in the Battle of Crete; the sole invaders were the Germans. The Germans permitted the Italians to occupy eastern Crete on May 28th, 1941, after the worst of the fighting in the Battle of Crete was over. The unit involved was the Siena Division, which had taken a hammering on the Albanian Front from the Cretan Division. The Cretans therefore loathed the Italians. The Italians occupied the Nomos (province) of Lassithi until 1943, when the Italians surrendered. Compared to the rest of Crete, this was a relatively quiet region in terms of the men on the run.

16 Patrick Leigh Fermor (1983): *Roumeli: Travels in Northern Greece*, Penguin, p. 133.

17 New Zealand Archives: WAII I: DA541: 22/19 POW in Crete and escape by S. D. Tisdall 13397.

18 McLagan Mss. (op. cit.), p. 12.

19 Foot & Langley, p. 21.

20 ibid., p. 25.

21 Lew Lind (1994): *The Battle of the Wine Dark Sea: The Aegean Campaign 1940–45*, Kenthurst, N.S.W: Kangaroo Press, p. 71.

22 This Appendix was written by M. B. McGlynn, not Dan Davin.

23 Letter from Arthur Lambert to John Irwin, 30th May, 1990. Our thanks to John for making this letter available to us.

CHAPTER 12

1 R. Davidson (1964): *With Courage High: The History of the 2/8th Field Company Royal Australian Engineers 1940–1946*. Melbourne, 2/8th Field Company, R.A.E. Association, pp. 171–172.

2 ibid.

APPENDIX 1

Summary of Major Escapes and Evacuations from Crete June 1941–December 1943

All escapes from occupied Crete were by sea. In the first two months of the occupation, this meant using whatever small craft could be found on the coast of Crete – abandoned motor landing craft (MLC), small fishing boats, and dinghies. Later on, a small number of escapers took advantage of Crete- or Greek-owned caiques. Beginning in late July 1941, most of those who escaped relied on clandestine evacuations organised by MI9/SOE using vessels – submarines, converted caiques, motor launches and motor torpedo boats – of the Royal Navy or the Royal Hellenic Navy.

The following two tables have estimates of the total number of troops who got off Crete between June 1941 and December 1943, with a breakdown of the main nationalities involved: Australian, New Zealand and British. The British figures include a small number of sailors of the Royal Navy and airmen from the Royal Air Force. The fourth column (Other), is made up primarily of soldiers from Mediterranean countries, mostly Palestinian, Cypriot and Greek personnel. Many of these evacuations also included civilians but they are not included in these figures. Both tables provide best estimates of the numbers involved in all the main escapes or evacuations; Table 1 is ordered chronologically, Table 2 according to the means of escape, whether they were carried out independently or relied on MI9 or SOE assistance.

Table 1: Escapes and Evacuations by Group, Date and Nationality

Escapes and Evacuations	Date of Return to Cairo	AIF	2 NZEF	British	Other	Total in Group
MLC 'Garrett Group'	9/6/41	25	8	99	8	140
MLC 'Day Group'	10/6/41	5	–	38	1	44
MLC 'Richards Group'	9/6/41	25	5	21	1	52
MLC 'Fitzhardinge Group'	5/6/41	29		30	9	68
Buchecker/Carter Group	20/7/41	2	2			4
Thrasher Group	31/7/41	39	3	25		67
Torbay Group	22/8/41	42	62	11	10	125
Redpath Group (October1941)	15/10/41	10	7	1		18
Hedgehog Group (Nov 1941)	29/11/41	28	28	11	19	86
Moir Group (April 1942)	14/4/42	3	5	1		9
MI9 Operation (May 1942)	25/5/42	4	9	15	3	31
MI9 Operation (June 1942)	8/6/42	5	8	5	1	19
Papanikolis (June 1942)	19/6/42		8			8
MI9 Operation (May 1943)	8/5/43	15	14	8	14	51
Miscellaneous	Various	22	17	48	60	147
Totals		254	176	313	126	869

Sources: PRO AIR 20/2330, AWM 3DRL 7974, AWM 535/4/3, Bishop (1998) Davin (1953), Folkand (1983), Johnson (2000), Long (1953), Macartney (1941)

Table 2: Escapes and Evacuations by Group, Date, Nationality and Means

Escapes and Evacuations	Date of Return to Cairo	AIF	2 NZEF	British	Other	Total in Group
	A. Independent					
MLC 'Garrett Group'	9/6/41	25	8	99	8	140
MLC 'Day Group'	10/6/41	5	–	38	1	44
MLC 'Richards Group'	9/6/41	25	5	21	1	52
MLC 'Fitzhardinge Group'	5/6/41	29	–	30	9	68
Buchecker/Carter Group	20/7/41	2	2	–	–	4
Redpath Group (October1941)	15/10/41	10	7	1	–	18
Moir Group (April 1942)	14/4/42	3	5	1	–	9
Sub-Total		99	27	190	19	335
	B. MI9/SOE Assisted					
Thrasher Group	31/7/41	39	3	25	–	67
Torbay Group	22/8/41	42	62	11	10	125
Hedgehog Group (Nov 1941)	29/11/41	28	28	11	19	86
MI9 Operation (May 1942)	25/5/42	4	9	15	3	31
MI9 Operation (June 1942)	8/6/42	5	8	5	1	19
Papanikolis (June 1942)	19/6/42		8	–	–	8
MI9 Operation (May 1943)	8/5/43	15	14	8	14	51
Sub-Total		133	132	75	47	387
	C. Miscellaneous					
Miscellaneous	Various	22	17	48	60	147
Total		254	176	313	126	869

Sources: Same as for Table 1

Table 3: Location of Escapes and Evacuations

Escapes and Evacuations	Date of Return to Cairo	Total in Group	Nome*	Per Cent
		A. Independent		
MLC 'Garrett Group'	9/6/41	140		
MLC 'Day Group'	10/6/41	44		
MLC 'Richards Group'	9/6/41	52		
MLC 'Fitzhardinge Group'	5/6/41	68	Hania	100
Buchecker/Carter Group	20/7/41	4		
Redpath Group (October 1941)	15/10/41	18		
Moir Group (April 1942)	14/4/42	9		
Sub-Total		335		100
		B. MI9/SOE Assisted		
Thrasher Group	31/7/41	67	Rethimnon	49.6
Torbay Group	22/8/41	125		
Hedgehog Group (Nov 1941)	29/11/41	86		
MI9 Operation (May 1942)	25/5/42	31	Heraklion	35.1
MI9 Operation (June 1942)	8/6/42	19		
Papanikolis (June 1942)	19/6/42	8		
MI9 Operation (May 1943)	8/5/43	51	Hania	15.3
Sub-Total		387		100.0
		C. Miscellaneous		
Miscellaneous	Various	147		
Total		869		

* *The island was divided into four nomes (prefectures) the names of which were (from west to east): Hania, Rethimnon, Heraklion and Lasithi*

Sources: Same as for Table 1

APPENDIX 2

Roll of Anzac Escapers and Evaders from Crete 1941–1943

In this roll we have restricted ourselves to the names of Australian and New Zealand soldiers only. The roll is organised chronologically, on the basis of the two tables in Appendix 1. The principal source of names for these lists are the Nominal Rolls that are available from the Public Record Office (PRO AIR 20/2330). Unfortunately, in its present state, this source is incomplete especially in respect to escapes that took place in June 1941. Where possible we have consulted other sources but we have not yet found complete lists for the early escapes. The names included under Miscellaneous are all known Australian and New Zealander evaders/escapers not included previously; mostly those who got away singly, or in small groups, at different times between June 1941 and December 1943.

1. MLC 'Garrett Group' (June 1941)

An abandoned MLC was commandeered on 1 June by Major Garrett of the Royal Marines with a party of 56 Royal Marines. They were joined by Australian, New Zealand and assorted other troops, giving a total of 5 officers and 134 other ranks. They picked up another New Zealander at sea. The barge stopped at Gavdos Island before heading south. They ran out of fuel on the second day and had to use improvised sails from then on. They made landfall on 9 June on the coast, 19 miles from Sidi Barrani (Other Sources: Davin, op. cit., p. 491; Long, op. cit., pp. 308-9; Macartney op. cit.).

AIF		
Camm, Sig l. K.	VX5641	
Cockman, Sgt G.	VX5833	
Edwards, Cpl A.	VX5552	2/7 Bn
Hall, Dvr A. B.	VX22904	
King, Pte R.	NX2191	
Kirby, Cpl R. F. W.	WX603	19 Bn HQ
Lang, L/Cpl	VX5801	2/7 Bn
Legge, Cpl K. A.	NX13358	2/1 Bn
Lester, Pte J.	VX5864	2/7 Bn
Macartney, Lt R. R.	VX115	2/2 Fd Regt
Nugent, Sgt H. G. B.	NX4358	2/2 Bn
Smith, Gnr R. T.	SX1019	3 Fd Regt
Steele, Pte C. H.	BX1338	
Wain, Dvr A. B.	VX5722	
Walker, Lt K. R.	VX4740	2/7 Bn
Walker, Cpl J. W.	VX4674	2/7 Bn
Wiles, Cpl J. E.	VX16067	2/7 Bn
2 NZEF		
Hancox, Pte W. A.		1 Gen Hosp
Peters, Gnr R. P. A.		29 Bn
Thompson, Pte		28 Bn

2. MLC 'Day Group' (June 1941)

A second abandoned MLC was commandeered on 1 June 1941 by Lt. G. M. Day of 1 Welch Regiment. He put to sea with a company of 44 men, including many from his own regiment. There were at least 5 Australians on the craft, all from the 2/7 Australian Infantry Battalion (Other Sources: Folkand, op. cit., pp. 111–13; Long, op. cit., pp. 308–9.).

AIF		
Bradfield, Pte R. P.	WX981	2/11 Bn
Gray, Pte C. M.	VX5600	2/7 Bn
Grosser, Pte L. L.	VX16095	2/7 Bn
Hansen, Pte I.	VX12399	2/7 Bn
Horne, Pte H. R.	VX11721	2/7 Bn

3. MLC 'Richards Group' (June 1941)

A third abandoned MLC [*96 SD 15*] was commandeered at Hora Sfakion on 1 June 1941 by Private Harry Richards of 2/11 Australian Infantry Battalion and hidden until the evening of that day. There were 50 men on board, including Australian, New Zealand and British troops, when they sailed on the night of 1 June. Richards named the barge *M.V. Leaving*. The barge was first taken to Gavdos Island. Worried about a shortage of fuel, Richards asked for volunteers to step down and reduce the load. Ten men volunteered to do so but another 4 who had got to the island independently, later asked to join the barge and were allowed on board. After leaving Gavdos they ran out of fuel on the third day, and had to use improvised sails for the rest of the journey, making landfall, near Sidi Barrani, on 9 June 1941 (Other sources: AWM 3DRL 7974; Davin, op. cit., p. 490; Folkand, op. cit., pp. 114–117; Long, op. cit., p. 309).

AIF		
Doran, Pte R. N.	VX8889	
Gordon, Pte J. A.	VX23474	
Holt, E. W.	VX23745	
Host, Pte E. J.	WX728	2/11 Bn
Jackson, A. C.	NX4603	
Lynch, R.	WX761	2/11 Bn
McMillan, L/Cpl G. J.	VX7141	
Richards, Pte H.	WX1944	2/11 Bn
Smith, Spr J. L.	NX5427	2/3 Bn
Thompson, Pte J.	VX5721	
2 NZEF		
Chappell, Dvr J.		ASC
Noonan, Dvr A. G.		ASC
Taylor, Pte A. H.		HQ NZ Div

4. MLC 'Fitzhardinge Group' (June 1941)

Two landing barges were abandoned at Ayia Galini. One of these craft was repaired and launched by a group led by Captain J. B. Fitzhardinge of 2/3 Field Regiment, Royal Australian Artillery. They embarked on 2 June with 11 officers and 66 other ranks. The craft was stopped by an

Italian submarine soon after leaving, and 9 of the 11 officers (including 3 Australians) were taken on board the submarine. One other officer drowned and one officer stayed on the barge which continued south. They made landfall on 5 June 1941, 10 miles south-east of Mersa Matruh (Other sources: Johnson, op. cit., pp, 115–17; Long, op. cit., p. 310).

AIF		
Avery, Sgt B. H.	WX349	2/11 Bn
Bedells, Major T. C.	WX14	2/11 Bn
Gillies, Pte E. A.	WX447	2/11 Bn
Lee, Sgt J. P.	VX5510	2/1 MG Bn
McDonald, Cpl R.	VX6508	2/1 MG Bn
Mitchell, WOII C.	WX456	2/11 Bn
Monger, P.	WX2052	2/3 RAA
Mortimer, W. A.	WX983	2/11 Bn
Quinlan, D. A.	WX746	2/11 Bn
Skinner, A. P.	WX1807	2/11 Bn
Smith, Sgt E.	WX387	2/11 Bn

5. Buchecker, McQuarrie, Gordon & Carter Group (July 1941)

This group seized a small boat from the beach near Souyia on 16 July 1941 and rowed and sailed it to the coast of North Africa arriving at Sidi Barrani on 20 July 1941. (Other Sources: Folkand, op. cit., pp. 106–110; AWM PROO723; NZA WAII DA447 22/2.)

AIF		
Buchecker, Pte H. R.	VX4712	2/7 Bn
Gordon, Sgt R. G.	VX4632	2/7 Bn
2 NZEF		
Carter, Pte B. B.	5399	27 Bn
McQuarrie, Pte D. N.	2983	18 Bn

6. Thrasher Group (July 1941)

Embarked 28 July 1941 at Limni Bay near Preveli, on submarine HMS *Thrasher*, reached Alexandria 31 July 1941.

AIF		
Baird, Pte R. J.	WX370	2/11 Bn
Bayley, Lt C. W.	WX334	2/11 Bn

Carter, Pte W. H.	WX1105	2/11 Bn
Cathery, Pte H.	VX5691	2/1 M G Bn
Cauley, Sgt J.	NX4243	2/5 Bn
Cook, Pte E.	WX1055	2/11 Bn
Dowling, Lt L. E.	WX274	2/11 Bn
Duncan, Pte J. H.	WX930	2/11 Bn
Edwards, Pte E. G.	WX778	2/11 Bn
Forrest, Pte A.	WX1133	2/11 Bn
Greenway, Lt G. J.	WX976	2/11 Bn
Hackshaw, Pte A. E.	WX2274	2/11 Bn
Haddock, Pte J.	WX1704	2/11 Bn
Jackson, Capt D. A. C.	WX32	2/11 Bn
Jewell, Pte W.	NX3242	2/2 Bn
Latham, Cpl W.	WX891	2/11 Bn
McCarrey, Pte W.	WX412	2/11 Bn
McEwan, Pte A.	WX330	2/11 Bn
McKerrow, Lt I.	VX15675	I.M.G. Bn
Melksham, Pte W. J.	QX3071	16 Bde HQ
Miller, Cpl D. L.	VX8876	2/1 M G Bn
Munro, Cpl R. B.	NX7160	2/2 Bn
Morrison, Pte S. N.	WX752	2/11 Bn
Nicholson, Pte G. L.	WX1938	2/11 Bn
O'Neill, Pte J. P.	WX426	2/11 Bn
Rigby, Pte A.	WX2088	2/11 Bn
Robertshaw, Pte J. McB.	VX11830	2/1 M G Bn
Ryan, WOII W.	NX8752	2/2 Bn
Shanahan, Capt P. M.	WX17	2/11 Bn
Sinclair, Pte N.	WX6142	2/11 Bn
Smith, Pte L. W.	WX1707	19 Bde HQ
Solomon, Pte V.	NX19649	2/2 Bn
Stirling, Sgt D. B.	WX606	2/11 Bn
Taylor, Sgt J. H.	VX7177	2/1 M G Bn
Thomas, Pte B. F.	WX6112	2/11 Bn
Wilde, Lt G. P.	VX908	2/11 Bn
Williams, Pte L. F.	WX863	2/11 Bn
Woods, Pte M. J.	QX3912	16 Bde HQ
Yoole, Pte K.	NX1590	2/2 Bn

2 NZEF		
Davis, Sgt F.	3774	18 Bn
Onyon, Cpl S.	3294	18 Bn
Reid, Gnr J.	20728	5 Fd Regt

7. Torbay Group (August 1941)

Embarked 20 August 1941 at Limni Bay near Preveli, on submarine HMS *Torbay*, reached Alexandria 22 August 1941.

AIF		
Baxter, Pte A. B.	VX41609	2/7 Bn
Blythman, L/Cpl C. A.	VX6804	2/7 Bn
Brosche, Spr W. J.	VX27882	2/8 Fd Coy
Burgoyne, Cpl R. B.	NX1258	2/2 Bn
Carse, Sgt A. J.	VX18484	2/8 Fd Coy
Cations, Pte H.	VX15827	2/7 Bn
Costello, Pte A.	NX7830	2/1 Bn
Curtain, Cpl C. A.	VX22193	2/8 Fd Coy
Elkins, Pte E. C.	WX325	2/11 Bn
Ericson, Pte A. H.	VX14546	2/7 Bn
Headford, Pte R.	VX16301	2/7 Bn
Hills, L/Cpl N. J. T.	WX9870	2/2 Bn
Honner, Capt R.	WX15	2/11 Bn
Hughes, Spr W. G.	VX21381	2/8 Fd Coy
Hutchinson, Pte R. E.	NX4288	2/3 Bn
Jarvis, Pte W. S.	WX920	2/11 Bn
Johnstone, Pte H. F.	VX14239	2/8 Bn
Keegan, Pte C. J.	QX2196	A.A.S.C.
Kelly, Pte C. A.	VX11861	2/7 Bn
Le Nevez, WOII R.	NX7965	2/3 Bn
Leonard, Cpl L. N.	NX4640	2/3 Bn
Lind, Bdr L. J.	NX8611	2/3 Fd Regt
Martin, Cpl H. H.	VX4611	2/7 Bn
McCosh, Pte T.	WX494	2/11 Bn
McDonald, Pte H. J.	NX9335	2/1 Fd Amb
McFarlane, Pte B.	VX13748	2/5 Bn
McGinty, Staff Sgt J. W.	VX4728	2/7 Bn
Megahey, Pte G.	NX9731	2/2 Bn
Morgan, Pte L. V.	WX567	2/11 Bn
Murray, Lt J. D.	WX244	2/11 Bn

O'Donnell, Pte L.	NX1295	2/2 Bn
Potter, Sgt J. G.	VX11979	2/7 Bn
Royce, Lt G. E.	WX248	2/11 Bn
Sandover, Major R. L.	WX5	2/11 Bn
Scott, Lt H. H.	WX980	2/11 Bn
Stapleton, Pte B. B.	WX919	2/11 Bn
Stephenson, Pte A. C.	VX3250	2/5 Bn
Stoneham, Lt A. C.	WX358	2/11 Bn
Unwin, Pte E. J.	QX3872	2/1 Fd Amb
Wallace, Pte J.	QX4000	2/2 Bn
Ward, Pte F. G.	VX44380	2/7 Bn
Yelland, Pte W.	VX7148	2/7 Bn

2 NZEF

Adams, Pte A. B.	4264	19 Bn
Anyan, Pte L.	4888	19 Bn
Bennett, Pte R. C.	6499	23 Bn
Bishell, Pte N. F.	5248	19 Bn
Boucher, Dvr A. J.	9123	
Brackenridge, Sgn H.	4576	Div Sigs
Burne, Spr L. R.	33604	4 Fd Amb
Casey, Pte R. T.	6635	NZASC
Casgoigne, Pte E. E.	37324	19 Bn
Cheynne, Cpl G.	9768	Div Sup Col
Clarke, Cpl A. C.	6278	Dev Pet Unit
Collins, L/Bdr P. L.	21151	
Cumming, Dvr J. M.	7511	4 RMT
Curtis, Cpl R.	8101	20 Bn
Day, Dvr J.	6077	Div Pet Coy
Diver, Gnr F.	25544	4th Fd Regt
Dorset, Pte J.	30322	22 Bn
Earnshaw, Cpl L. G.	6044	22 Bn
Hastings, Gnr W. N.	1869	4 Fd Regt
Hooker, Pte B. F.	8723	27 MG Bn
Irvine, Sgt S. R.	9571	23 Bn
Irving, Pte F. C.	10943	23 Bn
Johnson, Pte G. N.	31312	Div Pet Coy
Jones, Pte J. N.	11779	5th Fd Amb
Jupp, Cpl A. W.	34741	19 Bn
Kenny, Pte A. R.	31415	22 Bn
Manson, Gnr H. G.	21177	5 Fd Regt

Manuera, Pte W. P.	39779	28 Bn
Martin, Pte B. L.	33865	19 Bn
McHugh, Pte M. J.	7777	18 Bn
McKay, Spr L. W.	34479	19 Bn
McKenzie, Pte D. N.	5839	19 Bn
McKenzie, Spr D. M.	33235	
McLanachan, Pte F. W.	10548	Div Sup Col
Mitchell, Gnr W. N.	21647	5 Fd Regt
Norrie, Bdr S. P.	23337	19 Bn
Penhall, Pte I.	30592	22 Bn
Perry, Gnr C. C.	1632	4 Fd Regt
Phillips, Pte N. F.	7495	27 Bn
Phillips, Tpr K.	1259	Div Cav
Poole, Pte H. C.	8283	20 Bn
Porter, Pte P. V.	25986	28 Bn
Powke, Pte, B.H.	6735	22 Bn
Prebble, L/Bdr M.	24721	5 Fd Regt
Riddell, Pte R. E.	7064	27 MG Bn
Rule, Pte N. G.	22706	21 Bn
Ryan, Gnr P. C.	1820	4 Fd Regt
Sanders, Gnr L. F.	1647	4 Fd Regt
Sayers, Pte L. R.	30577	NZASC
Shand, Cpl A. J.	9039	4th RMT
Shirley, Sgn C. S.	5714	
Smith, Cpl A. G.	6776	22 Bn
Sneller, Pte E. G.	30394	22 Bn
Sollitt, Dvr L. R.	8911	2nd Div Supp
Taylor, Dvr W. G.	13506	Div Sup Col
Thompson, Pte J. H.	37409	Div Prov
Toho, Pte H.	5489	19 Bn
Toon, Dvr J. L. P.	8893	4 RMT
Walsh, Pte J.	3828	18 Bn
Wanoa, Pte T.	26082	28 Bn
Whitcombe, Gnr A. H.	29834	5 Fd Regt
Wikitera, Pte T.	39878	28 Bn

8. Redpath Group (October 1941)

After crossing from Crete to mainland Greece, this group commandeered a Greek caique in the vicinity of Cape Malea, S.E. Peloponnese. Under the command of Sergeant Redpath they embarked on 9 October and made landfall in North Africa close to Mersa Matruh on 15 October 1941. (Other Sources: ANZ WAII DA447 22/31; ANZ WAII i DA447 22/33; Jager, op. cit., p. 305)

AIF		
Cole, Gnr J. W.	WX179	2/2 Fd Reg
Hipwell, Pte R. J.	VX15848	2/7 Bn
Hosking, Lt. G. G. S.	WX399	2/11 Bn
Jager, Gnr C. H.	VX17073	2/2 Fd Reg
Laun, Gnr A. M.	VX10532	2/2 Fd Reg
McLaren, Pte I. A.	NX15437	2/2 Bn
Millman, Pte E.	VX15541	2/7 Bn
Murphy, Gnr K.	VX856	2/2 Fd Reg
Park, Cpl E. N.	NX8942	2/2 Bn
Travers, Gnr F. D.	VX14087	2/2 Fd Reg

2 NZEF		
Barrow, Dvr R. S.	955	Div Amm Co
Bristow, Sgt W. H.	2484	18 Bn
Empson, Sgt A. H.	2702	18 Bn
Redpath, Sgt J. A.	30836	19 Army Tps
Shearer, Pte T.	9375	20 Bn
Voyce, Gnr G. E.	21069	5 Fd Reg
Witting, Sgt R. R.	13358	19 Army Tps

9. Hedgehog Group (November 1941)

A group assembled by Captain J Smith-Hughes with the assistance of Lt. Jim Carstairs of the 2/7 Australian Infantry Battalion. They embarked on HMS *Hedgehog* at Treis Ekklessies on 23 November 1941. HMS *Hedgehog* was under the command of Lt. Campbell. It arrived in Alexandria on 29 November 1941.

AIF		
Bell, Pte A.	VX5407	2/7 Bn
Beyer, Pte F. E.	VX19853	2/7 Bn
Birch, Dvr T. C.	NX2911	2/1 Fd Amb
Brisbane, Pte R. J.	NX13076	2/1 Bn
Carstairs, Lt J. deM.	VX5423	2/7 Bn
Coffey, Cpl R. R.	VX5412	2/7 Bn
Cruikshank, Dvr W. A.	NX8795	2/1 Fd Amb

Delaney, Pte G. K.	NX8794	2/2 Bn
Fox, Pte H. S. A.	VX6820	2/7 Bn
Francis, Sig I. F.	VX1629	6 Div Sigs
Frawley, Pte T. I.	VX17556	2/7 Bn
Frawley, Sig J. C.	VX17558	2/7 Bn
Gildersleeve, WOII A. D.	NX1267	2/2 Bn
Hinton, Pte H. H.	NX18894	2/1 O.S.C.
Horsington, Dvr W. C.	NX4223	2/1 Fd Amb
Huggins, Dvr W. H.	NX9346	6 Div S.C.
Joiner, Pte S. W.	VX5634	2/7 Bn
Martin, Pte A. H.	VX36688	2/7 Bn
McKenzie, Cpl J.	VX7161	2/7 Bn
Murphy, Pte A. P.	NX2610	2/1 Bn
Oldfield, Pte R.	VX36685	2/7 Bn
Peck. L/Cpl L. L.	VX575	2/2 Fd Regt
Reiter, Sgt F. A.	VX4024	2/7 Bn
Savage, Pte G. A.	VX18824	2/5 Bn
Spark, Gnr D. F.	NX47054	2/2 Fd Regt
Walker, Pte J. H. D.	NX12875	2/3 Bn
Walker, Sgt L. G.	VX5870	2/7 Bn
Watkins, Pte S. E.	VX7115	2/7 Bn

2 NZEF

Archer, Pte G. R. J.	11547	6 Fd Amb
Aspinall, Gnr H. N.		4 Fd Reg
Bartlett, Dvr R. H.	31320	Div Pet Co
Bennie, Cpl F. D.	33116	Div Prov Co
Bodley, Spr J. N.	34103	19 Army Tps
Caiswell, L/Cpl F. R.	13481	6 Fd Amb
Check, Cpl S. H.	5190	19 Bn
Denny, Pte C.	9941	5 Fd Amb
Dewar, Pte J. P.	5614	Div HQ
Duncan, Pte J. A.	22077	21 Bn
Gosse, Spr C. W.	33141	19 Army Tps
Hughes, Pte S.	15083	20 Bn
Johnston, Pte J. J.	8724	27 MG Bn
Langdale, Pte A. H.	5047	19 Bn
Marshall, Pte J. G.	10436	Div Sup
McFarlane, Pte G.	9970	Div Sup
Moore, Dvr T. C.	32040	Div Sup
Mower, Pte J.	30561	22 Bn

Neilson, Pte D. R. S.	6890	22 Bn
Payne, Pte S. J.	4484	4 RMT
Pierce, Pte T. C. C.	22226	21 Bn
Robertson, Dvr T. C.	32037	Div Sup
Smith, Dvr J. W.	6641	Div Pet Co
Smith, Pte C. J.	11536	23 Bn
Smith, Pte L. A.	9012	4 RMT
Street, Cpl R. C.	5272	19 Bn
Tinning, Pte T.	7779	19 Bn
Todd, Sig G. E.	30478	Div Sigs

10. Moir Group (April 1942)

Led by Sergeant Tom Moir, this group stole a boat at Sfinari on the west coast of Crete, sailed south to Cape Krios, from where they left on 8 April 1942 for North Africa. They made landfall near Sidi Barrani on 14 April 1942. (Other Sources: Elliott, op. cit., pp. 61–3; McDevitt, op. cit. pp. 221–7; Rolfe, op. cit., pp. 95–100.)

AIF

Catley, Pte K. E.	NX7210	2/1 Fd Amb
McKergow, Pte J. W.	NX11463	2/1 Bn
O'Brien, Pte C.	VX40760	2/1 Bn

2 NZEF

Collins, Pte G. G.	13389	20 Bn
Gill, Pte H. W.	3260	18 Bn
Johnston, L/Bdr B. W.	20696	5 Fd Reg
Moir, Sgt T.	1481	4 Fd Reg
Rolfe, Pte R. W.	3715	4 RMT

11. MI9 Operation (May 1942)

Under the overall direction of SOE this group was taken from a small beach at Trofalos below the village of Krotos on 22 May 1942. They reached Alexandria on 25 May. (Other Sources: Kokonas, op. cit., pp. 41–2; Gordon, op. cit., pp. 98–9.)

AIF

Burgess, Cpl G.	NX9600	2/3 Bn
Dorney, Capt J. J. K.	VX327	2/2 Fd Amb

Saunders, Sgt R. W.	VX12843	2/7 Bn
Vincent, Pte L. C.	NX13043	2/1 Bn

2 NZEF

Delaney, Pte N. C.	8848	27 MG Bn
Dunbier, Dvr R. W.	12419	NZASC
Fitzsimmonds, Pte R. J.	9029	NZASC
Flynn, Dvr L. T.	8597	NZASC
MacKenzie, Dvr W. J.	9643	Div Sup Co
Penney, WO II W. G.	20837	17 LAD
Rogers, Gnr H. E. T.	20798	51 Fd Art
Spencer, Gnr G. A.	3353	4 Fd Reg
Washer, Dvr L. H.	12438	NZASC

12. MI9 Operation (June 1942)

Under the direction of SOE, this group was taken from a small beach at Trofalos below the village of Krotos. Embarked 6 June 1942 and reached Alexandria 8 June 1942. (Other Sources: Kokonas, op. cit., pp. 41–2.)

AIF

Delforce, Pte G.	NX1523	2/2 Bn
Doulis, Spr M.	WX3221	2/2 Fd Pk
Frazer, Lt L. T.	VX15205	2/8 Fd Coy
Gibson, Pte A. M.	WX5664	HQ Gd Bn
McAninly, Pte P. J.	VX19558	2/7 Bn

2 NZEF

Barrington, Sgt H. C.	4436	4 RMT
Catherwood, Pte D. M.	15227	4 Inf Bde
Christie, Cpl C. V.	7542	Div Sup Col
Cross, Gnr G. L.	29220	7 A/Tk 33 By
Fletcher, Sig J. D. H.	5636	Div Sig
McCaulay, Spr P.	33154	19 Army Tps Co
Stove, Dvr H.	8646	Div Sup Col
Whitfield, Pte J. W.	13155	Div HQ

13. Papanikolis (June 1942)

RHN *Papanikolis* was providing support for a sabotage operation in western Crete in June 1942. It embarked this group of NZ personnel as it was departing. (Other Sources: Elliott, op. cit., pp. 63–9; ANZ WAII I DA541 22/29)

2 NZEF		
Clarke, Pte C. E.	4837	19 Bn
Clutterbuck, Dvr J. L.	31929	Div Sup Col
Hoani, Pte W.	39337	28 Bn
Kerr, Dvr J. F.	4410	HQ NZASC
Mitchell, Gnr J.	20843	NZASC
Orr, Pte G. M.	6045	19 Bn
Perkins, Gnr G. C.	1772	4 Fd Regt
Tisdall, Dvr S. D.	13397	4 RMT

14. MI9 Group (May 1943)

The responsibility for assembling this group was taken by Xan Fielding and Tom Moir (until he was captured). The group assembled at Tripiti. They departed 6 May 1943 and arrived in Tobruk on 8 May. (Other Sources: Folkand, op. cit., 121–131; McDevitt, op. cit., pp. 266–81.)

AIF		
Allan, Pte W.	VX5873	2/7 Bn
Bertie, Pte J.	VX11941	2/5 Bn
Corbould, Sgt C. J.	VX4685	2/7 Bn
Duncan, Cpl A.	VX17061	2/7 Bn
Ezzy, Pte F.	NX15471	2/2 Bn
Grieves, Pte J.	VX7811	2/7 Bn
Howard, Pte V.	VX37362	2/7 Bn
Hunter, Pte C.	NX5452	16 Bde HQ
James, Gnr F.	NX3480	6 Bn 3 Fd Reg
Peck, Sgt C. H.	VX4662	2/7 Bn
Pettigrew, Pte D.	VX4663	2/7 Bn
Rankin, Pte C.	VX13409	2/6 Bn
Ruddick, Sgt C. N. N.	VX5567	2/7 Bn
Ruddick, Sgt G. C.	VX5550	2/7 Bn
Simcoe, Pte J.	NX5610	16 Bde HQ

2 NZEF		
Beere, Spr L.	33205	19 Army Tr, NZRE
Findlay, Pte J.	4613	1st Div Sup Col

Grant, Pte A.	8833	2 Coy 27 MG
Kelly, Pte L.	1434	26 Bn 4 Fd Reg
Knights, Pte M.	6486	1st Div Sigs
Little, Pte K.	20090	21 Bn 4 Fd Reg
Macdonald, Pte R.	1700	26 Bn 4 Fd Reg
McCallum, Pte D.	30096	22 Bn
McDevitt, Pte J.	7471	20 Bn
McLagan, Pte M.	2007	5 Fd Reg
Paulin, Pte A.	29854	18 Bn
Quinn, Pte J.	22436	28 Bn 5 Fd Reg
Symes, Pte J.	6633	1st Bn Pet Coy
Woods, Pte P.	13256	1st Div Sup Col

15. Miscellaneous (1941–1943)

	Service Number	Unit	Date Returned
AIF			
Bailey, Pte S. F.	NX11675	2/2 Bn	4/1/42
Baker, Pte A. C.	QX7784	2/2 Bn	10/11/41
Brown, Sgt S.	NX4120	2/1 Bn	6/5/42
Carroll, Sgn S. L.	WX953	2/11 Bn	19/6/41
Downing, Pte C.	VX5627	2/7 Bn	Dec-41
Dudley, Pte N. T.	NX5173	4 Bn	8/9/43
Dyer, WOII J.	2776	2/1 Bn	6/5/42
Embrey, Capt F. J.	NX127	2/1 Bn	4/9/41
Hosie, Pte A.	WX2522	2/11 Bn	Apr-42
Kilby, Sgt H. E.	NX8575	2/1 Bn	10/11/41
Ledgerwood, Sgt W.	VX4648	2/7 Bn	11/6/43
McCrane, Pte P. W.	VX6228	HQ Gds Bn	4/1/42
McGuiness, Sgt H.	NX7504	2/1 Bn	10/11/41
Nicol, Pte H.	WX2253	2/11 Bn	21/9/41
Poschalk, Pte	QX3874	AASC	8/9/43
Poultney, Pte H. T.	NX19604	2/2 Bn	10/11/41
Scott, Pte S. F.	NX1931	2/2 Bn	4/1/42
Shepherd, Pte W.	VX3333	2/5 Bn	Dec-41
Sheppeck, Cpl T. H.	VX5310	2/5 Bn	18/8/43
Spriggs, Pte T.	VX17570	2/7 Bn	1/7/43
Walker, Pte J. R.	VX4367	2/5 Bn	18/8/43
Watson, L/Cpl W.	NX15721	7th Div Pr	6/5/42

	Service Number	Unit	Date Returned
2 NZEF			
Amos, Sgn F.	915	Div Sigs	22/6/43
Brand, Pte J. M.	10430	23 Bn	10/11/41
Buchanan,L/Cpl W.T.F.	10065	23 Bn	10/11/41
Donovan, Sgt J. T.	22770	21Bty	11/11/41
Foley, Dvr E. F.	3654	4 RMT	4/5/42
Gilroy, Pte D. P.	7666	27 MG Bn	11/11/41
Howard, Pte E. A.	3153	18 Bn	2/11/41
Leleverr, Pte W.	5048	19 Bn	Dec-41
Loveridge, Dvr	5239	Div Sup Col	Nov-41
Marshall, Pte S.	7329	27 MG Bn	11/11/41
Morice, Dvr J. B.	3461	Div Amm Co	9/10/41
NcNab, Sgt D. G.	2124	6 Fd Cit	9/10/41
Nicholis, Sgt D.	4232	4 RMT	11/6/43
Rosson, Pte L. S.	35812	19 Bn	Nov-41
Thomas, Lt W. B.	9234	23 Rfe Bn	5/5/42
Swinburne, Pte W. H.	4381	Pet Coy	8/9/43
Westgate, Cpl J.	3316	18 Bn	11/11/41

APPENDIX 3

Alphabetical Lists of All Known Anzac Evaders and Escapers from Crete June 1941–December 1943

A. All Known Australian Evaders/Escapers

Name	Number	Unit	Date Returned
Allan, Pte W.	VX5873	2/7 Bn	May-43
Avery, Sgt B. H.	WX349	2/11 Bn	Jun-41
Bailey, Pte S. F.	NX11675	2/2 Bn	Jan-42
Baird, Pte R. J.	WX370	2/11 Bn	Jul-41
Baker, Pte A. C.	QX7784	2/2 Bn	Nov-41
Baxter, Pte A. B.	VX41609	2/7 Bn	Aug-41
Bayley, Lt C. W.	WX334	2/11 Bn	Jul-41
Bedells, Major T. C.	WX14	2/11 Bn	Jun-41
Bell, Pte A.	VX5407	2/7 Bn	Nov-41
Bertie, Pte J.	VX11941	2/5 Bn	May-43
Beyer, Pte F. E.	VX19853	2/7 Bn	Nov-41
Birch, Dvr T. C.	NX2911	2/1 Fd Amb	Nov-41
Blythman, L/Cpl C. A.	VX6804	2/7 Bn	Aug-41
Bradfield, Pte R. P.	WX981	2/11 Bn	Jun-41
Brisbane, Pte R. J.	NX13076	2/1 Bn	Nov-41
Brosche, Spr W. J.	VX27882	2/8 Fd Coy	Aug-41
Brown, Sgt S.	NX4120	2/1 Bn	May-42
Buchecker, Pte H. R.	VX4712	2/7 Bn	Jul-41
Burgess, Cpl G.	NX9600	2/3 Bn	May-42

Name	Number	Unit	Date Returned
Burgoyne, Cpl R. B.	NX1258	2/2 Bn	Aug-41
Camm, Sig I. K.	VX5641		Jun-41
Carroll, Sgn S. L.	WX953	2/11 Bn	Jun-41
Carse, Sgt A. J.	VX18484	2/8 Fd Coy	Aug-41
Carstairs, Lt J. deM.	VX5423	2/7 Bn	Nov-41
Carter, Pte W. H.	WX1105	2/11 Bn	Jul-41
Cathery, Pte H.	VX5691	2/1 M G Bn	Jul-41
Cations, Pte H.	VX15827	2/7 Bn	Aug-41
Catley, Pte K. E.	NX7210	2/1 Fd Amb	Apr-42
Cauley, Sgt J.	NX4243	2/5 Bn	Jul-41
Cockman, Sgt G.	VX5833		Jun-41
Coffey, Cpl R. R.	VX5412	2/7 Bn	Nov-41
Cole, Gnr J. W.	WX179	2/2 Fd Reg	Oct-41
Cook, Pte E.	WX1055	2/11 Bn	Jul-41
Corbould, Sgt C. J.	VX4685	2/7 Bn	May-43
Costello, Pte A.	NX7830	2/1 Bn	Aug-41
Cruikshank, Dvr W. A.	NX8795	2/1 Fd Amb	Nov-41
Curtain, Cpl C. A.	VX22193	2/8 Fd Coy	Aug-41
Delaney, Pte G. K.	NX8794	2/2 Bn	Nov-41
Delforce, Pte G.	NX1523	2/2 Bn	Jun-42
Doran, Pte R. N.	VX8889		Jun-42
Dorney, Capt J. J. K.	VX327	2/2 Fd Amb	May-42
Doulis, Spr M.	WX3221	2/2 Fd Pk	Jun-42
Dowling, Lt L. E.	WX274	2/11 Bn	Jul-41
Downing, Pte C.	VX5627	2/7 Bn	Dec-41
Dudley, Pte N. T.	NX5173	4 Bn	Sep-43
Duncan, Cpl A.	VX17061	2/7 Bn	May-43
Duncan, Pte J. H.	WX930	2/11 Bn	Jul-41
Dyer, WO II J.	NX2776	2/1 Bn	May-42
Edwards, Cpl A.	VX5552	2/7 Bn	Jun-41
Edwards, Pte E. G.	WX778	2/11 Bn	Jul-41
Elkins, Pte E. C.	WX325	2/11 Bn	Aug-41
Embrey, Capt F. J.	NX127	2/1 Bn	Sep-41
Ericson, Pte A. H.	VX14546	2/7 Bn	Aug-41
Ezzy, Pte F.	NX15471	2/2 Bn	May-43
Forrest, Pte A.	WX1133	2/11 Bn	Jul-41
Fox, Pte H. S. A.	VX6820	2/7 Bn	Nov-41
Francis, Sig I. F.	VX1629	6 Div Sigs	Nov-41
Frawley, Pte T. I.	VX17556	2/7 Bn	Nov-41

Name	Number	Unit	Date Returned
Frawley, Sig J. C.	VX17558	2/7 Bn	Nov-41
Frazer, Lt L. T.	VX15205	2/8 Fd Coy	Jun-42
Gibson, Pte A. M.	WX5664	HQ Gd Bn	Jun-42
Gildersleeve, WO II A. D.	NX1267	2/2 Bn	Nov-41
Gillies, Pte E. A.	WX447	2/11 Bn	Jun-41
Gordon, Pte J. A.	VX23474		Jun-41
Gordon, Sgt R. G.	VX4632	2/7 Bn	Jul-41
Gray, Pte C. M.	VX5600	2/7 Bn	Jun-41
Greenway, Lt G. J.	WX976	2/11 Bn	Jul-41
Grieves, Pte J.	VX7811	2/7 Bn	May-43
Grosser, Pte L. L.	VX16095	2/7 Bn	Jun-41
Hackshaw, Pte A. E.	WX2274	2/11 Bn	Jul-41
Haddock, Pte J.	WX1704	2/11 Bn	Jul-41
Hall, Dvr A. B.	VX22904		Jun-41
Hansen, Pte I.	VX12399	2/7 Bn	Jun-41
Headford, Pte R.	VX16301	2/7 Bn	Aug-41
Hills, L/Cpl N. J. T.	WX9870	2/2 Bn	Aug-41
Hinton, Pte H. H.	NX18894	2/1 O.S.C.	Nov-41
Hipwell, Pte R. J.	VX15848	2/7 Bn	Oct-41
Holt, E. W.	VX23745		Jun-41
Honner, Capt R.	WX15	2/11 Bn	Aug-41
Horne, Pte H. R.	VX11721	2/7 Bn	Jun-41
Horsington, Dvr W. C.	NX4223	2/1 Fd Amb	Nov-41
Hosie, Pte A.	WX2522	2/11 Bn	Apr-42
Hosking, Lt. G. G. S.	WX399	2/11 Bn	Oct-41
Host, Pte E. J.	WX728	2/11 Bn	Jun-41
Howard, Pte V.	VX37362	2/7 Bn	May-43
Huggins, Dvr W. H.	NX9346	6 Div S.C.	Nov-41
Hughes, Spr W. G.	VX21381	2/8 Fd Coy	Aug-41
Hunter, Pte C.	NX5452	16 Bde HQ	May-43
Hutchinson, Pte R. E.	NX4288	2/3 Bn	Aug-41
Jackson, A. C.	NX4603		Jun-41
Jackson, Capt D. A. C.	WX32	2/11 Bn	Jul-41
Jager, Gnr C. H.	VX17073	2/2 Fd Reg	Oct-41
James, Gnr F.	NX3480	6 Bn 3 Fd Reg	May-43
Jarvis, Pte W. S.	WX920	2/11 Bn	Aug-41
Jewell, Pte W.	NX3242	2/2 Bn	Jul-41
Johnstone, Pte H. F.	VX14239	2/8 Bn	Aug-41
Joiner, Pte S. W.	VX5634	2/7 Bn	Nov-41

Name	Number	Unit	Date Returned
Keegan, Pte C. J.	QX2196	A.A.S.C.	Aug-41
Kelly, Pte C. A.	VX11861	2/7 Bn	Aug-41
Kilby, Sgt H. E.	NX8575	2/1 Bn	Nov-41
King, Pte R.	NX2191		Jun-41
Kirby, Cpl R. F. W.	WX603	19 Bn HQ	Jun-41
Lang, L/Cpl	VX5801	2/7 Bn	Jun-41
Latham, Cpl W.	WX891	2/11 Bn	Jul-41
Laun, Gnr A. M.	VX10532	2/2 Fd Reg	Oct-41
Le Nevez, WO II R.	NX7965	2/3 Bn	Aug-41
Ledgerwood, Sgt W.	VX4648	2/7 Bn	Jun-43
Lee, Sgt J. P.	VX5510	2/1 MG Bn	Jun-41
Legge, Cpl K.A.	NX13358	2/1 Bn	Jun-41
Leonard, Cpl L. N.	NX4640	2/3 Bn	Aug-41
Lester, Pte J.	VX5864	2/7 Bn	Jun-41
Lind, Bdr L. J.	NX8611	2/3 Fd Regt	Aug-41
Lynch, R.	WX761	2/11 Bn	Jun-41
Macartney, Lt R. R.	VX115	2/2 Fd Regt	Jun-41
Martin, Cpl H. H.	VX4611	2/7 Bn	Aug-41
Martin, Pte A. H.	VX36688	2/7 Bn	Nov-41
McAninly, Pte P. J.	VX19558	2/7 Bn	Jun-42
McCarrey, Pte W.	WX412	2/11 Bn	Jul-41
McCosh, Pte T.	WX494	2/11 Bn	Aug-41
McCrane, Pte P. W.	VX6228	HQ Gds Bn	Jan-42
McDonald, Cpl R.	VX6508	2/1 MG Bn	Jun-41
McDonald, Pte H. J.	NX9335	2/1 Fd Amb	Aug-41
McEwan, Pte A.	WX330	2/11 Bn	Jul-41
McFarlane, Pte B.	VX13748	2/5 Bn	Aug-41
McGinty, Staff Sgt J. W.	VX4728	2/7 Bn	Aug-41
McGuiness, Sgt H.	NX7504	2/1 Bn	Nov-41
McKenzie, Cpl J.	VX7161	2/7 Bn	Nov-41
McKergow, Pte J. W.	NX11463	2/1 Bn	Apr-42
McKerrow, Lt I.	VX15675	I.M.G. Bn	Jul-41
McLaren, Pte I. A.	NX15437	2/2 Bn	Oct-41
McMillan, L/Cpl G. J.	VX7141		Jun-41
Megahey, Pte G.	NX9731	2/2 Bn	Aug-41
Melksham, Pte W. J.	QX3071	16 Bde HQ	Jul-41
Miller, Cpl D. L.	VX8876	2/1 M G Bn	Jul-41
Millman, Pte E.	VX15541	2/7 Bn	Oct-41
Mitchell, WOII C.	WX456	2/11 Bn	Jun-41

Name	Number	Unit	Date Returned
Monger, P.	WX2052	2/3 RAA	Jun-41
Morgan, Pte L. V.	WX567	2/11 Bn	Aug-41
Morrison, Pte S. N.	WX752	2/11 Bn	Jul-41
Mortimer, W. A.	WX983	2/11 Bn	Jun-41
Munro, Cpl R. B.	NX7160	2/2 Bn	Jul-41
Murphy, Gnr K.	VX856	2/2 Fd Reg	Oct-41
Murphy, Pte A. P.	NX2610	2/1 Bn	Nov-41
Murray, Lt J. D.	WX244	2/11 Bn	Aug-41
Nicholson, Pte G. L.	WX1938	2/11 Bn	Jul-41
Nicol, Pte H.	WX2253	2/11 Bn	Sep-41
Nugent, Sgt H. G. B.	NX4358	2/2 Bn	Jun-41
O'Brien, Pte C.	VX40760	2/1 Bn	Apr-42
O'Donnell, Pte L.	NX1295	2/2 Bn	Aug-41
O'Neill, Pte J. P.	WX426	2/11 Bn	Jul-41
Oldfield, Pte R.	VX36685	2/7 Bn	Nov-41
Park, Cpl E. N.	NX8942	2/2 Bn	Oct-41
Peck, Sgt C. H.	VX4662	2/7 Bn	May-43
Peck. L/Cpl L. L.	VX575	2/2 Fd Regt	Nov-41
Pettigrew, Pte D.	VX4663	2/7 Bn	May-43
Poschalk, Pte	QX3874	AASC	Sep-43
Potter, Sgt J. G.	VX11979	2/7 Bn	Aug-41
Poultney, Pte H. T.	NX19604	2/2 Bn	Nov-41
Quinlan, D. A.	WX746	2/11 Bn	Jun-41
Rankin, Pte C.	VX13409	2/6 Bn	May-43
Reiter, Sgt F. A.	VX4024	2/7 Bn	Nov-41
Richards, Pte H.	WX1944	2/11 Bn	Jun-41
Rigby, Pte A.	WX2088	2/11 Bn	Jul-41
Robertshaw, Pte J. McB.	VX11830	2/1 M G Bn	Jul-41
Royce, Lt G. E.	WX248	2/11 Bn	Aug-41
Ruddick, Sgt C. N. N.	VX5567	2/7 Bn	May-43
Ruddick, Sgt G. C.	VX5550	2/7 Bn	May-43
Ryan, WO II W.	NX8752	2/2 Bn	Jul-41
Sandover, Major R. L.	WX5	2/11 Bn	Aug-41
Saunders, Sgt R. W.	VX12843	2/7 Bn	May-42
Savage, Pte G. A.	VX18824	2/5 Bn	Nov-41
Scott, Lt H. H.	WX980	2/11 Bn	Aug-41
Scott, Pte S. F.	NX1931	2/2 Bn	Jan-42
Shanahan, Capt P. M.	WX17	2/11 Bn	Jul-41

Name	Number	Unit	Date Returned
Shepherd, Pte W.	VX3333	2/5 Bn	Dec-41
Sheppeck, Cpl T. H.	VX5310	2/5 Bn	Aug-43
Simcoe, Pte J.	NX5610	16 Bde HQ	May-43
Sinclair, Pte N.	WX6142	2/11 Bn	Jul-41
Skinner, A. P.	WX1807	2/11 Bn	Jun-41
Smith, Gnr R. T.	SX1019	3 Fd Regt	Jun-41
Smith, Pte L. W.	WX1707	19 Bde HQ	Jul-41
Smith, Sgt E.	WX387	2/11 Bn	Jun-41
Smith, Spr J. L.	NX5427	2/3 Bn	Jun-41
Solomon, Pte V.	NX19649	2/2 Bn	Jul-41
Spark, Gnr D. F.	NX47054	2/2 Fd Regt	Nov-41
Spriggs, Pte T.	VX17570	2/7 Bn	Jul-43
Stapleton, Pte B. B.	WX919	2/11 Bn	Aug-41
Steele, Pte C. H.	BX1338		Jun-41
Stephenson, Pte A. C.	VX3250	2/5 Bn	Aug-41
Stirling, Sgt D. B.	WX606	2/11 Bn	Jul-41
Stoneham, Lt A. C.	WX358	2/11 Bn	Aug-41
Taylor, Sgt J. H.	VX7177	2/1 M G Bn	Jul-41
Thomas, Pte B. F.	WX6112	2/11 Bn	Jul-41
Thompson, Pte J. C.	VX5721		Jun-41
Travers, Gnr F. D.	VX14087	2/2 Fd Reg	Oct-41
Unwin, Pte E. J.	QX3872	2/1 Fd Amb	Aug-41
Vincent, Pte L. C.	NX13043	2/1 Bn	May-42
Wain, Dvr A. B.	VX5722		Jun-41
Walker, Cpl J. W.	VX4674	2/7 Bn	Jun-41
Walker, Lt K. R.	VX4740	2/7 Bn	Jun-41
Walker, Pte J. H. D.	NX12875	2/3 Bn	Nov-41
Walker, Pte J. R.	VX4347	2/5 Bn	Aug-43
Walker, Sgt L. G.	VX5870	2/7 Bn	Nov-41
Wallace, Pte J.	QX4000	2/2 Bn	Aug-41
Ward, Pte F. G.	VX44380	2/7 Bn	Aug-41
Watkins, Pte S. E.	VX7115	2/7 Bn	Nov-41
Watson, L/Cpl W.	NX17521	7th Div Prov Co	May-42
Wilde, Lt G. P.	VX908	2/11 Bn	Jul-41
Wiles, Cpl J. E.	VX16067	2/7 Bn	Jun-41
Williams, Pte L. F.	WX863	2/11 Bn	Jul-41
Woods, Pte M. J.	QX3912	16 Bde HQ	Jul-41
Yelland, Pte W.	VX7148	2/7 Bn	Aug-41
Yoole, Pte K.	NX1590	2/2 Bn	Jul-41

B. All Known New Zealand Evaders/Escapers

Name	Number	Unit	Date Returned
Adams, Pte A. B.	4264	19 Bn	Aug-41
Amos, Sgn F.	915	Div Sigs	Jun-43
Anyan, Pte L.	4888	19 Bn	Aug-41
Archer, Pte G. R. J.	11547	6 Fd Amb	Nov-41
Aspinall, Gnr H. N.		4 Fd Reg	Nov-41
Barrington, Sgt H. C.	4436	4 RMT	Jun-42
Barrow, Dvr R. S.	955	Div Amm Co	Oct-41
Bartlett, Dvr R. H.	31320	Div Pet Co	Nov-41
Beere, Spr L.	33205	19 Army Tr, NZRE	May-43
Bennett, Pte R. C.	6499	23 Bn	Aug-41
Bennie, Cpl F. D.	33116	Div Prov Co	Nov-41
Bishell, Pte N. F.	5248	19 Bn	Aug-41
Bodley, Spr J. N.	34103	19 Army Tps Co	Nov-41
Boucher, Dvr A. J.	9123		Aug-41
Brackenridge, Sgn H.	4576	Div Sigs	Aug-41
Brand, Pte J. M.	10430	23 Bn	Nov-41
Bristow, Sgt W. H.	2484	18 Bn	Oct-41
Buchanan, L/Cpl W. T. F.	10065	23 Bn	Nov-41
Burne, Spr L. R.	33604	4 Fd Amb	Aug-41
Caiswell, L/Cpl F. R.	13481	6 Fd Amb	Nov-41
Carter, Pte B. B.	5399	27 Bn	Jul-41
Casey, Pte R. T.	6635	NZASC	Aug-41
Casgoigne, Pte E. E.	37324	19 Bn	Aug-41
Catherwood, Pte D. M.	15227	4 Inf Bde	Jun-42
Chappell, Dvr J.		ASC	Jun-41
Check, Cpl S. H.	5190	19 Bn	Nov-41
Cheynne, Cpl G.	9768	Div Sup Col	Aug-41
Christie, Cpl C. V.	7542	Div Sup Col	Jun-42
Clarke, Cpl A. C.	6278	Dev Pet Unit	Aug-41
Clarke, Pte C. E.	4837	19 Bn	Jun-42
Clutterbuck, Dvr J. L.	31929	Div Sup Col	Jun-42
Collins, L/Bdr P. L.	21151		Aug-41
Collins, Pte G. G.	13389	20 Bn	Apr-42
Cross, Gnr G. L.	29220	7 A/Tk 33 By	Jun-42
Cumming, Dvr J. M.	7511	4 RMT	Aug-41
Curtis, Cpl R.	8101	20 Bn	Aug-41

Name	Number	Unit	Date Returned
Davis, Sgt F.	3774	18 Bn	Jul-41
Day, Dvr J.	6077	Div Pet Coy	Aug-41
Delaney, Pte N. C.	8848	27 MG Bn	May-42
Denny, Pte C.	9941	5 Fd Amb	Nov-41
Dewar, Pte J. P.	5614	Div HQ	Nov-41
Diver, Gnr F.	25544	4th Fd Regt	Aug-41
Donovan, Sgt J. T.	22770	21Bty	Nov-41
Dorset, Pte J.	30322	22 Bn	Aug-41
Dunbier, Dvr R. W.	12419	NZASC	May-42
Duncan, Pte J. A.	22077	21 Bn	Nov-41
Earnshaw, Cpl L. G.	6044	22 Bn	Aug-41
Empson, Sgt A. H.	2702	18 Bn	Oct-41
Findlay, Pte J.	4613	1st Div Sup Col	May-43
Fitzsimmonds, Pte R. J.	9029	NZASC	May-42
Fletcher, Sig J. D. H.	5636	Div Sig	Jun-42
Flynn, Dvr L. T.	8597	NZASC	May-42
Foley, Dvr E. F.	3654	4 RMT	May-42
Gill, Pte H. W.	3260	18 Bn	Apr-42
Gilroy, Pte D. P.	7666	27 MG Bn	Nov-41
Gosse, Spr C. W.	33141	19 Army Tps Co	Nov-41
Grant, Pte A.	8833	2 Coy 27 MG	May-43
Hancox, Pte W. A.		1 Gen Hos	Jun-41
Hastings, Gnr W. N.	1869	4 Fd Regt	Aug-41
Hoani, Pte W.	39337	28 Bn	Jun-42
Hooker, Pte B. F.	8723	27 MG Bn	Aug-41
Howard, Pte E. A.	3153	18 Bn	Nov-41
Hughes, Pte S.	15083	20 Bn	Nov-41
Irvine, Sgt S. R.	9571	23 Bn	Aug-41
Irving, Pte F. C.	10943	23 Bn	Aug-41
Johnson, Pte G. N.	31312	Div Pet Coy	Aug-41
Johnston, L/Bdr B. W.	20696	5 Fd Reg	Apr-42
Johnston, Pte J. J.	8724	27 MG Bn	Nov-41
Jones, Pte J. N.	11779	5th Fd Amb	Aug-41
Jupp, Cpl A. W.	34741	19 Bn	Aug-41
Kelly, Pte L.	1434	26 Bn 4 Fd Reg	May-43
Kenny, Pte A. R.	31415	22 Bn	Aug-41
Kerr, Dvr J. F.	4410	HQ NZASC	Jun-42
Knights, Pte M.	6486	1st Div Sigs	May-43
Langdale, Pte A. H.	5047	19 Bn	Nov-41

Name	Number	Unit	Date Returned
Leleverr, Pte W.	5048	19 Bn	Dec-41
Little, Pte K.	20090	21 Bn 4 Fd Reg	May-43
Loveridge, Dvr	5239	Div Sup Col	Nov-41
Macdonald, Pte R.	1700	26 Bn 4 Fd Reg	May-43
MacKenzie, Dvr W. J.	9643	Div Sup Co	May-42
Manson, Gnr H. G.	21177	5 Fd Regt	Aug-41
Manuera, Pte W. P.	39779	28 Bn	Aug-41
Marshall, Pte J. G.	10436	Div Sup	Nov-41
Marshall, Pte S.	7329	27 MG Bn	Nov-41
Martin, Pte B. L.	33865	19 Bn	Aug-41
McCallum, Pte D.	30096	22 Bn	May-43
McCaulay, Spr P.	33154	19 Army Tps Co	Jun-42
McDevitt, Pte J.	7471	20 Bn	May-43
McFarlane, Pte G.	9970	Div Sup	Nov-41
McHugh, Pte M. J.	7777	18 Bn	Aug-41
McKay, Spr L. W.	34479	19 Bn	Aug-41
McKenzie, Pte D. N.	5839	19 Bn	Aug-41
McKenzie, Spr D. M.	33235		Aug-41
McLagan, Pte M.	2007	5 Fd Reg	May-43
McLanachan, Pte F. W.	10548	Div Sup Col	Aug-41
McQuarrie, Pte D. N.	2983	18 Bn	Jul-41
Mitchell, Gnr J.	20843	NZASC	Jun-42
Mitchell, Gnr W. N.	21647	5 Fd Regt	Aug-41
Moir, Sgt T.	1481	4 Fd Reg	Apr-42
Moore, Dvr T. C.	32040	Div Sup	Nov-41
Morice, Dvr J. B.	3461	Div Amm Co	Oct-41
Mower, Pte J.	30561	22 Bn	Nov-41
NcNab, Sgt D. G.	2124	6 Fd Cit	Oct-41
Neilson, Pte D. R. S.	6890	22 Bn	Nov-41
Nicholis, Sgt D.	4232	4 RMT	Jun-43
Noonan, Dvr A. G.		ASC	Jun-41
Norrie, Bdr S. P.	23337	19 Bn	Aug-41
Onyon, Cpl S.	3294	18 Bn	Jul-41
Orr, Pte G. M.	6045	19 Bn	Jun-42
Paulin, Pte A.	29854	18 Bn	May-43
Payne, Pte S. J.	4484	4 RMT	Nov-41
Penhall, Pte I.	30592	22 Bn	Aug-41
Penney, WO II W. G.	20837	17 LAD	May-42
Perkins, Gnr G. C.	1772	4 Fd Regt	Jun-42

Name	Number	Unit	Date Returned
Perry, Gnr C. C.	1632	4 Fd Regt	Aug-41
Peters, Gnr R. P. A.		29 Bn	Jun-41
Phillips, Pte N. F.	7495	27 Bn	Aug-41
Phillips, Tpr K.	1259	Div Cav	Aug-41
Pierce, Pte T. C. C.	22226	21 Bn	Nov-41
Poole, Pte H. C.	8283	20 Bn	Aug-41
Porter, Pte P. V.	25986	28 Bn	Aug-41
Powke, Pte, B. H.	6735	22 Bn	Aug-41
Prebble, L/Bdr M.	24721	5 Fd Regt	Aug-41
Quinn, Pte J.	22436	28 Bn 5 Fd Reg	May-43
Redpath, Sgt J. A.	30836	19 Army Tps Co	Oct-41
Reid, Gnr J.	20728	5 Fd Regt	Jul-41
Riddell, Pte R. E.	7064	27 MG Bn	Aug-41
Robertson, Dvr T. C.	32037	Div Sup	Nov-41
Rogers, Gnr H. E. T.	20798	51 Fd Art	May-42
Rolfe, Pte R. W.	3715	4 RMT	Apr-42
Rosson, Pte L. S.	35812	19 Bn	Nov-41
Rule, Pte N. G.	22706	21 Bn	Aug-41
Ryan, Gnr P. C.	1820	4 Fd Regt	Aug-41
Sanders, Gnr L. F.	1647	4 Fd Regt	Aug-41
Sayers, Pte L. R.	30577	NZASC	Aug-41
Shand, Cpl A. J.	9039	4th RMT	Aug-41
Shearer, Pte T.	9375	20 Bn	Oct-41
Shirley, Sgn C. S.	5714		Aug-41
Smith, Cpl A. G.	6776	22 Bn	Aug-41
Smith, Dvr J. W.	6641	Div Pet Co	Nov-41
Smith, Pte C. J.	11536	23 Bn	Nov-41
Smith, Pte L. A.	9012	4 RMT	Nov-41
Sneller, Pte E. G.	30394	22 Bn	Aug-41
Sollitt, Dvr L. R.	8911	2nd Div Supp	Aug-41
Spencer, Gnr G. A.	3353	4 Fd Reg	May-42
Stove, Dvr H.	8646	Div Sup Col	Jun-42
Street, Cpl R. C.	5272	19 Bn	Nov-41
Swinburne, Pte W. H.	4381	Pet Coy	Sep-43
Symes, Pte J.	6633	1st Bn Pet Coy	May-43
Taylor, Dvr W. G.	13506	Div Sup Col	Aug-41
Taylor, Pte A. H.		HQ NZ Div	Jun-41
Thomas, Lt W. B.	9234	23 Rfe Bn	May-42
Thompson, Pte		28 Bn	Jun-41

Name	Number	Unit	Date Returned
Thompson, Pte J. H.	37409	Div Prov	Aug-41
Tinning, Pte T.	7779	19 Bn	Nov-41
Tisdall, Dvr S. D.	13397	4 RMT	Jun-42
Todd, Sig G. E.	30478	Div Sigs	Nov-41
Toho, Pte H.	5489	19 Bn	Aug-41
Toon, Dvr J. L. P.	8893	4 RMT	Aug-41
Voyce, Gnr G. E.	21069	5 Fd Reg	Oct-41
Walsh, Pte J.	3828	18 Bn	Aug-41
Wanoa, Pte T.	26082	28 Bn	Aug-41
Washer, Dvr L. H.	12438	NZASC	May-42
Westgate, Cpl J.	3316	18 Bn	Nov-41
Whitcombe, Gnr A. H.	29834	5 Fd Regt	Aug-41
Whitfield, Pte J. W.	13155	Div HQ	Jun-42
Wikitera, Pte T.	39878	28 Bn	Aug-41
Witting, Sgt R. R.	13358	19 Army Tps Co	Oct-41
Woods, Pte P.	13256	1st Div Sup Col	May-43

Index

Afrika Corps 130
Agrofilichas 174–5, 242 n.31
Ahladiakes 90, 113–4
Akhendria 124, 192
Al Ajaila 141
Albania 21, 22
Alevizakis, Father John 101
Alexandria 23, 97, 100, 104, 116, 126, 129, 133, 158, 166, 167, 196, 204
Aliakianou 111
Allen, Wally 185
Allied forces
  air drops of personnel and supplies 149
  German execution of 114, 115
  military support in Crete
    unavailable during North African campaign 163, 168
    retreat and evacuation from Crete 25–31, 51
  surrender on Crete 31–3, 40–1, 46, 48
  training, in event of being taken prisoner 33, 70–1, 139
  withdrawal from Greece 22–3, 202
  See also Australian forces; British forces; escapers; evacuees; evaders; evaders and escapers on the run; New Zealand forces; prisoners of war
Alones 101
Amari district 83–6, 100, 105, 124, 157, 160, 177, 186, 203
Andrew, L. W. 25
Angell, Joe 44, 45, 80, 149–54, 209
Anotate Epitrope Apelevtheroseos Kritis (AEAK) 124
Antiparos 72
Anzacs, *see* Allied forces; Australian evaders and escapers; Australian forces; New Zealand evaders and escapers; New Zealand forces
Apodoulou 100, 177
Apokoronas district 133, 169
1 Argyll and Sutherland Highlanders 41
Army Interrogation Office (AIO) 139
Arolithi 101
Artsidakis, Alexandra 217
Asfendiles 122
Asi Gonia 101, 160, 236 n.3
Askyfou 25, 77, 113, 131, 236 n.3, 239 n.63, 243 n.8
Asomatos 84

Athens 20, 51, 140, 152, 197
Atkinson, G. D. 72
atrocities 109–12, 114, 138, 165, 167, 169, 171, 177, 190
Australian evaders and escapers 201, 246, 247, 250, 251, 252–3, 254–5, 257–8, 259–60, 261, 262, 264–9. *See also* specific names
Australian forces 21, 22
  actions, Rethimnon and Heraklion 40
  units
    1 Australian Battalion 58
    2/1 Australian Battalion 39, 40, 73, 105
    2/2 Australian Battalion 39, 85, 101
    2/3 Australian Battalion 125
    2/5 Australian Battalion 72
    2/6 Australian Battalion 216
    2/7 Australian Battalion 32, 35, 37, 80, 89, 125, 194
    2/8 Australian Battalion 132
    2/11 (City of Perth) Australian Battalion 39, 40, 41, 42, 84, 100, 217
    2/3 Australian Field Regiment 42, 143
    2/8 Field Company 39, 102
    Royal Regiment of Australian Artillery 25–6
  See also Allied forces
Avery, Basil 41
awards 240–1 n.40
  Distinguished Conduct Medal 72, 156
  Mentioned in Dispatches 152, 156
  Military Medal 44, 89, 156
Ayia Galini, evasions from 40–4, 41, 43, 46, 100
Ayia Irini 80, 90, 91, 107, 180, 235 n.73
Ayia Prison 151, 188, 189, 190, 198–9
Ayia Roumeli 39, 65, 66
Ayios Apostolis 51
Ayios Vasileios, 84–5, 94
Azoyires 136, 140–3

Baigent, L. S. 234 n.26
bandits 117, 131, 147, 165, 171–2, 179, 208
Bandouvas, Manoli 125
Bardia 140, 158
Battle of Crete 19, 23–5, 27, 45, 168, 202, 212ß–3, 244 n.15
  anniversaries 216, 217
  casualties 24–5
  memorials 214
Bavie, Lt 36
Bazely, Pte 72
Bedells, T. C. 42
Beere, Len 120, 209
Beirakis, Katina 191–2, 193–4, 195, 202
Belchem, R. F. K. 231 n.2
Benghazi 140, 141
Bishop, Pte 42
Black Watch 40, 41, 42
Blamey, Sir Thomas 22
Boileau, D. R. C. 56, 234 n.26
boots of evaders and escapers 119, 123, 126, 127, 134, 137, 145, 154, 160, 170, 179, 211–2
Bougaros, George 143
bridle paths 64, 77, 117, 235 n.60
Britain, support of Greece 19, 20–2
British forces 22, 137
  actions, Rethimnon and Heraklion 40
  units 21, 40
    1 Argyll and Sutherland Highlanders 41
    Black Watch 40, 41, 42
    King's Royal Rifle Corps 56
    Royal Army Service Corps 124
    Sherwood Rangers 105
    2 York and Lancaster Regiment 41
  See also Allied forces; Royal Air Force; Royal Marines; Royal Navy

Buchecker, R. G. 89, 90, 201, 236 n.10, 246, 247, 248, 252
Bulgaria 20
Burgess, George 125–6, 127
Burgoyne, R. B. 101, 103

caiques, *see* escapes (by small boat from Crete)
Cairo 124, 138, 158, 175, 176, 204
Campbell, Alistair Te Ariki, *Retreat* 26–7
Campbell, Ian 40–1
Campbell, John 125
Canea 57, 143, 156, 209
Cape Krios 115–9, 120, 121, 135
Cape Maleas 108
'Captain George' 116–9, 149, 164–5
capture / recapture of evaders and escapers 114, 115, 129, 151–2, 174–6, 186–9, 197, 198–9, 202, 219
Carroll, S. L. ('Tich') 42–4
Carta, General 202
Carter, B. B. 89
Carter, C. S. M. 66, 201
Caselli, Tom 56
caves, as dwelling and hiding places 208
  Ahladiakes area 113–4
  Lambert and Goodall in 174–5
    Nerospili 181, 183, 185
  Norm Scott in 132–3, 172–3, 189, 197
  northern Crete 93, 94, 86–7, 130–3, 144–5, 146, 170, 178
  Potamida 209
Chambers, Ron 39
Christmas
  1941 134–6
  1942 178, 181
Churchill, Randolph 205, 243–4 n.13
Churchill, Winston 205
Clarabut, G. S. 97, 98, 99
Clarke, Dudley 70, 71
Clothing for Crete Appeal 215
Collins, Tom 154, 156
Colvin, F. B. 39
Colwell, Sgt 35
Cook, Athol 58
Corbould, C. J. 184
Cosgrave, Sig. 50
Costa Rica 133
counter-espionage, *see* German counter-intelligence
Cowell, P. J. 96
Craig, J. W. C. 72
Creforce 19, 24
Cretan Associations 214
Cretan forces 107, 244 n.15
Cretan generosity to evaders and escapers 62–3, 64–5, 91, 108, 115, 117, 119–21, 137–8, 205–10
  Christmas and New Year 1941–2 134–6
  medical assistance 44, 45, 69, 121, 206, 208
  north-western Crete 145–6
    organisation of hiding and guiding 62, 64, 83, 84, 85, 100–1, 124, 203, 206, 209
  supply of clothing 82, 124, 206
  supply of food 62, 82, 83, 85, 90, 108, 115, 124, 179, 186, 189, 197, 206, 207, 209
  supply of identity cards 143–4, 152, 206
  supply of money 90, 153, 164, 179, 206
  tributes to 214–6
  See also Resistance
'Cretan wireless' 110, 113, 208
Cretans
  as British agents 191–2, 194, 195, 202
  as German agents 137, 158, 167, 168, 169, 174–5, 177–8, 190, 242 n.31
  characteristics of 75–6
  costume 80

Cretans (*continued*)
- diet 76, 82, 85, 90, 129, 132
- family networks 208
- German reprisals against 50, 109–12, 114–5, 138, 141, 153, 165, 167, 168–9, 173, 174, 175, 177, 190
- habit of telling people what they wanted to hear 68
- postwar links with Australia and New Zealand 214–8
- refugees 67, 136
- 'Returned Yanks' 63, 79, 117, 135, 179
- risk of helping evaders and escapers 86, 90, 91–2, 93, 108, 138, 145, 148, 150, 173, 207–8
- supply of food to POW camp 55, 56, 61
- tributes to 214–6
- unfriendly 134, 174
- women 27–9, 40, 61, 68, 77, 78–9, 92, 132, 206, 207, 208. *See also* names of specific women
- *See also* guerillas; Resistance

Crete
- Allied troops disembarked on, after withdrawal from Greece 23
- as supply base for German North African campaign 139
- code name *Never-Never Land* 236 n.3
- communications 77
- in 1941 74–81
- peasant society 74–5
- retreat and withdrawal of Allied troops from 25–31
- rural houses 76, 77–8
- terrain 211
- *See also* Battle of Crete

Cross, Gil 176
Crouch, Cecil 124
Cumberlege, Mike 125
Cunningham, Sir Andrew Browne 23, 96, 167
Curtain, Con 39, 219
Cypriots 201, 202, 245
Cyrenaica 138–9

Damer, Helen 239 n.63
Damer, Seán 50, 77, 79, 129, 131, 183, 207, 211, 218, 234 n.30, 243 n.22
Daoundakis, Manolis 114
Davis, F. 139
Davis, Gordon 144, 145, 178–9, 186, 187, 188
Day, G. M. 246, 247, 248, 250
Day, Ron 219
Debache 177
debriefing, *see* interrogation of evacuees
Delaney, Norm 79–80
Demonyaris 186
Derna 156
Dieppe Raid 205
diet
- Cretans 76, 82, 85, 90, 129, 132
- prisoners of war 53, 54–5

diet, evaders and escapers on the run, 63, 66, 67–8, 82, 90, 94, 108, 117, 134, 140–1, 151, 159–60, 170, 179, 198, 212
- carob beans 129
- *horta* 91, 129, 132, 133, 134, 179, 188, 189, 239 n.63
- olive oil 82, 85, 132
- seafood 152
- snails 129, 130, 132, 133, 170, 179, 188, 189, 198

Dikti range 74, 133–4, 211
Dimirakis, Manoli 216
Dimirakis, Yiorgo 216
Drakona 124
Drimiskos 84
'Dulag Kreta', *see* prisoner-of-war camp, Crete
Dunbabin, Tom 129, 139, 185
Duncan, John 'Papastratos' 184, 185

Earnshaw, Leonard 53, 57, 62, 103–4
Edwards, Geoffrey 59, 99–100, 217

Egypt
evaders and escapers reach 37, 42, 44, 66, 70, 82, 89, 100, 104, 105, 141, 155–6, 158, 167
Rommel's advance on 163
troops landed in, after withdrawal from Greece 23
El Alamein 163, 167, 176–7
Elafonissos 86, 116, 121, 153, 236 n.9
Elliott, Murray 166–7, 189–90, 199
Elos 44
Embrey, F. J. 73, 105, 242 n.28
Empson, A. P. 72
Epanohori 80, 107, 235 n.73
HMS *Escampador* 125
escape routes 83
escapers (from POW camp) 34, 56–69, 74, 100, 123, 210–1
escapes (by small boat from Crete) 45–6, 82, 83, 89–90, 121–2, 201
alphabetical list of all known Anzac evaders and escapers 264–74
Buchecker / Carter Group 86, 89, 246, 247, 248, 252
'Captain George' 115–9, 149
MLC 'Day' Group' 246, 247, 248, 250
MLC 'Fitzhardinge Group' 41–2, 246, 247, 248, 251–2
MLC 'Garrett Group' 34–7, 46, 246, 247, 248, 249–50
MLC 'Richards Group' 246, 247, 248, 251
Moir Group 153–6, 246, 247, 248, 259
Redpath Group 107–8, 246, 247, 248, 256–7
roll of Anzac escapers and evaders 249–63
summary of major escapes and evacuations 245–8
'Tich' Carroll 42–4
Vernikos' Group 105
See also evacuations, of evaders and escapers
evacuations, after Battle of Crete 19, 22–3, 25, 27, 29–31, 39, 40, 51, 52, 65
evacuations, of evaders and escapers 82, 83, 85, 149
activity on south coast alerts Germans 147
Len Frazer 160–3
MI9 use of ex-escapers 72, 176
roll of Anzac escapers and evaders 249–63
SOE gives low priority to 139, 203–5
summary of major escapes and evacuations 245–8
See also escapes (by small boat from Crete); *Hedgehog*; MI9; *Papanikolis*; Royal Navy; Special Operations Executive; *Torbay*; *Thrasher*
evacuees
alphabetical list of all known Anzac evaders and escapers 264–74
interrogation of 139, 156, 158–9, 167, 176, 196
numbers of 200–3
roll of Anzac escapers and evaders 249–63
evaders
alphabetical list of all known Anzac evaders and escapers 264–74
from Ayia Galini 40–4, 46
from Sfakia 34–40, 46
in 'Lotus Land' (Amari district) 83–6
mental attributes necessary 210–1
numbers of 200–1
roll of Anzac escapers and evaders 249–63
wounded 44–5, 69, 121
evaders and escapers on the run 70
boots 119, 123, 126, 127, 134, 137, 145, 154, 160, 170, 179, 211–2

evaders and escapers on the run (*continued*)
capture / recapture 114, 115, 129, 151–2, 174–6, 186–9, 197, 198–9, 202, 219
clothing 79, 70, 206, 211, 212
Cretan girlfriends and wives 125, 194, 208
death by misadventure 202–3
dispersal 82–3
execution 114, 115, 202
Greek language use 80, 94, 131, 145
Greek names 79–80
health 125, 148, 151, 152–3, 154, 164, 172–3, 178–9, 197–8, 212, 219
help with farm work 103, 120, 145–6, 150–1, 208–9
identity cards 143–4
in central Crete 123–30, 173–6
in eastern Crete 65, 133–4
in north-western Crete 83, 92–4, 105–8, 130–2, 144–8, 170–2, 178–9, 186–7
in south-western Crete 83, 86–92, 137, 138, 147, 148–54, 158–9, 164–7, 179–80
left to own devices 33, 71
living off the land 91, 207
local difficulties experienced 211–3
mental attributes necessary 210–1, 212
numbers of 73–4, 156, 169, 185–6, 196, 200–3
risk to Cretans of helping 86, 90, 91–2, 93, 108, 138, 145, 148, 150, 173, 207–8
surrender to Germans 119, 123, 129, 202, 219
tributes to Cretans 214–6
use of ex-escapers to rescue 72
See also awards; caves, as dwelling and hiding places; Cretan generosity to evaders and escapers; diet, evaders and escapers; evacuations, of evaders and escapers; and names of individual evaders and escapers
Ezzy, Frank 181, 183–4, 193, 211

Farley, Driver 31
Fielding, Xan
and Len Frazer 159, 160
and Norm Scott 172
comments on disappointment of men who missed evacuation 128
describes fate of Komnas 177
Dudley Perkins works with 199
negotiations with Cretan Resistance 159
organisation of last evacuation 181–3, 190, 191, 192–3 195
praises resilience and strength of men on the run 212
reports on German counter-espionage 168–70
SOE agent for western Crete 73, 126, 138, 159
Fitzhardinge, J. B. 246, 247, 248, 251–2
'folboat' 96, 97, 237 n.27
footwear, *see* boots of evaders and escapers
Fournes 92, 111, 145
Frati 84, 105
Frazer, Ian 67, 159, 218, 221–2
Frazer, Kevin 69
Frazer, Len 219–22
advised to go to south-central Crete 149
and evacuation promised by 'Captain George' 116, 117–9
calculation of distances across Libyan Sea 86, 88
Christmas celebrations 1941 135–6
diagram of hand loom 135, 207
diary to be published 218, 220
evacuation of 159–63, 211–2, 220
evasion from Skafia 39-40, 219, 220

in Azoyires 140–3
in cave in Ahladiakes area 113–4
involvement in attempts to buy boat 90
map of evasion route 38
mentions 'Returned Yanks' 79
on the run, June–July 1941 65–9
walks over mountains 211
Frazer, Renee 67, 69, 119, 141
Freyberg, Bernard Cyril Freyberg, Baron 22, 24, 25
Friend, John 45

Galatas 25, 33, 51, 59, 62, 64, 91, 102, 117
Garrett, R. 34–5, 37, 46, 246, 247, 248, 249
Gavdos Island 35, 89, 97, 143, 155, 166
Geneva Convention 56
Georgiakis, Petros 184
Georgioupolis 64
Gerakari 124
German counter-intelligence 137, 167–70, 180
agents provocateurs 150, 158, 169
Cretan agents 137, 158, 167, 168, 169, 174–5, 177–8, 190, 242 n.31
German forces 22
fall in morale after El Alamein 176–7
garrison forces 108, 113, 177
invasions
Battle of Crete 24–5, 40
Greece 20, 22, 107
leaflet drop 118, 119
listening/observation posts 113, 114, 147, 165, 181
patrols 41, 46, 103, 113, 119, 131, 133, 136, 137, 145, 148, 155, 169, 186–7, 190, 209–10
raids 126, 127, 167, 168–9, 170, 177
Omalos Plateau 114
Preveli Monastery 104–5
'Waterview' 179–80
reconnaissance flights 92, 113, 119, 155
reinforcements 137
reprisals against Cretans 67, 86, 109–12, 114–5, 138, 141, 143, 165, 167, 168–9, 173, 174, 175, 177, 190
'Tribunals' 114–5
units
5 Mountain Division 32
100 Mountain Regiment 48
Gianiou 84
Gilby, Pte 202–3
Gill, Bert 62, 120, 121–2, 153–4, 156, 240–1 n.40
Glabedakis, Yiannis 117, 165, 179
Goodall, Ted 173–6, 211, 212, 241 n.26
Gordon, R. R. 89
'Great Flap' 163
Greece
boat crossings from Crete to 105, 107–8
British support of 19, 20–2
German invasion of 20, 22, 107
Italian invasion of 20–1
withdrawal of Allied troops from 22–3, 202
Greek forces 21, 22, 25
1 Greek Regiment 44
5 Greek Regiment 25
Greek Orthodox Church 78, 84, 217. *See also* Preveli Monastery
Greenway, Lt 72
guerillas 60, 66, 124, 125, 129, 146–7, 199, 202, 211
Gullet, Jo 216

Hancox, W. A. 35
Hania 24, 40, 50, 51, 75, 77, 84, 92, 100, 121, 141, 143, 145, 149, 151, 177, 187–8, 191, 209, 217, 248
Hargest, James 25
Harokopos, Yorgos 105
Hartmann, Capt. 168
HMS *Hedgehog* 125, 126, 158, 241 n.52, 246, 247, 248, 257–9

Heka, Adam 62
Heraklion 24, 40, 46, 75, 109, 113, 124, 129, 165, 201, 248
'High Spy Route' 83
Hildyard, Miles 63–4, 105–7, 242 n.28
Hitler Youth 58
Hoani, Bill 152
Hora Sfakion
  evacuation from 19, 25, 27–31, 205
  evasions from 34–40, 46
  German shooting of Cretans at 50
  road to 77
  surrender at 31–3, 48
Horham VI, Operation 196
hospitals
  No. 7 General [Army] Hospital 51
  POW Camp Hospital 51, 54–5
Hunter, Charlie 181, 184, 185, 191, 193, 194, 195
Huston, Dick
  and 'Returned Yanks' 79
  capture and imprisonment 186–9, 198–9
  careful not to risk Cretan families 108, 145
  comments on fate of traitors 177–8
  documentary about 213
  Huston Manuscript 237 n.18
  in northern Crete 92–4, 130–2, 144–8, 170–2, 178–9
  learns Greek 80
  lives off land 207
  recruited into secret organisation 147, 240 n.20
  works on land with locals 209

Ida (Psiloritis) range 74, 84
identity cards 143–4, 152
Imbros 25
Independent Organisation of Escape and Intelligence 84
Inter-Service Liaison Department (ISLD) 71, 124, 181, 192, 193, 202, 203, 204
interrogation of evacuees 139, 156, 158–9, 167, 176, 196
Irene Vernikos 105
Irving, Fred 49–50, 53, 58, 107
Irwin, John, 'In Rich Regard' 213, 218, 237, 242 n.13
Italian garrison, Lasithi district 134
Italy
  invasion of Greece 20–1
  occupation of eastern Crete 244 n.15

Jackson, D. A. C. 84
Jager, Charles 25, 49, 62, 77, 79, 91–2, 107, 216
James, H.F. 143
Johnston, Bruce ('Bella') 60, 77, 80, 122–3, 151, 153, 154, 155–6, 214, 217, 240–1 n.40
Johnston, Peter 217
Jones, Flap 184

Kakodiki Stream 179
Kalamata 133
kalderimi (bridle paths) 64, 77, 117, 235 n.60
Kali-Sykia 101
Kandanos 67, 109–10
Kassamo 143
Kastelli 25, 44, 83, 110, 113, 165
Kastellos 93, 132, 186
Keble, Brigadier 204
Kedros, Mt 84
Kerr, John 121, 152–3, 154, 157, 158, 164, 165, 166, 167
Kinder, James 19
King's Royal Rifle Corps 56
Kiriakos (bandit) 131, 147
Kissamo district 156
Knight, Milton 144, 145, 186, 187, 213, 242 n.13
Knossos 40
Kokonas, Alexandros 124
Kontomari 109
Koukonara 192

Koundoura 120
Kouroutes 177
Koustoyerako 66, 67, 80, 90, 121, 181, 182, 183, 184, 185, 192, 199, 203, 211
Kreipe, General 202
Krotos 163
Kroussonas 168
Ktista 154, 179, 240 n.35

Lagonikakis, Dimitris 172–3
Lagonikakis family 239 n.65
Lagonikakis, Irini 133, 172–3, 189, 198, 208
Lagouvardos, Father Agathangelos 84, 95, 100, 124
Lakkoi 183, 184
Lambert, Arthur
  betrayal and arrest 174–5
  comments on failure of British High Command to help 204
  describes Woodhouse's comments on failure of authorities to help 129
  help at Galatas after escape from POW Camp 62, 64
  escape from POW Camp 58–9, 61
  Greek name, Thanassis 80
  in eastern Crete 65, 133–4
  in Lambini district 125, 173
  in Messara district 173–4
  misses out on evacuation 127–8
  reaction to surrender at Hora Skafion 32
  Reg Saunders refuses to abandon 213
  surrounded by mob in Zaros 174
  transported to Germany 176
  tribute to Cretan people 216
  without boots 212
  writes to John Irwin 213
Lambini 125, 127, 173
Lasithi prefecture 134, 173, 185, 196, 244 n.15
Layforce 32, 56, 205
Le Souef, Leslie 31, 54–5
Ledaki family 145
Leigh Fermor, Patrick 168, 176, 202, 206, 240 n.20
Levant Schooner Flotilla 204
Levka Ori 74
Libyan Sea 66, 86
Limni Beach 94, 96, 97, 217
Lind, Lew 50, 53, 61, 77, 79, 90–1, 101–2, 104, 105, 112, 215–6
Liparakis, Sratis 94
Little, Ken 44–5, 69, 79, 80, 116, 143, 152, 204–5, 215
Loutro 39
Lustre force 19, 133. *See also* 'W' Force
Lyons, Doug 219

Macartney, Lt. 36–7
Mahurangi College, Warkworth 217
Makrakis, Alex 117, 135, 179
Makrakis family 120, 121, 135–6, 221–2
Maleme 24–5, 40, 56, 58, 63, 66, 102, 121, 129, 147, 149, 165, 177, 189
  Hill 107 25
Maori Battalion 25, 26–7, 29, 44, 62, 80, 121, 149
Marathon 22
Marmaras 64
Masters, Harry 190, 198
Mauthausen Concentration Camp 199
Mazower, Mark 115
McDevitt, Jim
  and Fifi Papantonakis 121, 134–5, 152, 208
  at Koustoyerako before evacuation 181, 183, 184, 190
  at Therisso 63
  at 'Waterview' 179–80
  describes evacuation of John Medley 204–5
  describes German agent 168

McDevitt, Jim (*continued*)
  describes reaction to request to evacuate Norm Scott 191
  escape from POW camp 61
  evacuation from Crete 194, 195–6
  Greek name, Dimitris 80
  in Ahladiakes cave 113–4
  in western Crete 65, 121, 134–5, 148–9, 157, 158, 164–6, 167, 183
  learns Greek 80
  lives off land 91, 207
  meets Katina Beirakis 193–4
  meets 'Returned Yanks' 79
  Tom Moir asks to help organises evacuation 185
  walk over mountains to Lakkoi 183–4
  witnesses attack on *Papakinolis* 167
  works on land with locals 209
McDonough, Paddy 129
McDonough, Roisin 129
McIntyre, Peter 37
McLagan, Murray
  and 'Captain George' 117
  at Koundoura 120
  at Therisso 62, 65
  comments on surrender of men on the run 119
  describes friends drinking with German soldiers 209–10
  describes German troops returning from El Alamein 176–7
  evacuation from Crete 192, 194
  feelings on hearing of Pearl Harbor and fall of Singapore 130
  in western Crete 157, 159
  makes and sells stock chains 120
  notes progress of German North African Campaign 139
  sketch of yoke and plough 122
  works on land with locals 190–1, 207, 209
McQuarrie, D. N. 89
McWilliam, Sgt 42
Medley, John 165, 204–5, 243–4 n.13
Meiers, A. C. C. 100, 126
Mersa Matruh 42, 44
Mesara Bay 240 n.35
Meskla 64, 78, 80, 82, 92, 145, 180
Messara Plain 105, 173
MI6, *see* Inter-Service Liaison Department (ISLD)
MI9 34, 70–3, 138
  Escape Section 139
  evacuations assisted by MI9 / SOE 83, 85, 94–104, 125, 126–7, 139, 163, 181–3, 185, 189, 190–6, 198, 203–5, 246, 247, 248, 259–60, 261–2
  Greek personnel 72–3, 105
  'N' Section 71, 139
  Preventive Training Section 139, 203
  See also Special Operations Executive
Middle East Headquarters 70, 71, 124, 129, 130, 139, 149, 156, 168, 202, 205
Mirthios 84
Moir, Dudley 189
Moir, Tom
  and Fifi Papantonakis 148, 208
  awarded DCM 72, 156
  capture by Germans 190, 198, 199
  escape attempt from Crete 121–2
  escape from Crete 153–6, 157, 240 n.35, 246, 247, 248, 259
  escape from POW camp 61
  in western Crete 63, 65, 148, 149, 152
  interrogation after escape from Crete 156, 164
  return to Crete as MI9 recruit 185, 189–90
Moni 181
Moorman, Charles 49
Mortimer, W. A. 41–2
Moss, Billy 202
Motor Landing Craft, *see* escapes (by small boat from Crete)

Moustakos 121
Munro, Darby 39
Mussolini, Benito 20

Nathan, Ned
  at Sklavopoula 121, 134–5, 148–9
  evasion of capture 44, 45, 69, 73
  Greek name, Andreas 80
  on walkabout in western Crete 149
  reunion with Joe Angell 149–52
Neapolis 108
Neo Horio 133
Nerospili 181, 183, 185
New Zealand evaders and escapers 201, 246, 247, 250, 251, 252, 254, 255–6, 257, 258–9, 260, 261–2, 263, 270–4. *See also* specific names
New Zealand forces 21, 22, 102–3
  defence of Maleme sector 25, 44
  units
    11 Battalion 144
    18 Battalion 29, 62, 72, 89, 139
    19 Battalion 92
    21 Battalion, 23, 44
    22 Battalion 49, 53, 72
    23 Battalion 107
    27 (MG) Battalion 89
    28 (Maori) Battalion 25, 26–7, 29, 44, 62, 80, 121, 149
    1 General Hospital 35
  New Zealand Army Service Corps 31
  New Zealand Army Service Corps, Divisional Petrol Co. 92
  New Zealand Artillery, 4 Field Regiment 121
  New Zealand Divisional Signals 144
  5 New Zealand Infantry Brigade 29
  Royal New Zealand Artillery, 5 Field Regiment 60, 61, 117
  See also Allied forces
Nicholl, C. C. 202–3
Nicholls, D. 196
Nithavris 177
Nomos prefecture 84, 244 n.15
North Africa 86, 108, 122, 137, 153, 204. *See also* Egypt
North African Campaign 139–40, 141, 163, 167, 168, 176–7, 190

Omalos Plateau 66, 114, 183, 184, 202
Ottoman Empire 64, 170, 235 n.60

Paleochora 77, 90, 110, 114, 143
  German occupation 86, 113, 122–3, 141, 151, 180
Papadakis, Andreas 101, 124, 159, 202
Papaderos, Stelios 181, 182
Papanikolis 68, 165, 181, 205, 246, 247, 248, 260–1
Papantonakis family 121, 148, 153
Papantonakis, Iphigenia (Fifi) 121, 135, 148, 152, 168, 181, 193, 208
Paratiritis 149
Parish, Michael Woodbine 105–7, 242 n.28
Paterakis, Kostas 68
Paterakis, Manolis 68, 199, 203
Paterakis, Vasilis 66, 199
Patsos 105
Pauling, Arthur 149
Pearl Harbor 130
Pediada 185
Peloponnese 108
Perivolia 92
Perkins, Dudley
  and Fifi Papantonakis 148, 208
  escape attempt from Crete with 'Captain George' 164–5
  escape attempts from Crete on stolen / abandoned boats 121–2
  escape from POW Camp 60–1
  evacuation on *Papanikolis*, 165, 166, 167
  falls down rock face 152–3
  in western Crete after escape 63, 65, 149, 158

Perkins, Dudley (*continued*)
killed in action 145, 199
misses escape from Crete with Moir's group 154, 157
return to Crete as SOE guerilla leader 199
Petrakoyorgos, Yorgos 124, 125
Platanos 177
Polentas, Andreas 177
Pondikakis family 120
Pool, Francis 94–5, 96, 97, 100, 124
Poole, Cliff 58
Porto Rafina 22
Potamida 209
Preveli Monastery 84, 85, 86, 124, 217
German raid of 104–5
rescue from 94–104, 128
Prevelly, Western Australia 217
Prison Valley 25
prisoners of war 31–3, 48–56
deaths 56
diet 53, 54–5, 139
health 53, 54–6, 59
morale 53, 139
officers and badly wounded airlifted to Athens 51
return from Hora Skafion to camp 49–50
use on German military works 56
See also escapers
prisoner-of-war camp, Crete 51–5, 100, 123, 132, 133, 139, 209
Australian area 51, 53, 66
British areas 51
Camp Hospital 51, 54–5
Cypriot area 51
Greek area 51
map of camp and nearer villages 52
New Zealand area 51, 53, 54
sanitation 53–4
prisoner-of-war camps, Germany 175, 180, 197, 199
Prodromi 121
Psilafi Ridge 183
Psiloritis (Ida) range 74, 84
Psychoundakis, George 100–1, 129, 160, 220

Qattara Depression 167
Quinn, Jim 179, 185

Raftis 22
Rankin, 'Aussie' 144, 145, 170, 186, 187
Ratcliffe, Colin 92–4, 132, 145, 186, 188
Reade, Arthur 181
Rebellion, 1905 64–5
Redpath, J. A. 72, 107–8, 246, 247, 248, 256–7
Regan, Major 39
rescue, *see* evacuations
Resistance 66, 67, 83, 84, 85–6, 95, 100, 109, 124, 137–8, 139, 151–2, 157, 159, 167–8, 169, 177, 183, 203
Rethimnon 24, 40, 46, 50, 75, 84, 100, 124, 248
Rethymo 39, 50
'Returned Yanks' 63, 79, 117, 135, 179
Reynolds, Des 179
Richards, Harry 37, 246, 247, 248, 251
Ringel, Julius 109
Riza 64, 92
Robinson, Elevtheria 194
Robinson, Sid 194
Rockefeller Foundation study 74, 79
Rodopos Peninsula 105, 107–8
Rolfe, Estelle 216
Rolfe, Jim 216
Rolfe, Reg 53, 60, 62, 120, 121–2, 152, 153–4, 156, 216, 240 n.35, 240–1 n.40
Rommel, Erwin 140, 163
Royal Air Force 21, 22, 41, 51
Royal Army Service Corps 124
Royal Hellenic Navy 202
Royal Marines 32, 34, 35, 41, 46
Royal Navy
casualties 31

evacuations by 19, 22–3, 25, 27, 29–31, 39, 40, 51, 52, 65, 82, 94–104, 202, 203, 236 n.5
Ruddick, Geoff 79, 194–5, 196
Rumania 20
'Ruperts' 106
Ryan, Bill 39, 40

safe houses and villages 83, 85, 124, 139
Salmon, Joe 179
Salonika 219
Samaria 66, 183, 211
Samonas 132, 133, 172, 189
Sandover, Ray 40, 41, 42, 46, 100
Satanas (guerilla kapitan) 125
Saunders, Reg 73, 80, 125–6, 127, 157–8, 213, 216, 236 n.5, 241 n.52
scholarships for Cretan students 217
Scott, Norman 132–3, 172–3, 189, 191, 196–8, 208, 212, 239 n.65
Scott, Phyllis 239 n.65
Selino 66, 90–2, 102, 105, 107, 114, 115, 120, 136, 143, 156
Sewell, Sonny 29
Sfakia / Sfakion, *see* Hora Sfakion
Sfinari 153
Sfinarion 45
sheep-stealing 75–6
Sherwood Rangers 105
Sidi Barrani 37, 89, 155–6, 236 n.10
Simcoe, John 181, 183, 184, 193, 195, 242 n.4
Simonds, A. C. 71, 139
Simpson, Tony, *Operation Mercury* 22
Singapore 130
Sitia range 74
Skafi 91
Skines 51, 53, 111, 216
Sklavopoula 44, 121, 134–5, 151, 152, 168, 181
Smith-Hughes, Jack 124–5, 128, 204, 240 n.20
Solomon, Vic 39, 85
Souda Bay 23, 25, 105, 111–2, 133, 141, 147, 189
Souris, Nikos 195, 240 n.20
Souyia 67, 90, 113, 181, 236 n.10
Special Boat Squadron (SBS) 97, 165
Special Operations Executive (SOE)
British agents 84, 101, 168
Cretan agents 191–2, 194, 195, 202
documents mentioning men on the run 156–7
Dudley Perkins volunteers for service 199
evacuations assisted by MI9 / SOE 83, 85, 94–104, 125, 126–7, 139, 163, 181–3, 185, 189, 190–6, 198, 203–5, 246, 247, 248, 259–60, 261–2
Greek operations 204
low priority given to evacuation 139, 203–5
MI9 borrows personnel from 71, 95
report on Cretan Resistance 137–9, 169, 176
See also Dunbabin, Tom; Fielding, Xan; MI9; Smith-Hughes, Jack; Woodhouse, Monty
Spinalonga 95
Spinarion 215
Spriggs, Tom 196
St Nicolas 216
Stephanides, Theo 26
Stockbridge, Ralph 124
Stomiou 165
Stove, Herb 50, 79, 161, 162, 220
Strifomadi pass 183
Strovles 120
Student, Kurt 109, 115, 234 n.26
Sudetenland 19
Supreme Committee for the Liberation of Crete 124
Swinburne, Wally 196
Symes, Jack 92–4, 132, 145, 146, 147–8, 170, 186

Tarrant, Sgt 29
Tarves, Alec 195
Tavronitis River 25
Tavroulakis, Stamati 101
Taylor, A. H. 37
Therisso 62, 63–4, 80–1, 92, 124, 131, 180
arms dump at 65
Thomas, Sandy 33
Thompson, J. H. 53–4, 57, 58, 233 n.18
HMS *Thrasher* 94, 96–100, 102, 139, 201, 217, 246, 247, 248, 252–4
HMS *Thunderbolt* 124
Timbaki 165, 173, 201
Timbakion 41
Tisdall, S. D. 209
Tobruk 140, 163, 167, 196
Torakis family 121
HMS *Torbay* 100, 102–4, 124, 126–7, 219, 246, 247, 248, 254–6
Treis Ekklessies 125, 126, 127, 129, 133, 137, 138, 204
Tripiti 181, 185, 201
Trofalos 163
Tsamandaki family 145
Tsamandaki, Nico 145
Tsifakis, Christos 203
Tsitsiridis, Yiannis 50
Tsouliadakis clan 168
Tsoutsouros Bay 124
Turkey 23, 75, 80, 105, 170, 208

Ulrick, Jack 32
ULTRA intelligence 24

Vafes 177
Vakakis, Spiro and Anastasia 120
Varipetro 64, 93, 94, 132, 145–6, 170, 178, 186
Vasilis, Kapetan, *see* Perkins, Dudley
Vassilakis, Manolis 105
Vatos 84
Venizelos, Eleftherios 64
Vernikos, Emmanuel 105, 107, 235 n.73
Vickers, Eric 62
Vine, Lt 99
Vlithia 179
Vothiana 117, 120, 121, 135–6, 221–2
Vourvoure 101
Vrisses 25

'W' Force 19, 23
Wachter, Hans 168
Walker, Ian 35, 36
Walker, Keith 35, 37
Walker, T. G. 48
'Waterview' 179–80
Waugh, Evelyn 27, 30–1
Wavell, Sir Archibald 20, 21, 22
Weston, C. E. 46
White Mountains 64, 65, 66, 67, 74, 77, 83, 92, 105, 129, 156, 183, 199, 211, 236 n.3
Wilson, Loraine 183
winter (1941–42) 119, 129, 130, 131–2, 133, 134, 137, 143, 221
Winter, Peter 31, 48, 49, 54, 57–8, 61, 63, 78–9, 80–1, 82–3, 111
Wiseman, Norm 39, 219
women, Cretan 27–9, 40, 61, 68, 77, 78–9, 92, 132, 206, 207, 208. *See also* names of specific women
Woodhouse, Monty 125, 126, 127, 128, 129, 133, 138, 163, 169, 175, 204, 240 n.20

Xyloskalo 184

Yannina 22
2 York and Lancaster Regiment 41

Zaros 174
Zourva 64